The Work of Reading

"Taking off from a challenge to what one of the editors appositely calls the empirico-historicism of contemporary criticism, the writers here analyze the contemporary critical scene with a highly enjoyable wit and searching, iconoclastic energy. Close reading, the place of knowledge, the neoliberal university, historicism, are topics that come within the sights of a buoyantly refreshing scrutiny. A must read for anyone interested in our discipline and those seeking a new and enlivening understanding of it."

—Isobel Armstrong, *Professor Emeritus of English, Birkbeck, University of London, UK*

"Why read? Why describe what we've read? What counts as a good description, and for whom and what can we do with a work we've described? Each generation of readers—and of academics in literary studies, as long as there is such a thing—must ask these questions over again: this thoughtful, trustworthy and well-assembled volume gives a generation's answers. Poems display art, or artfulness; close reading has a history, and involves—rather than negating—history. Higher education isn't neutral: it can sustain, or discourage, reading for form—and for justice. Reading means seeking surprise—and noticing motives. Critique may emerge as "radical defiance," unbowed by premature declarations of its death. Critics can work by example, not just by manifesto; we may persuade (as William Empson did) by our own style. We ought to know (like Frank Kermode; unlike Polonius) what we don't know. And we can find ways forward not just in philosophy but in the literary works we purport to love—from Milton's syntax to Lydia Millet's ellipsis.

This collection knows it's not the first to raise these queries—indeed, its contributors ably and repeatedly respond to Rita Felski and to others who ask whether we can live by critique alone (N-O) or whether we're done with it (also nope), whether we already know what we mean by form (we will keep trying). And that knowledge—alongside the ample skills of its many contributors, from multiple continents and generations—makes it perhaps the best high-level introduction to how and why we read now."

—Stephanie Burt, *Professor of English, Harvard University, USA*

"Here is a spirited new defense of literature, close reading and critique in the era of the neoliberal university. This stimulating new volley in the 'method wars' brings together a range of sharp thinkers, both renowned and fresh to the field, spanning generations."

—Caroline Levine, *David and Kathleen Ryan Professor of Humanities, Cornell University, USA*

"In the wake of historicism, post-critique and surface reading, how should literary studies conceive itself? In *The Work of Reading*, lively essays by British and American scholars, junior and senior, provide answers, including a spirited defense of critique itself, but primarily encouraging a broader vision of the possibilities of close reading as a fundamental humanist activity."

—Jonathan Culler, *Class of 1916 Professor of English and Comparative Literature, Cornell University, USA, and author of* Literary Theory: A Very Short Introduction *(2nd edition, 2011)*

Anirudh Sridhar · Mir Ali Hosseini ·
Derek Attridge
Editors

The Work of Reading

Literary Criticism in the 21st Century

Editors
Anirudh Sridhar
University of Oxford
Oxford, UK

Mir Ali Hosseini
University of Freiburg
Freiburg, Germany

Derek Attridge
University of York
York, UK

ISBN 978-3-030-71138-2 ISBN 978-3-030-71139-9 (eBook)
https://doi.org/10.1007/978-3-030-71139-9

This Palgrave Macmillan imprint is published by the registered company Springer Nature Switzerland AG
The registered company address is: Gewerbestrasse 11, 6330 Cham, Switzerland

Preface

There seems to be a growing recognition in literature departments of the Anglophone world and beyond that the work of reading must proceed from the "ground up"; that is to say, the study of literature should return to manifest facts—words and texts—from the grand speculations that preoccupied previous decades. While the new orientation renders possible a reemergence of the literary, reaction as mere neutrality has always been fraught with danger. This volume argues that the return to fact announced in recent "turns" has largely obscured, perhaps more than the regimes they sought to topple, the work as work and reading as reading.

The problems facing literary criticism today emerge from pressures to which all the humanities are subjected by an age that prizes, above all, the value of use. In answering the wants of the market, there is no doubt that the fields of science and technology surpass their peers with ease. Propagating in a strange admixture, a loss of authority—vis-à-vis STEM—coupled with ostensible autonomy—as regards self-governance—the field of literary studies has in this millennium proliferated a mass of competing methodological processes. Vincent Leitch has identified in literary studies today "94 subdisciplines and fields circling around 12 major topics."[1] Although such levels of disaggregation would normally indicate a pattern of dissolution, some tacit agreement about a generally desirable orientation seems to have crystallized. Inspired, no doubt, by

[1] Leitch, *Literary Criticism*, vi.

the cultural and academic successes of STEM, literary studies has assumed some key axioms of the former's methodologies: we have thus come to be governed today, above a transient shelf of diverse options, by what Derek Attridge in the Introduction to this volume calls "empirico-historicism." Safe in the illusion of "progress" and "diversity" that the cocoon of data most often grants, we seem to have become unequal to the simple questions repeatedly posed by other disciplines, colleagues, and even friends: "what sets your discipline apart, and what, if any, unique insights can your methods yield?"

The present work seeks to challenge the hegemony of empirico-historicism, while at the same time proposing ways to emerge from our current state of disciplinary entropy. This requires us to think past the assembly line to the foundational natures of our quarry, which the few existing challenges to empirico-historicism have often passed over. We thus revisit those basic questions that divided the discipline in the past century but have been eschewed in the recent rush to relevance.

Is the text whole? Is it part of history? Is the text an external occurrence? Is it an event in the reading experience? Or both? Does the text stand outside history? Is it inimical to psychology? Is form politically interested? Do texts have instrumental value? Does close reading? Is a canon necessary for literary criticism? How can it be selected and extended? And to step back even further, what does it mean to be a literary professional? What is, in other words, the work of reading?

To address these questions, the volume has been divided into three sections, "Criticism Today," "Critical Styles," and "Close Reading." In section I, we look at the barriers in the discipline today that prevent attention to works of art as works of art. Staten considers the gradual disintegration of the artwork-as-functional-whole, beginning with the death of the author, and resulting now in an "anything goes" attitude to close reading. Hosseini zooms out to the neoliberal conditions of the contemporary university, which constantly draws the discipline of reading into the logic of markets—postcritique, its affect and attachment, being an unexpected case study in this regard. Rooney is against the artificial restriction to the apparent as demanded by recent interventions such as surface reading, postcritique, and new formalism, arguing that the hidden forces in artworks, how unexpected meanings emerge from symptomatic readings, is foreclosed by sealing the text from its social origins. Battersby argues that, given the salability of polemic tone, the discipline has come to be possessed by an attitude of one-upmanship, resulting in a series of self-styled interventions in recent years that have contributed little to further through demonstration the task of reading.

Section II considers the craft of critical writing. The neoliberal principles organizing production in the humanities have come to reflect—despite the "freedom" that those principles ostensibly celebrate—in a uniformity of critical style that, since Adorno's bombed volley on intellectual mass production, far from being challenged, has become a mark of pride amongst the historians of literature. Rasch protests. He argues that although we can no longer write in the vigor of metaphysical conviction, given the gradual loss of certainty in modern philosophy, we can, and indeed should, attempt to win most lasting sympathy from readers by measuring the weight and examining the poise of our judgments. McDonald draws from Frank Kermode an ethics of humility embedded in the critical style, a recognition of our fallen state that precludes final answers (and meaning) from written interpretation. Eisendrath distils from Hamlet a mode of close reading that values slowness and intimacy with the text, as opposed to the efficiency and objectivity celebrated by empiricism. Grimble recommends that professors of the humanities, to counter expectations from their courses of utility and employability, should attempt to display in their teaching and writing, a fineness and subtlety unattainable to the more instrumental courses of study.

Battersby's call for argument by demonstration is followed up in section III, where the writers defend close reading through demonstrative readings. They counter through their unique modes of analysis and attention the main arguments against the practice of close reading of the past half-century, namely, the supposed indifference to history, politics, and psychology. Wolfson conducts a form of close reading better described as close hearing, wherein a poem is understood historically through the sounds of past poems invoked in its words. Sridhar argues against the reification of the poetic artefact and the instrumentalization of the canon by performing a reading that treats the poem as a live field of semantic and syntactic forces—forces which he then argues can be traced to past poems to retroactively construct "functional" canons. Eyers proposes an understanding of history that deviates from the archival fact-based historicism that dominates the academy today by inferring from the development of narrative form the journey of the subject in its struggles with socio-political and historical forces. Kornbluh explains how a re-objectification of the artwork (from the various subjectivisms of vogue) can set off a wholesale re-structuring of political thought from the prevailing instrumental logic—that texts should be flowery tools of propaganda—to more oblique connections between thought and environment that can be forged through formal innovations.

Most chapters, however, transcend the sections in which they are placed. Rasch's essay, for instance, collapses the question of close reading onto the question of how interpretation is to be articulated. His argument is also carried out via demonstration, of well-weighed style, in Eliot's and his own prose. Wolfson, on other hand, wants to dispel the lumbering myths in literary studies today, that close reading does away with history, and that new formalism is in any way "new." Because most texts thus transgress their sections, the organization must be understood as determined by that with which each essay is chiefly, rather than only, concerned.

The essays are also in dialogue with one another. For instance, Hosseini, Kornbluh, and Eisendrath attack in complementary ways the instrumental reason animating recent methodological interventions. Hosseini brings out the allure of employability lurking in the clamor for "attachment," Kornbluh repudiates the demand that literary works be instruments of rhetorical persuasion, and Eisendrath challenges the notion that a good study is one from which action can immediately spring.

McDonald and Rooney both affirm that knowledge of meaning will always remain incomplete. Rooney uses the Miltonic paradox, "darkness visible," to argue that the question of origin can be shrouded in mystery but must nonetheless be comprehended as an integral part of a text's meaning. McDonald, on the other hand, shows that in the writings of Kermode, the poststructuralist notion of deferred meaning and the proscription from finality in the doctrine of Original Sin combined to form a critical style that says just enough to stimulate further dialogue.

Many chapters are also dialectically interlocked. Let us take the question of whether a literary artefact is a whole. We noted that for texts to engender surprise, they must for Rooney be seen as having mysterious origins. But Staten argues that the only way to teach close reading, to ensure the selection of relevant connotations, rather than the stream of consciousness now accepted in classrooms, is to treat the literary text as a functional—as opposed to metaphysical—whole. That is, for Staten, the interpretation of a line can only be confirmed by whether it hangs together with all others.

Some pedagogical tools developed in individual chapters also supplement one another. Wolfson and Sridhar, for instance, suggest that in reading poetry, full meaning can only be understood historically. For Wolfson, meaning in a present poem is informed by the sounds of phrases invoked from the past. Sridhar, on the other hand, argues that a poem often points to a past poem as its semantic precursor, and that close reading must account for the lyric history brought to bear on the poem's use of words. By identifying the resonances of sound and sense—as McDonald also shows Kermode arguing—canons can thus come together as world-systems that can be studied through links of shared meaning.

The essays in this volume make a case for close reading neither by acquiescence to the positivist demands of the contemporary university nor by dispensing with the actual, but by demonstrating new ways of understanding history and politics that can emerge through a close and committed engagement with the artwork. Eyers, for instance, shows how narrative form can be read "as recording device or fever chart, not of history as an external, public, empirically verifiable procession of events, and not of subjective interiority as the private counterpart to, or denial of, the latter, but of some hitherto obscure admixture of, or alchemical solution beyond, the two."[2] And Wolfson states that "close reading has been derogated as anti-context, especially anti-history; yet here is Brooks facing a past critic-self with remorse, and [Mary] Shelley provoking close reading sharpened not only by literary history but also by her historical moment."[3] Such arguments are essential if literary criticism is to assert some form of disciplinary autonomy—lest we, in the hope of remaining relevant, end up second-order historians or programmers, looking constantly to methodological innovations upstream for our renewing mandate.

Wolfson's derivation of method from Keats's poetry, Eisendrath's, from the follies of the "anti-close reader," Polonius, and Rooney's, from the pregnant paradoxes of *Paradise Lost*, show the authors' willingness to continue learning the craft of reading from literature rather than the popular discourses of the moment. Indeed, most essays in this volume ask the question "how to read?" with a sincerity that might have attended its first posing. Our focus on the brass tacks of reading is a reminder that despite the tumult of the past century, from the modernist debates on method to our own times, we have gotten no closer to answering the

[2] Chapter 12, 243–260.

[3] Chapter 10, 195–218.

fundamental questions of our discipline. And perhaps they will always be out of reach, and, as Empson says, we will, in the end, have to "rely on each particular poem" to show us "the way in which it is trying to be good."[4] Nevertheless, as Attridge insists in the Introduction, writing as we are under the fog of plague, it is crucial that we examine honestly what it is we are actually doing and why it is important.

Oxford, UK — Anirudh Sridhar
Freiburg, Germany — Mir Ali Hosseini

References

Empson, William. *Seven Types of Ambiguity*. London: Chatto and Windus, 1949.

Leitch, Vincent B. *Literary Criticism in the 21st Century: Theory Renaissance*. New York: Bloomsbury, 2014.

[4] Empson, *Seven Types of Ambiguity*, 7.

Acknowledgments

This collection grew out of conversations that we had with Derek Attridge in the quaint German town of Freiburg at a conference on method in literary studies, which we organized in 2017. Although this volume is a separate endeavour, we remain indebted to the institutions that sponsored the conference for setting us in train, especially the Faculty of Philology and the English Department at the University of Freiburg, and all the participants thereof. We would particularly like to thank those at the time who supported us in our disaffected musings: from our department, Laura Bieger, Benjamin Kohlamnn, Gert Fehlner, Nicole Bancher, and Wolfgang Hochbruck, and among our friends, Tara Akbari, Rahil Zabihi, and Michaela Frey. We are also grateful for the support and trust that Allie Troyanos and Rachel Jacobe at Palgrave Macmillan have shown us over the past two years, as this volume has slowly taken shape from its amorphous beginnings. The author of our Afterword, Heather Dubrow, deserves special mention for her heroic efforts to assimilate all the essays and return priceless feedback, all through the stabs of broken bones. Finally, we remain to this day puzzled as to why Derek Attridge had such faith as to embark on this journey with us, and continue guiding us, unfailingly, at each straying step. What you are about to read would not have come about without his generosity of spirit.

Anirudh Sridhar
Mir Ali Hosseini

Contents

Notes on Contributors

Derek Attridge has written books which include *Peculiar Language: Literature as Difference from the Renaissance to James Joyce*, *The Singularity of Literature*, *J.M. Coetzee and the Ethics of Reading: Literature in the Event*, *Reading and Responsibility: Deconstruction's Traces*, *The Work of Literature*, *The Craft of Poetry* (with Henry Staten), and *The Experience of Poetry: From Homer's Listeners to Shakespeare's Readers*. Among the volumes he has edited or co-edited are *The Cambridge Companion to James Joyce*, *Theory after "Theory,"* and *The Cambridge History of South African Literature*. He has taught in the UK, the USA, France, and Italy, and received a Guggenheim Fellowship and a Leverhulme Research Professorship. He is Emeritus Professor at the University of York, UK.

Doug Battersby is a Leverhulme Early Career Fellow at the University of Bristol. His research interests fall broadly in the fields of modern and contemporary fiction and literary theory, with a particular focus on theories and practices of close reading. Dr. Battersby's recent work is published or forthcoming in *The Cambridge Quarterly*, *English: The Journal of the English Association*, *MFS: Modern Fiction Studies*, *Modernism/modernity*, *Philosophy and Literature*, and *Textual Practice*.

Heather Dubrow is John D. Boyd, SJ, Chair in Poetic Imagination at Fordham University; among the institutions where she taught previously are Carleton College and the University of Wisconsin-Madison. Her publications include seven single-authored volumes of literary criticism, a co-edited collection of essays, an edition of *As You Like It,* and essays on higher education and teaching. Two full-length collections and two chapbooks of her own poetry have also appeared.

Rachel Eisendrath is the Tow Associate Professor of English and director of the Medieval and Renaissance Studies Program at Barnard College, Columbia University. She specializes in English Renaissance poetry. Her first book, *Poetry in a World of Things: Aesthetics and Empiricism in Renaissance Ekphrasis* (University of Chicago Press, 2018), was co-winner of the Elizabeth Dietz Award for the best publication in English early modern literary studies. Recent articles have appeared in *English Literary History*, *Literary Imagination*, and *Spenser Studies*. She also writes creative nonfiction; *Gallery of Clouds*, her experimental meditation on Arcadia, memory, and reading, is forthcoming from New York Review Books.

Tom Eyers is Associate Professor of Philosophy, and Affiliated Faculty in English, at Duquesne University. His three books to date are *Lacan and the Concept of the Real* (Palgrave, 2012); *Post-Rationalism: Psychoanalysis, Epistemology, and Marxism in Postwar France* (Bloomsbury, 2013); and *Speculative Formalism: Literature, Theory, and the Critical Present* (Northwestern University Press, 2017). He recently completed a new book manuscript with the title *Romantic Abstraction: Language, Nature, Historical Time.*

Simon Grimble is Associate Professor in the Department of English Studies at Durham University. He is the author of *Landscape, Writing and 'The Condition of England': 1878–1917, Ruskin to Modernism* (2004), and editor of *Lives of Victorian Literary Figures: John Ruskin* (2005) as well as of an online collection of essays and poems on *Brexit and the Democratic Intellect* (2017). He has written widely on critics and intellectuals in Britain from the mid-nineteenth century to the present and is currently writing a book on intellectuals and the politics of style.

Mir Ali Hosseini is a doctoral candidate at the University of Freiburg, where he is working on his dissertation on the essay form and mid-twentieth-century intellectual history, with a scholarship from the Studienstiftung des Deutschen Volkes. Previously, he completed an M.A. in Philosophy at KU Leuven and an M.A. in English Literatures and Literary Theory at the University of Freiburg. He is the author of an award-winning study of "style" in the works of Wittgenstein, Heidegger, and

Derrida. Among other topics, he has written on Wallace Stevens's and T. S. Eliot's poetry, the self in Augustine and Nietzsche, the city and the soul in Plato's *Republic* and *Symposium*, theories of democracy, and the history of humanism.

Anna Kornbluh is Professor of English at the University of Illinois, Chicago, where her research and teaching center on the novel and theory, especially formalism, Marxism, and psychoanalysis. She is the author of *The Order of Forms: Realism, Formalism, and Social Space* (Chicago, 2019), *Marxist Film Theory and Fight Club* (Bloomsbury, 2019), and *Realizing Capital* (Fordham, 2014), and the founding facilitator for The V21 Collective (Victorian studies for the 21st Century) and InterCcECT (The Inter Chicago Circle for Experimental Critical Theory).

Ronan McDonald holds the Gerry Higgins Chair of Irish Studies at the University of Melbourne. He is President of the Irish Studies Association of Australia and New Zealand. He has research interests in Irish literature, the history of criticism, and the value of the humanities. His books include *Tragedy and Irish Literature* (2002), *The Cambridge Introduction to Samuel Beckett* (2007) and *The Death of the Critic* (2008). Edited collections include *The Values of Literary Studies: Critical Institutions, Scholarly Agendas* (Cambridge University Press, 2015) and *Flann O'Brien and Modernism* (2014). He is the series editor for *Cambridge Themes in Irish Literature and Culture*. He is joint CI (with Simon During) on an Australian Research Council-funded project "English: The History of the Discipline 1920–70."

William Rasch is Professor Emeritus of German Studies at Indiana University. He has published extensively on the German intellectual tradition—philosophy, social theory, political theory—concentrating on the work of Niklas Luhmann, Carl Schmitt, and aspects of German idealism. He is author of *Niklas Luhmann's Modernity: The Paradoxes of Differentiation* (2000), *Sovereignty and Its Discontents* (2004), and *Carl Schmitt: State and Society* (2019), as well as editor of several volumes concentrating on the work of Luhmann, Schmitt, German film, and aerial bombing during World War II. His long-standing pleasure in reading the works and criticism of Anglo-American modernism is reflected in the essay included in this volume.

Ellen Rooney is the Royce Family Professor of Teaching Excellence at Brown University, where she teaches literary and cultural theory and the nineteenth-century novel in the Departments of English and Modern Culture and Media and in Gender and Sexuality Studies. She is Co-editor (with Elizabeth Weed) of *differences: a journal of feminist cultural studies* and Associate Editor of *Novel.* Rooney is the author of *Seductive Reasoning: Pluralism as the Problematic of Contemporary Literary Theory* and editor of the *Cambridge Companion to Feminist Literary Theory.* Her current project, *The Reading Effect and the Persistence of Form,* examines the recently reanimated questions of literary form and formalization in relation to contemporaneous work, often on a parallel track, addressing theories of surface reading and the postcritical.

Anirudh Sridhar recently completed his D.Phil. in English from the University of Oxford. His thesis was on the uses of mathematics and mathematical physics in second-generation modernist poetry. Through a series of close readings, he argued that poets literate in mathematics, in the early to mid-twentieth century, used new mathematical ideas ironically and playfully to suggest a lack in the mathematical description of reality and to assert poetry's own truth-telling powers. Anirudh has also written on John Ruskin's theory of labour, W.H. Auden's mid-century assault on the social sciences, and Tintoretto's paintings. Before starting his D.Phil., he took an M.A. in Literature and Theory at Freiburg University, and a BS in Environmental Law and Policy at the State University of New York.

Henry Staten is Lockwood Professor in the Humanities at the University of Washington. Beginning with his first book, Wittgenstein and Derrida (1984), he has worked across the boundaries between literature and philosophy and between Continental and analytic philosophy. Among his recent publications are *The Craft of Poetry: Dialogues on Minimal Interpretation,* co-authored with Derek Attridge, and *Techne Theory: A New Language for Art.* He is currently writing about neuroscientist-philosopher Terrence Deacon's *Incomplete Nature*, a work that promises to open a new era in thinking about the nature of mind and about the way that forms of all kinds emerge from initially inanimate processes.

Susan J. Wolfson Professor of English at Princeton University, has published widely in Long Romanticism, with interest in the theoretical stakes and pressures of close reading for aesthetics, social inflections, and historical informings of literary formations. She is completing *A Greeting of the Spirit,* an array of careful engagements with Keats's poems. Recent books include *The Annotated Northanger Abbey, by Jane Austen* (2012), the award-winning *Reading John Keats* (2015), and *Romantic Shades and Shadows* (2018). Past President of the Association of Literary Scholars and Critics, and Clark Lecturer at Trinity College, Cambridge, she has also received awards from the Guggenheim Foundation and the National Endowment for the Humanities, and the Phi Beta Kappa Teaching Award at Princeton.

CHAPTER 1

Introduction: Criticism Today—Form, Critique, and the Experience of Literature

Derek Attridge

1 Literary Criticism and the Academy

Writing this introduction when half the world is deprived of many of its too easily taken-for-granted privileges, I am conscious more than ever of the huge role played by the arts, including literature, in the lives of millions: during this pandemic, newspapers, magazines, and web publications are filled with recommendations for reading; online editions of literary works and recorded performances of plays are being made available free of charge; and countless homes have become sites of literary encounters (not to mention the enjoyment of film and video). No doubt only a small proportion of the books being read would count as "great literature," or even as inventive rather than formulaic literary works, but still it seems likely that large numbers of people are discovering, or rediscovering, the deeply pleasurable experience of engaging with the kind of literature that offers challenges and surprises, that inspires admiration for its craft and subtlety, and that takes the reader into unaccustomed realms

D. Attridge (✉)
University of York, York, UK
e-mail: derek.attridge@york.ac.uk

A. Sridhar et al. (eds.), *The Work of Reading*,
https://doi.org/10.1007/978-3-030-71139-9_1

of thought and feeling. In the discussion that follows, it's to such works I will be referring when I use the term *literature*. (A consideration of the function of the more general body of "imaginative writing" would be valuable but would run along different lines.)

These unparalleled and unforeseen circumstances raise in particularly telling form an old question: what is the role of the academic literary critic in the fostering and diffusion of literature? The role of the weekly or monthly reviewer is clear, and the role of the literature teacher is, on the surface at least, easy to understand. But what is the purpose, and what are the benefits, of publishing articles and books on works of literature written by others? (The question is of course hardly without self-interest on my part.) If we could answer this question, it would be an easy step from there to favoring certain kinds of articles and books over others—but of course no simple answer is available. Much scholarly writing in the field of literary studies could be said to add to the store of the world's knowledge, but this in itself carries no necessary positive value; it would have to be shown that any given increase in information was beneficial to readers and perhaps to the culture more generally. Other academic works seek to expose the systematic injustices of the past as revealed, unconsciously, in literary texts; the authors of works of this type perhaps expect that through such exposure, similar injustices in the present can be avoided—an expectation that could only be fulfilled if literary criticism were to become an influential genre with wide public appeal. A third variety of academic publication has as at least part of its ambition to enhance the experience of readers in their engagement with literary works; although admirable, this remains a problematic goal, given that most of the publications in question will be read only by other academics. (If the aim is to enlarge the reading public for literature, good, cheap editions and well-written, insightful introductions are the most obviously worthwhile books.)

This is a harsh estimate of the value of what I and thousands of others have devoted a large part of our lives to, but at times like this one is driven to be as honest as possible about what it is we do—especially when that occupation is one we can carry on in relative safety, while many people are risking their health and even lives to establish and prolong the conditions that make such safety possible. My hope, and it can only be a hope, is that my academic publications have served the writers and writings they have been concerned with; that they have gained new readers for literary works of substance and deepened the enjoyment and enlightenment those works are able to offer. The more purely theoretical texts I have written belong more to the discipline of philosophy than to literary criticism and, like all philosophical endeavors, aim at general truths (though I would disclaim any notion of timeless universals); but even these I would like to think have a potential role in enhancing understanding of not just the nature but also the value of literature.

My fear, however, is that the institution of academic literary scholarship has become too inward-looking and self-perpetuating to be a strong force for good in the wider world; too much of our energy goes into ever more ingenious interpretations and theories, or increasingly detailed investigations of historical minutiae, or expanding accumulations of footnotes in "definitive" editions, or quarrels among ourselves over issues of interest to very few. It is true that our efforts help to sustain a number of publishers and contribute to the profits of booksellers and the livelihood of librarians; and the vast merry-go-round of "research funding" relies on reputations made by publication in order to fund yet more publication and gain promotion for individuals. But these are relatively limited benefits, and the professionalization of the literary academy, together with the creeping dominance of the science model of research, has had many deleterious consequences. As the mountain of published work grows, so does the task of exhaustive referencing; and the likelihood of saying what has already been said increases accordingly—but so does the likelihood of any given reader's knowing that it has already been said. The huge expansion of online materials only compounds the problem, making the amassing of references much easier than in the days when the laborious maintaining of handwritten index cards (I still have boxes and boxes of them) made selection imperative, but at the same time reducing the careful reading of the works referred to. Moreover, the abstracts now required by many journals and presses offer tempting short-cuts. At the same time, under the pressure of the neoliberal privileging of monetary reward and utilitarian training over a broader understanding of education, the numbers enrolling in literature courses are in decline in many places—a phenomenon undoubtedly exacerbated by the insular preoccupations of the profession.

There are signs of growing dissatisfaction with this situation, and I take the present volume to be one of them. The contributors have responded to a call to return to the work of art, neither roaming in the abstract realms of "Theory" nor rummaging through the hoard of contextual particulars. Whether revaluing the practice of close reading, assessing the current wave of "postcritical" theorizing, revisiting the arguments of earlier critics and theorists, challenging the dogmas of critical practice, calling for renewed attention to the language of criticism, or exemplifying the rewards of close attention to the literary work, these essays demonstrate both a willingness to resist the forces—political, institutional, ideological, or simply inertial—that govern and distort our critical and pedagogical practice and a creative commitment to the exploration of methods and approaches more attuned to the needs and aspirations of today's writers and readers.

2 Attending to Form

If one were to risk an adjective to describe the dominant mode of literary studies in the English-speaking world at the start of the current millennium it might be "empirico-historical": the wave of high theory had passed, the principle of canonical expansion had been accepted, and questions of literary evaluation had been put on the back burner. Trend-conscious graduate students in all periods were exploring archives, examining historical contexts, and excavating little-read authors. No doubt classroom teaching still included a fair amount of formal analysis, consideration of the major works of the canon, and discussion of what makes a successful literary work, but these concerns were not greatly in evidence beyond the undergraduate curriculum. However, there were indications that the great ship of academic literary discourse was beginning, slowly, to change course. To pick out a few: 2000 was the year in which Isobel Armstrong's *The Radical Aesthetic* was published, arguing that a concern with the aesthetic was not inimical to progressive thought, and the same year saw the special issue of *Modern Language Quarterly* titled "Reading for Form," edited by Susan Wolfson and Marshall Brown.[1] Among the many books and essays advocating and illustrating attention to literary form that followed in a steady stream were Peter de Bolla's *Art Matters* (2001); *Aesthetic Subjects* (2003), a substantial collection of essays edited by Pamela R. Matthews and David McWhirter; my own short volume *The Singularity of Literature* (2004); and Jonathan Loesberg's study *A Return to Aesthetics* (2005). By 2007, the situation had changed sufficiently for *PMLA* to include in the journal section

[1] *Reading for Form* was later published as a book.

headed "The Changing Profession" an article by Marjorie Levinson with the heading "What is New Formalism?"

This stream was joined by another torrent that could be said to have begun in 2003 with Eve Sedgwick's book *Touching Feeling*—more specifically with her chapter "Paranoid Reading and Reparative Reading"[2]—and to have received a further boost the following year with Bruno Latour's essay "Why Has Critique Run Out of Steam?" This approach, which also helped to open the way for fresh attention to form, queried the tendency of critics to treat literary works with suspicion as symptomatic of societal and ideological ills, emphasizing instead the affirmative dimension of literary reading. As is remarked by the editors of the volume *Critique and Postcritique*, published in 2017 and confirming the arrival of yet another "post-" in the parade of posts that has marked recent decades, "There is little doubt that debates about the merits of critique are very much in the air and that the intellectual or political payoff of interrogating, demystifying, and defamiliarizing is no longer quite so evident."[3] This mode of reading was often carried out in conjunction with a new appreciation of the importance of *affect*—the rapid dissemination of this word, in place of the unscientific-sounding "feeling," being itself an indicator of the success of the new trend. Other voices in the debate proposed a shift of metaphors in literary analysis from depth to surface, or called for "just" or "generous" reading, or advocated "thin description," or argued for the value of "minimal interpretation."[4]

On the one hand, then, by the second decade of the new millennium there was a growing awareness that questions of literary form had been ignored in the rush to history that marked the last decades of the previous one, and, on the other, an increasing skepticism about the widespread assumption that literary works were to be read against the grain and in the service of ideological unmasking. These twin shifts became especially evident, in different combinations, in a number of books over the past

[2] Sedgwick, *Touching Feeling*, Chap. 4, "Paranoid Reading and Reparative Reading, or, You're So Paranoid, You Probably Think This Essay Is About You"; Sedgwick's essay was first published in 1997 under a slightly different title.

[3] Anker and Felski, *Critique and Postcritique*, 1.

[4] See Best and Marcus, "Surface Reading"; Marcus, *Between Women*, 75; Bewes, "Reading with the Grain"; Love, "Thin Description"; Attridge and Staten, *Craft of Poetry*. For an assessment of the "postcritique" school as it impacts art history, see Callahan, "Post-Critique in Contemporary Art History."

few years that have garnered considerable attention. In 2015, Caroline Levine's *Forms* proposed a fresh look at the role of form while in the same year Rita Felski's *The Limits of Critique* followed Sedgwick and Latour in advocating the replacement of suspicious by affirmative reading. Two years later Tom Eyers, in *Speculative Formalism*, offered a different account of the role of literary form, while Joseph North, adopting I. A. Richards as his guiding light, raised the banner of close reading in *Literary Criticism: A Political History*. Both Eyers and North see their task in part as escaping from the strait-jacket of history: as Eyers puts it, "history, instead of being a question to be answered, has threatened to become a catch-all *explanans* to be passively assumed, bringing with it an obfuscation of what makes literature, literature"[5]; or in North's words, the "central logic that has dictated so much of the last three decades of literary study" is "the rejection of the project of criticism—aesthetic education for something resembling, in aspiration if not in fact, a general audience—and the embrace of the project of scholarship—the production of cultural and historical knowledge for an audience of specialists."[6] North makes a strong case for regarding the shift to empiricism, under the guise of "scholarship," as a shift to a conservative mode of literary study in conformity with the instrumental urgings of neoliberal capitalism, and for the progressive credentials of the kind of criticism he is advocating.

Now it should go without saying that a great deal of the literary criticism that appeared during the decades prior to 2000 did in fact take formal matters into consideration, and that not everyone in literary studies was engaged in empirical investigation or ideological critique. Many literary critics, for instance, took their bearings from continental philosophers who placed a high value on the contribution literature can make to thought and ethical understanding (and I include myself in this category). Literary form remained central to stylistic studies influenced by linguistic theory (another category to which I confess membership), to narratology, and to Anglo-American analytic aesthetics, all of which continue to thrive. Moreover, the picture I have drawn reflects only the trends most in evidence in such places as high-profile critical journals, conferences on the state of literary studies, and leading publishers' lists of

[5] Eyers, *Speculative Formalism*, 7.

[6] North, *Literary Criticism*, 115.

new books; a full survey of the day-to-day work of the college or university teacher might yield a rather different picture. But even though a shift of focus in these elite sites is not necessarily representative of the great quantity of work being done in literary departments around the world, it remains significant as a possible pointer to more widespread changes of emphasis in literary studies ahead.

I welcome this fresh attention to issues I've been interested in for several decades, though it remains important to subject the newly emerging accounts of literary form and affect to careful assessment. I applaud the fact that most of these accounts attempt to stay true to the principle of social relevance that lay at the heart of the tradition of critique by attempting to build a bridge of some sort between formal questions and the needs of the world in which we live, as long as this admirable desire doesn't impede accurate reporting on the way literary form actually works. The question of pleasure, for instance, the fundamental spur to the devotion of time and energy to literary works on the part of readers, gets short shrift in many of these accounts.

Caroline Levine's project in *Forms* is to show how the forms that characterize aesthetic objects are also at work in cultural and political institutions and practices, a correlation that she achieves by restricting the notion of "form" to the most general structuring features of both domains: as Levine's subtitle has it, *Whole, Rhythm, Hierarchy, Network.* Form in literary works is understood largely in terms of the relations among elements of content according to these four principles and, in the world outside literature, in terms of the corresponding relations among real entities. While it is undoubtedly valuable to understand the formal structures that enable the social, economic, and political spheres to function as they do, it's not clear that one has to turn to literature to discover the primary modes of such ways of connecting; nor is it clear that the homologies traceable between certain literary works concerned with relations in these spheres and those spheres themselves is generalizable to an account of the operation of literary form across a wider range of works.

One of the strengths of Levine's approach is her emphasis on the *experience* of form, whether in the literary work or in the world, and I shall be returning to this issue. This emphasis emerges especially clearly in her treatment of rhythm, where she offers a telling critique of the spatialization of time in much literary criticism. Her analysis of the rhythms of Elizabeth Barrett Browning's poem "The Young Queen" marks perhaps her closest approach to a concern with form as distinct from content:

rightly resisting the notion that "prosody is political insofar as it mirrors rhythms in the world," she argues that the unusual metrical structure of the poem, a conflation of short meter and poulter's measure,[7] adds a further rhythm to the historical rhythms described in the poem, namely, the announcement of William IV's death, his funeral, and the accession of the young Victoria. Yet in saying that "the state and the poet are actually at work on one and the same project—the struggle to impose temporal order" she falls back on the unhelpful notion of a parallel between aesthetic and political forms that runs through the book.[8] It's also perhaps significant that the example Levine chooses is a remarkably bad poem—a fact which Browning seems to have acknowledged, as she omitted it from her collected works later in life.

The idea that the forms of literature and those of the world exhibit parallels is also present in Tom Eyers's *Speculative Formalism*, though the shared qualities he finds in the two spheres are not the same as Levine's. Eyers's book is studded with phrasal variations on one central paradox concerning what he calls the "peculiar kind of reference that literature performs": its "nonrelational referentiality," its "nonmimetic connective function"; or its "productive incommensurability."[9] An early formulation of this paradox reads: "The resonance of world and word is to be found in the *non*-mimetic, *non*-correlational but nonetheless *shared* moments of incompletion that define text and materiality, literature and history."[10] The aim of the book's argument is "to render history and text alike as complex forms, imperfectly and awkwardly interlaced in various agonistic combinations."[11] We hear of "the fleeting contact of the act of imagination and the sheer facticity of worldly density"[12] and are told that Francis Ponge's poetry "wishes to find in the very impossibility of any transitive

[7] The meter can be regarded either as poulter's measure with the first line divided or short metre with the third and fourth lines running together. There is a further metrical allusion not mentioned by Levine: the rhymes echo those of the traditional tail rhyme stanza (*aabccb*), though the disposition of long and short lines is diametrically opposed to the usual arrangement.

[8] Levine, *Forms*, 79.

[9] Eyers, *Speculative Formalism*, 61, 69, 83, 96.

[10] Eyers, 14.

[11] Eyers, 29.

[12] Eyers, 102.

movement between the essence of things and their linguistic apprehension the possibility, nonetheless, of their fragile resonance."[13] Although Eyers finds fault with Levine for lacking a theory of literary reference, and his critique of mimetic accounts of the operation of form is spot-on, his own theory does not emerge with sufficient clarity from the constantly reiterated statement of the paradox that, for him, governs the relation between text and world. What does it mean for textual and non-textual realities to "resonate," to "share" properties, to make "fleeting contact," to "spark in affinity"[14]—and to do so without any suspicion of mimesis? If these suggestive metaphors could be grounded in an account of what happens when the reader encounters, say, narrative surprises, or metrical variations, or rapid stichomythia, it would be easier to understand how the connection between formal arrangement and worldly realities is made.

Rita Felski, in *The Limits of Critique*, is largely concerned to offer a critique of critique,[15] but in her final full chapter, "'Context Stinks!,'" she advances some constructive suggestions by hitching her cart to Latour's "actor-network theory" in order to claim for literary works the capacity to act as agents in the world.[16] Although this approach necessitates treating metaphors as realities (ignoring, for instance, the fact that literary works as material objects are nothing but ink on paper or perturbations in the air requiring human agents to bring them into being), it does at least pay some attention to the experience of reading literature, a topic that comes to the fore in Felski's earlier book, *Uses of Literature*, where, pondering the "mysterious event of reading," she rightly observes that "we are sorely in need of richer and deeper accounts of how selves interact with texts."[17] However, neither of these books shows any deep engagement with questions of form, an absence which may be connected to the curious hostility

[13] Eyers, 70.

[14] Eyers, 99.

[15] Felski's arguments are addressed at many points in this volume; see, in particular, the chapters by Battersby, Grimble, and Hosseini.

[16] Actor-network theory has connections with the philosophical movement known as "OOO" ("object-oriented-ontology"), which in turn has links to the "anti-correlationist" school of Quentin Meillassoux and, more fuzzily, to the work of Alain Badiou. All these approaches involve a questioning of the fundamental Kantian insight that the human mind has no direct access to the world in itself; this skepticism plays out in different ways in literary studies, all of which undervalue (fatally, to my mind) the role of the reader's experience of the powers of language and artistic invention.

[17] Felski, *Uses of Literature*, 11.

Felski shows toward all attempts to specify what is peculiar to literature as a use of language or to pursue what it might mean to read a literary work as literature and not something else. When she points out that the recent revival of formal criticism "shows scant interest in the puzzle of how texts resonate across time" and that "we sorely need alternatives to seeing [artworks] as transcendentally timeless on the one hand and imprisoned in their moment of origin on the other,"[18] she touches on a significant problem in literary studies but has no solution to offer. In particular, the question of how a literary work can continue to strike the reader as inventive, as broaching new possibilities of thought and feeling hundreds of years after it was written, needs to be addressed; as Eliot noted in a 1940 radio broadcast, without, however, offering an explanation of the phenomenon, "No good poet wants novelty or eccentricity for its own sake: the element of surprise in good poetry is something which remains for ever, and is not only valid for its own time."[19]

In contrast to Levine and Eyers, Joseph North, in *Literary Criticism*, addresses directly the question of the reader's engagement with the literary work and the value of this experience.[20] He defends the tradition of close reading and attention to form but calls for an approach that neither attempts to "reinvigorate an idealist aesthetics" nor to "use form as a way to reinvigorate the dominant historicist/contextualist methods."[21] His third way, drawing on the work of Armstrong, Sedgwick, D. A. Miller, and Lauren Berlant, is the way of "aesthetic education," "cultural intervention," and "subject formation": in other words, a critical method that sees as its task the heightening of literature's capacity to contribute beneficially to the lives of its readers and the society of which they are part. He is well aware of the danger that his proposals will sound like a conservative appeal to return to a type of criticism aimed at enhancing liberal subjecthood, and stresses that he is looking for a mode of radical criticism. He is surely right to stress the importance not

[18] Felski, *Limits of Critique*, 154.

[19] T. S. Eliot, "A New Tradition of Poetic Drama," quoted in Eliot, *Poems*, 1:361–62. I have discussed the transtemporal nature of artistic inventiveness in *The Work of Literature* and *The Singularity of Literature*.

[20] See the discussions of North's book in the essays by Battersby, Grimble, and Hosseini in this volume.

[21] North, *Literary Criticism*, 147.

only of the context of production in the literary sphere but the context of reception—what he calls "real, living readers."[22]

As his subtitle, *A Political History*, suggests, North is largely concerned with the history of Anglo-American literary criticism, and his positive recommendations remain undeveloped. His vision of what a newly invigorated literary criticism would be like is appealing, however; take this summary of what North feels is an emerging consensus in literary studies, for instance:

> It seems the method being called for would be deeply concerned with the aesthetic and the formal; sensitive to feeling and affect both as forms of cognition and in their own right as crucial determinants of individual, collective, and historical changes; able to move broadly, in something like a generalist fashion, across times, places, and cultures; willing to use the literary as a means of ethical (or political?) education; have its emphasis on therapeutic rather than merely diagnostic uses of the literary; and would be committed in a deep and rigorous but still fairly direct way to a public role.[23]

Whether or not North is correct in his claim that these requirements are being increasingly accepted, they constitute a good basis for thinking about a desirable future for literary studies. They leave many questions unasked, however. What kind of attention to the specificity of literature would be needed to implement them? What needs to be said about the pleasures and insights offered to readers by form? What can be said about formal features that don't contribute to meaning? And what kind of education can the literary provide that is not available from other sources?

3 The Experience of Literature

I would like to refocus the discussion around the question of *experience*. If the text becomes a work of literature only in the event of reading, as I and others have argued,[24] it is the reader's experience of the event that brings

[22] North, 232.

[23] North, 193–94.

[24] See, for instance, Attridge, *Work of Literature* and *Singularity of Literature*, *passim*; Rosenblatt, *Literary Work*; Szafraniec, *Event of Literature*. Toril Moi argues for a related conception of a "poem, a play, a novel as a particularly complex action" ("'Nothing Is

the literary work into being as a *literary* work, rather than the many other things it can be for a reader, from historical document to moral treatise to autobiographical revelation. The notion of experience figures centrally in a number of philosophical schools, notably empiricism (with its assumption that knowledge derives from sensory experience), phenomenology (which is often labeled the "philosophy of experience"), and existentialism (with its emphasis on personal decisions). Locke, Berkeley, Hume, Husserl, Bergson, Merleau-Ponty, and many others appeal to experience, and it's an important idea for Descartes, Kant, Hegel, and Walter Benjamin. John Dewey, in the significantly named *Art as Experience*, uses the concept in extending aesthetics to everyday life. Several literary theorists find the word essential—a list would include Hans Robert Jauss, Hans-Georg Gadamer, and Louise Rosenblatt, as well as Stanley Fish and many others associated with reader-response criticism.[25] In an anthology with the title *The Experience of Literature*, Lionel Trilling explains that his commentaries "have one purpose only—to make it more likely that the act of reading will be an experience, having in mind what the word implies of an activity of consciousness and response."[26] Jacques Derrida states that "the interest of deconstruction [...] is a certain experience of the impossible: that is, [...] of the other"[27], and Foucault wished to develop a non-phenomenological account of experience.[28] I've found myself using the term frequently, and it figures in the title of my most recent book.[29]

It remains a problematic word, however, because of its mercurial variety of meaning. Modern German distinguishes between *Erlebnis*, internally directed experience in the moment, and *Erfahrung*, externally directed, accumulated experience, a distinction that was important for Benjamin and Heidegger. French, on the other hand, complicates matters in the other direction by using the same word—*expérience*—to mean not

Hidden,'" 36) which she derives from Wittgenstein; but her account pays insufficient attention to the role of the reader in performing that action.

[25] In *Against Democracy: Literary Experience in the Age of Emancipations*, Simon During foregrounds experience in arguing for the contribution made by literature to the rise of democracy. During sees the emphasis placed on experience in democratic systems as benefitting from the novel's power as a describer of experience in society (*passim*).

[26] My thanks to Mir Ali Hosseini for bringing this work to my attention.

[27] Derrida, "Psyche," 328.

[28] See Gutting, "Foucault's Philosophy of Experience."

[29] Attridge, *Experience of Poetry*.

only "experience" but also "experiment." Martin Jay begins an essay titled "Experience without a Subject" with quotations from Gadamer and Michael Oakeshott on the obscurity and unmanageability of the term, summing up the ubiquity of the concept in philosophical debate as follows:

> Obscurity and unmanageability notwithstanding, 'experience' remains a key term in both everyday language and the lexicons of esoteric philosophies. Indeed, Gadamer, Oakeshott, and a host of other twentieth-century thinkers, from Martin Buber to Georges Bataille, from Edmund Husserl to John Dewey, from Ernst Jünger to Jean-François Lyotard, have felt compelled to mull over its multiple meanings and contradictory implications.[30]

I don't intend to join this vast and frequently muddy conversation, though it's inevitable that it should be heard in the background. I propose to use the term in a fairly colloquial sense to refer to what happens, mentally, emotionally, and physically, in the process of literary reading. By emphasizing experience, I am resisting the familiar discourse of meaning: literary works, of course, mean, but what makes them literary is that it's the *process* of meaning that's important rather than any meaning that may be extracted. If the reader gains any knowledge from the experience of a literary work, it is knowledge as know-how, not information.

What I don't want to imply by using the term is that a theory of the literary work as event is primarily an empirical—that is to say, a psychological or neurological—theory interested in what goes on in reader's brain (or, for that matter, a physiological theory interested in what goes on in the rest of the body), even though any conclusions that might be drawn about the reader's experience might be mappable onto these domains. As a response to the inadequacies of literary studies in the latter part of the twentieth century, the turn to empirical science in cognitive or data-driven approaches seems to me a move in precisely the wrong direction; these approaches may bring in funding from science-oriented universities and foundations, but they move even further away from what is distinctive about literary experience and do little to enrich that experience for others. Nor does my focus on experience imply a phenomenological theory; although my approach has much in common with the arguments

[30] Jay, *Cultural Semantics*, 47.

of Mikel Dufrenne, Roman Ingarden, Gadamer, and Wolfgang Iser in their examination of the reader's relation to the text, it's less interested in generalizing about the subject or the implied reader and more interested in the singularity of every reading, and the implications of that singularity.[31]

My fundamental question is: what can we deduce from the accounts given by writers and readers, and from individual introspection tested against the reports of others, about the components of the singular experience—conscious and unconscious—whereby a text (as a set of linguistic signs) is brought into being as a literary work, understood from the reader's perspective? In what ways might an engagement with a powerful work effect changes in an individual? The act-event[32] of reading involves the introduction into the sphere of the familiar and habitual an element—a way of thinking or feeling, a piece of reality, a formal arrangement—that is unexpected but, because it makes good an absence in that sphere, has a feeling of rightness about it.[33] As Barbara Johnson puts it, "What the surprise encounter with otherness should do is lay bare some hint of an ignorance one never knew one had."[34] Mere novelty isn't sufficient to produce the sense of the opening up of new horizons characteristic of powerful literary experience.

I've suggested elsewhere that the power of the artwork may be viewed according to three perspectives, exploring its singularity, its otherness, and its inventiveness (each of which is dependent on the other two). The complexity of the reading process when these properties of a work of literature are fully engaged with is often underestimated; to focus on

[31] In *The Work of Literature* I give a brief account of the importance of phenomenological approaches to my thinking about the experience of literary works (Attridge, *Work of Literature*, 90–93).

[32] Reading is a variety of perception, which always has a dual active and passive character; to see, for example, is to exercise the faculty of sight and to allow light rays to enter the eyes. But literary reading demands both heightened activity—the bringing to bear on a verbal text a complex set of strategies—and enhanced receptivity to what is unfamiliar and unpredictable.

[33] For G. H. Hardy, mathematical theorems such as Euclid's or Pythagoras's also exhibit "a very high degree of *unexpectedness*, combined with *inevitability* and *economy*." Hardy, *Mathematician's Apology*, 29. My thanks to Anirudh Sridhar for alerting me to this connection.

[34] Johnson, *World of Difference*, 16. See also Ellen Rooney's discussion of surprise in her contribution to this volume.

experience is not to simplify but rather to complicate our account of the literary. When I read a novel I respond to the author's use of language, the exploitation of generic properties, the occurrence of tropes, the examination of moral issues, the representation of characters, the description of places and objects, the development of the plot, the implied attitudes of the narrator, and many more elements. Many of these dimensions of my response are also relevant to the reading of poetry or plays (or the watching of a performance), together with others peculiar to the particular genre. And in experiencing these events, simultaneous processes occur as part of the reading. Among these are semantic interpretation, allowing the words to generate meanings; generic interpretation, creating expectations based on the kind of work it signals itself as; intertextual resonances, bringing other works into relation with this one; engagement with plot developments, producing overlapping sequences of tension and release; affective responses to reported feelings, utterances, and happenings; registration of historical or cultural difference, surprise or shock (or boredom) when the work does (or doesn't) move into unexpected terrain; evaluation of the artistic success or otherwise of the work; forays into new realms of knowledge; the testing of moral positions; and—when the work is successful—admiration for the achievement of the writer.

What would a literary criticism founded on such a notion of literary experience look like? (I am using the term *criticism* to include the kinds of literary research and scholarship whose purpose is to illuminate particular works or oeuvres, which I take to be the aim of most historical studies in the literary field; studies that are wholly concerned with the presentation of information for its own sake are not my concern here.) And, to return to my opening questions, how would it contribute to wider and fuller appreciation of literature, and thus to the individual and perhaps cultural and social changes of which literature is capable? Let me say at once that much of the most valuable critical writing of the past has, at least in part, depended on a scrupulous rendering of the critic's experience, whether of particular literary works or of literature more generally. And I must stress that in using the term *experience* I'm not relying on a notion of the reader as a pure subjectivity, but as a singular node within the cultural network at a given moment, or what I prefer to call an "idioculture."[35] The best literary analysis is produced by a reader who is, while engaging with the

[35] See Attridge, "Context, Idioculture, Invention," 682–83, for a concise account of this term.

work, channeling the rich resources of the culture of which he or she is a product.

The kind of critical commentary I have in mind resists the temptation to impress the reader with ingenious feats of interpretation or sallies of recondite scholarship, abstains from one-upmanship and points-scoring, and understands that what may be said about a literary work is never final. Its aim is to deepen and enhance the experience of other readers, an aim which will be fulfilled only if the critic is able to bring to the work a degree of expertise and an appropriate fund of knowledge. These qualities differ from critic to critic, which means that every critical account has something different to offer; critical styles are equally various, ranging from the poetic to the analytic. Such variety is a strength of the critical enterprise, and it would be impossible to set out the ingredients of a successful critical commentary, other than the very basic ones. Sensitivity to language and to literary form (at least in the genre in question) would seem to be a *sine qua non*, and one would expect any good reading to have at least a modicum of relevant historical knowledge and theoretical sophistication. In addition to these minimal requirements, an openness to the new, the surprising, the challenging, is important. Together with the responsiveness all of these qualities suggest, there is a kind of responsibility involved: responsibility not just *to* the work, but *for* the work (since strong commentary keeps works alive); and a responsibility to do justice to the work for the sake of the author, known or unknown, whose labor and creativity the work represents. There is also the matter of responsibility to the present: a critical reading is addressed to an audience *now*, and ought to reflect the needs and demands of the time. Evaluation is also a characteristic of good commentary, though this need not be explicit: the selection of a particular work implies a judgment, and an account of its working inevitably carries with it a sense of the work's singularity and inventiveness. And finally, the critical commentary itself, as a piece of writing, needs to be inventive and to bear the singular marks of its writer.

This may sound like a detailed prescription, but it's not; it allows for any number of different ways of doing criticism, depending on the critic's experience of the work, the style of criticism, and the assumed audience. It might take the form of a first-person account of that experience, but it might equally be impersonal and analytic. The account may concentrate on the work's sedimentation of history, on its use of formal properties, on its challenge to the political and moral norms of its time or of our time. It may be a reading designed to bring out a particular theoretical point. But by emphasizing experience, we emphasize that a full engagement with the work, intellectual and emotional and often somatic, is the foundation of any successful critical writing. This kind of reading, it should be added, is not as different from the kinds of reading that take place in non-academic settings as is the case with many of the approaches currently enshrined in academic literary studies.[36] Rather than symptomatic reading, affirmative reading; in place of critical distance, critical engagement; instead of the affective fallacy, the exploration of feelings.

An emphasis on the reader's experience allows form to be analyzed as something that *happens*, not as a static property of the text, and as an aspect that contributes to the arousal of emotion as much as to the perception of satisfying structures or the appreciation of verbal beauty. Readers don't seek homologies between rhyme-schemes and political structures or between plot arrangements and economic hierarchies. The question of form's connection to the world or to history becomes only a part of the question of the work's impact on the reader, since it is only through individual responses that any such connection is made. And if literature effects a certain kind of education, it's not through any truths, morals, or injunctions that readers carry away from their reading, but changes brought about—sometimes consciously, though more often unconsciously—by the remarkable experience of the literary work.

References

Anker, Elizabeth S., and Rita Felski, eds. *Critique and Postcritique*. Durham: Duke University Press, 2017.

Best, Stephen, and Sharon Marcus. "Surface Reading: An Introduction." *Representations* 108, no. 1 (2009): 1–21.

Bewes, Timothy. "Reading with the Grain: A New Word in Literary Criticism." *Differences* 21, no. 3 (2010): 1–33.

Armstrong, Isobel. *The Radical Aesthetic*. Oxford: Blackwell, 2000.

[36] "Suspicious reading," notes Eric Hayot, is "driven always to overmaster the text by locating it within a historical context that it itself could not have grasped or managed as such, a style of reading, it is worth noting, that also defined itself strongly in opposition to what one might think of as 'ordinary' or 'amateur' reading" ("Then and Now," 288). In his challenging essay "Uncritical Reading," Michael Warner suggests that the kinds of reading that happen outside academic contexts are too easily dismissed by academic critics and teachers.

Attridge, Derek. "Context, Idioculture, Invention." *New Literary History* 42, no. 4 (2011): 681–99.

———. *The Experience of Poetry: From Homer's Listeners to Shakespeare's Readers.* Oxford: Oxford University Press, 2019.

———. *The Singularity of Literature.* Abingdon: Routledge, 2017.

———. *The Work of Literature.* Oxford: Oxford University Press, 2015.

Attridge, Derek, and Henry Staten. *The Craft of Poetry: Dialogues on Minimal Interpretation.* Abingdon: Routledge, 2015.

Callahan, Sara. "Critique and Post-Critique in Contemporary Art History: Excessive Attachment to Suspicion in Academia and Beyond." *Arts and Humanities in Higher Education*, November 14, 2019. https://journals.sagepub.com/doi/abs/10.1177/1474022219885785.

Bolla, Peter de. *Art Matters.* Cambridge, MA: Harvard University Press, 2001.

Derrida, Jacques. "Psyche: The Invention of the Other." In *Acts of Literature*, edited by Derek Attridge, 310–43. New York: Routledge, 1992.

Dewey, John. *Art as Experience.* London: George Allen & Unwin, 1934.

During, Simon. *Against Democracy: Literary Experience in the Era of Emancipations.* New York: Fordham University Press, 2012.

Eliot, T. S. *The Poems: The Annotated Text.* Edited by Christopher Ricks and Jim McCue. London: Faber & Faber, 2015.

Eyers, Tom. *Speculative Formalism: Literature, Theory, and the Critical Present.* Evanston: Northwestern University Press, 2017.

Felski, Rita. *The Limits of Critique.* Chicago: University of Chicago Press, 2015.

———. *Uses of Literature.* Malden, MA: Blackwell, 2008.

Gutting, Gary. "Foucault's Philosophy of Experience." *boundary 2* 29, no. 2 (2002): 69–85.

Hardy, G. H. *A Mathematician's Apology.* Edmonton: University of Alberta Mathematical Society, 1940.

Hayot, Eric. "Then and Now." In Anker and Felski, eds., *Critique and Postcritique*, 279–95.

Jay, Martin. *Cultural Semantics: Keywords of Our Time.* Amherst: University of Massachusetts Press, 1998.

Johnson, Barbara. *A World of Difference.* Baltimore: Johns Hopkins University Press, 1987.

Latour, Bruno. "Why Has Critique Run Out of Steam? From Matters of Fact to Matters of Concern." *Critical Inquiry* 30, no. 2 (2004): 225–48.

Levine, Caroline. *Forms: Whole, Rhythm, Hierarchy, Network.* Princeton: Princeton University Press, 2015.

Levinson, Marjorie. "What Is New Formalism?" *PMLA* 122, no. 2 (March 2007): 558–69.

Loesberg, Jonathan. *A Return to Aesthetics: Autonomy, Indifference, and Postmodernism.* Stanford: Stanford University Press, 2005.

Love, Heather. "Close Reading and Thin Description." *Public Culture* 25, no. 3 (2013): 401–34.

Marcus, Sharon. *Between Women: Friendship, Desire, and Marriage in Victorian England*. Princeton: Princeton University Press, 2007.

Matthews, Pamela R., and David McWhirter, eds. *Aesthetic Subjects*. Minneapolis: University of Minnesota Press, 2003.

Moi, Toril. "'Nothing Is Hidden': From Confusionm to Clarity; or, Wittgenstein on Critique." In Anker and Felski, eds., *Critique and Postcritique*, 31–49.

North, Joseph. *Literary Criticism: A Political History*. Cambridge: Harvard University Press, 2017.

Rosenblatt, Louise. *The Reader, the Text, the Poem: The Transactional Theory of the Literary Work*. Carbondale: Southern Illinois University Press, 1978.

Sedgwick, Eve Kosofsky. "Paranoid Reading and Reparative Reading, or, You're So Paranoid, You Probably Think This Introduction Is About You." In *Novel Gazing: Queer Readings in Fiction*, edited by Eve Kosofsky Sedgwick, 1–37. Durham: Duke University Press, 1997.

———. *Touching Feeling: Affect, Pedagogy, Performativity*. Durham: Duke University Press, 2003.

Szafraniec, Asja. *Beckett, Derrida, and the Event of Literature*. Stanford University Press, 2007.

Warner, Michael. "Uncritical Reading." In *Polemic: Critical or Uncritical*, edited by Jane Gallop, 13–37. New York: Routledge, 2004.

Wolfson, Susan J., and Marshall Brown, eds. "Reading for Form." Special issue, *Modern Language Quarterly* 61, no. 1 (2000).

———. *Reading for Form*. Seattle: University of Washington Press, 2006.

Criticism Today

CHAPTER 2

Is the Author Still Dead?

Henry Staten

1 Part One

The evidence of critical pragmatics yields two apparently contradictory principles of poetry criticism.

The first principle is that readings must respect the words on the page, maintaining a sharp boundary between what is in the poem and what is "extrinsic" to it. Without such a restriction, the poem loses its identity as just this poem, this group of words organized as a unified—or, as we might more modestly say, coherent—whole.

Yet, as everyone today is acutely aware, the boundary between the inside and the outside of a poem, the boundary that would define a putative "text itself" or "poem itself" that might possess the quality of coherence is impossible to define in a rigorous, non-metaphysical way. Thus, the second principle is that the boundary between what is *inside* and what is *outside* a poem—*if there is one at all*—is indeterminate and indeterminable, in constant flux, subject to complex, evolving negotiations among readers. The second principle renders the first principle problematic (to say the least); and yet, to give up the idea of a text itself,

H. Staten (✉)
University of Washington, Seattle, WA, USA
e-mail: hstaten@uw.edu

A. Sridhar et al. (eds.), *The Work of Reading*,
https://doi.org/10.1007/978-3-030-71139-9_2

one with determinate boundaries of some sort, would leave us in a situation in which "anything goes"—or at least, one in which we have no principled way to deny that anything goes.

Perhaps we can reconcile these two principles by conceiving the boundary between inside- and outside-the-text as indefinitely elastic—stretchable, perhaps quite far, yet not without limit. This would give us a sense of boundary, while allowing for a continuing process of negotiation about what counts as "inside." But how could we translate such a notion into guidelines for criticism? It's hard to see on what, besides the idea of a text itself, the notion of a boundary to interpretation—be it ever so elastic—can be grounded; but many critics since the late 1970s have rejected this as a naïve notion. The 1970s saw the rise of a vague, sociologically inflected quasi-Kantianism, according to which the objects of interpretation are not simply given to perception, as in empiricism, or even, as in Kant, shaped by transcendental forms of rational mind, but "constructed" according to predetermined interpretive grids that are *culturally determined*. Commentators like Stanley Fish established the idea that texts don't have "inherent" qualities that constrain interpretation, but are ascribed them by "interpretive communities" each of which sees the text its own way. This kind of thinking was thrown together with a poorly understood deconstructionism and then blended with the identity-politics approach to form the dominant critical ideology, one that categorically rejects the notion of the poem itself.

The New Critics, and in particular Cleanth Brooks, must bear much of the blame for this rejection because of the way they defined poems as *unified objects*. Taking his cue from John Donne on one side and Coleridge on the other, Brooks mixed literary criticism with certain supernaturalist notions, arguing that the poem-making imagination is a "magic power" that unifies the conflicts and contradictions of human experience in a way comparable to that by which "the soul is unified with God."[1] Nothing could have been more effectively formulated to make critics in the 1970s and 1980s run the other way, especially under the influence of doctrines of the "death of the author" that I will consider in the second part of this essay. These critics learned, on the one hand, to revel in fragmentation, internal fissures, and non-unity in literary texts, and, on the

[1] Brooks, *Well-Wrought Urn*, 18–19.

other hand, they learned to dissolve the boundaries of the text into whatever sort of historical or sociological context their particular interpretive method favored.

Strangely ignored in all these debates is the obvious reason a poem should be treated as a whole: not because it's magically unified, or because it's a natural object with inherent or intrinsic qualities, but because it's an *artifact*, something made by one or more human beings by means of a culturally evolved know-how, an art or *techne*, and who was trying, as artificers of all kinds do, to make a complete, optimally functioning artifact, like a whole chair or a whole basketball game. To treat poems as artisanal wholes is to remain within the rules of social constructionism, in the most basic way. After all, before a poem can be constructed by an interpretive community, it must have been constructed, also according to culturally determined conventions, by a poet. Even if we think of this original construction as essentially a product of historical influences, if the result is to be recognized as a *poem* those influences must exert their constructive force through the funnel of poetic conventions.

But somehow the applicability of the notion of social construction to poem-making was never noticed. Even stranger is the fact that the notion of *close reading*, which is, strictly speaking, meaningless in the absence of a *text itself*, survived the demise of the text itself, no longer as a genuine term of art but as an abstract honorific, an ill-defined title to which every self-respecting literary critic lays claim. I've never met a contextualist who did not take pride in being an accomplished "close reader," even though for new-fangled contextualism there is no formal boundary defining the arena of readerly attention, and therefore no "text itself"; the inside of the poem, on this conception, is the direct, or only modestly mediated, product of the psychological or sociohistorical outside. But what is close reading without a *poem itself*, considered as a coherent whole? Close reading didn't mean "careful" or "skillful" reading; it meant precisely the kind of reading that aimed at "the words on the page," "these words in this order," and tried to keep context on the periphery of the reading. One can read any kind of text, including context, very attentively, and one can be very sharp in revealing how the sociohistorical outside permeates the inside of the literary text—but what, in the absence of a poem itself, qualifies this kind of thing as *close reading*, in the technical literary-critical sense of the term?

No doubt the term needs updating; very few of us today believe in the poem as verbal icon. But any redefinition that wouldn't make close reading an empty notion, one that just means "very attentive reading," needs to posit a boundary of some sort between the poem's inside and outside.

Brooks didn't only contribute to the current critical disarray by his notions of unity; a more active factor was his particular *method* of close reading, the insidious potential of which was perceived, and decried, by John Crowe Ransom already in 1947, the year *The Well-Wrought Urn* was published. Ransom worried that the "centrifugal energy" discovered in individual words or phrases of poems by the "new critics" (the name that Ransom himself had bestowed on them) created a "spread of meaning" that could meander "away from that of the poem as a whole." "And the critic goes straight from one detail to another, in the manner of the bee who gathers honey from the several blossoms as he comes to them, without noticing the bush that supports the whole."[2] Ransom stressed the importance of what he called "logical structure" in poems, as against Brooks's focus on the "ironic" or "paradoxical" "texture" of the poem's imagery. Logical structure, on Ransom's account, is what primarily holds the thought of an entire poem together—the basis of whatever "unity" it might have; whereas Brooks's practice of looking for a poem's unity in its texture of imagery opened the way to the interpretation of isolated images and metaphors as a primary focus.[3]

To be fair, Brooks himself didn't just read isolated words or images; he looked for "chains of imagery" that come together in a "total pattern" constituted by "the poem as a whole"; but for readers who, unlike Brooks, had not already been trained into the sense of the whole poem, Brooks's readings yielded too fuzzy a sense of structure to resist the centrifugal energy that Ransom detected in his brand of interpretation.[4] No doubt one of the main reasons in the ensuing breakdown of close reading had to do with the remarkable adaptability of blossom-visiting to poetry pedagogy, where it spread like wildfire in the 1970s because it's so easily teachable to undergrads. One need only take a word, an image,

[2] Ransom, "Poetry," 36.

[3] Ransom did not mean by "logical structure" the kind of logical structure that Brooks rejected in "The Heresy of Paraphrase." Brooks used the term casually to refer to the purported "content" of a poem that could be paraphrased in a logical proposition; but Ransom meant the whole evolving thought, with its logical connections, that led from beginning to end of a poem.

[4] Brooks, *The Well-Wrought Urn*, 28, 194.

a metaphor, a stylistic feature, anything notable in a poem, and free associate with it, bringing to light all the things it brings to our minds by however loose a connection. In the classroom, this results in spontaneous, freewheeling discussion; everybody wants in on this entertaining game that doesn't require too much thinking, either from student or teacher. I know how much fun this game is because that's how I too started out teaching poetry.[5]

It's true that the influential recent critics who have blurred the notion of close reading have not practiced *pure* free association; rather, they have channeled their free associations, and taught their acolytes to channel theirs, in specific and highly structured directions. One could, for example, train one's imagination to free associate about history from a vaguely Left standpoint, as Jerome McGann did in his influential reading of Tennyson's "Charge of the Light Brigade"; or one could train it to hear traditional philosophical struggles with intelligibility and sensibility, as Paul de Man did in his pseudo-deconstructive reading of Hugo's "Written on a Flemish window-pane."[6] In these readings McGann and de Man exemplified a practice carried on by many other critics of diverse stripes: grabbing hold of those isolated features of a poem they could most readily yoke to their particular styles of free association, and then changing the topic from the poem we thought they were discussing to the topography of the new conceptual landscape into which they led us. This looks to the unwary reader like *extremely* close reading, carrying what was once described as the "lemon squeezer school of criticism" to new extremes; yet this meaning is produced with little or no regard for the architecture of the whole linguistic artifact under consideration. Thus McGann hangs a panoramic tour of post-Napoleonic European history and of the iconography of French painting of the period, from the thin thread of the single image, "flashed all their sabers bare." And de Man, with his incomparable chutzpah, does him one better, producing a murky disquisition on time and the mind (mired in the Cartesian worries over "the certainty of sense perception" that de Man, despite his purported rebirth as a Derridean,

[5] Centrifugal reading received another major boost from Stephen Booth's great commentary on Shakespeare's sonnets; an interesting case, because Booth actually stressed both logical structure and imagistic texture, and *the former's priority of structure over texture*. But it was texture, predictably, that caught on.

[6] McGann, *Beauty of Inflections*, 193–201; de Man, *Resistance to Theory*, 47–49. I have criticized McGann's reading in close detail in Staten, "How Not to Historicize."

never outgrew) out of a single phrase *that doesn't even occur in the poem.* He declares *ex cathedra* that Hugo's "l'esprit [...] Entende [...] son pied sonore" means "l'esprit entend le temps," and squeezes this lemon of his own invention for all it's worth, yielding a philosophically obscure meditation on perception and intellection that leaves very little of the poem still breathing.

In these readings neither McGann nor de Man tries to justify, or even notes, the fact that they're ignoring the poem as a whole, but Stephen Greenblatt made reading isolated bits of work into a principle of the "New Historicism" in his remarks on Queen Elizabeth's reaction to a performance of *Richard II*.[7] Elizabeth got upset about the representation in the play of regicide, without noticing that the play as a whole treated regicide as a bad thing, and the historicizing critic, according to Greenblatt, should focus on how the play was historically received, not on what a critic today, studying how the regicide fits into the overall architecture of the play, can see it as. This is sound doctrine for the critic who is not concerned with literary works as, loosely speaking, "stand-alone" objects but with their historical entanglements; from a formalist standpoint, however, Greenblatt's maneuver accords primacy to the understandings of untrained and careless readers like Elizabeth, who are given the authority to set the critic's interpretive agenda. How could students trained *exclusively* in such an agenda ever begin to value, or even have any practical notion of what a "poem itself" might be, considered as an artisanal whole?[8]

Once close reading evolved to the point that it set the critical imagination free from the discipline of the whole poem, the idea spread that there was no limit to interpretation. Individual critics might think their own

[7] See Greenblatt, "Introduction."

[8] At this point it's necessary to re-state an obvious point that is continually ignored by critics of formalism: that no formalist critic has ever treated a text as, in Greenblatt's words, "an iconic object whose meaning is perfectly contained within its own formal structure" (Greenblatt, "Introduction," 4). Not even Wimsatt, who popularized the notion of the verbal icon, read poems this way; yet this characterization of formalism is practically universal. In fact, such a treatment is impossible in principle. Even a glance at Brooks's readings shows that he is constantly bringing in various kinds of contextual knowledge (such as the sexual meaning of "die" in the Renaissance). Of course, Brooks was not a rigorous formalist, but even the Russian Formalists, who were very rigorous indeed, according to Boris Eichenbaum, quickly realized that individual works had to be treated in light of the history of works from which they follow.

readings were uniquely compelling, as McGann and de Man no doubt did; and if one was an acolyte of such work, one shared this conviction; but for the larger academic public that consumed an endless series of new readings, these were just two more of a limitless number of lenses through which poems could be viewed, each one of them producing a different poem from the same text, each lens equally optional, equally arbitrary, and equally valid.

The idea flourished that *the production of imaginative new interpretations*, as many as possible, was the main purpose of literary criticism, and the new interpretations that were most valued, sometimes the *only* ones valued, were those that least resembled the poem we thought we had read, and which undermined or subverted or deconstructed whatever we had previously thought about it.

That's why Fish could make such a splash in 1980 with the arguments of "How to Recognize a Poem When You See One." In this piece he reported a human experiment he had performed, in which he presented to a class of unsuspecting students as a religious poem what was in fact a list of names, left over from a preceding class, that Fish had found on the blackboard; at which they unprotestingly proceeded to brainstorm a whole plethora of poetico-religious meanings that could be attributed to this list. Nobody asked, "What kind of religious poem is it? Is it Jewish, Catholic, Protestant, Cathar? When was it written? What school of poetry does it belong to, or is it influenced by?" Or, most important, "Is this really a poem *at all?*" Fish's students knew how to *close read*, so they didn't need any such information. They weren't bothered by the lack of any recognizable conventional form to the poem, or even of any kind of visible connection among its parts. They were so accustomed to taking isolated bits of a poem and then brainstorming the connections among them that they saw these absences simply as challenges to their critical ingenuity—critical ingenuity, after all, being what it's all about.

What we should learn from Fish's experiment is not, however, as he triumphantly claimed, that interpretive communities make poems, but that he was having his fun with a pathetically naïve audience, one that had been trained in the new style of "close reading," the style that soars free of most of the constraints on interpretation that give sense to the idea of close reading.

2 Part Two

The deracination of close reading dovetailed nicely with the French assault on the author. As everyone knows, the two most influential blasts of this assault were Foucault's "What is an Author?"[9] and Barthes's "The Death of the Author," both written in the late 1960s, but the influence of which crested in the United States in the 80s. These dazzling, very muddled essays completed the demolition of the text itself that had begun with the internal decay of the New Criticism.

Foucault's overarching claim is concisely stated in his final paragraphs: "the subject (and its substitutes) must be stripped of its creative role and analyzed as a complex and variable function of discourse" (Bouchard, 138). His main target throughout is the old-fashioned criticism that posits a psycho-biographical individual, a "genius," as the text's origin, but he additionally criticizes previous expositors of the "death of the author," claiming that they have not been radical enough. Among these failed attempts is formalism, which pretends to address only the *internal* architecture of literary works yet keeps covertly alive the fantasy of the *author as origin*. Formalists "evade [*esquiver*]" that which "ought to have been elucidated [*dégager*]"—the "privilege" that criticism has accorded the figure of the author.

There's no reason in principle why his claim about formalism couldn't be right. But in place of a forthright demonstration of this claim, Foucault wraps his argument in vagueness and equivocation, centering on two crucial concepts, "author-function" and "work." "Author-function" primarily refers to the psychological individual that critics' imaginations project as absolute creative origin of the text, but takes a mysterious turn

[9] There are two versions of "What is an Author?": (a) the original 1969 version, published in the *Bulletin de la Société Fraincaise de philosophie* and subsequently in *Littoral*, no. 9 (1983): 3–23 (cited in text parenthetically as *Littoral*; available online at http://www.epel-edition.com/fichiers/telecharger/Littoral9.pdf) and (b) a 1970 version delivered at SUNY Buffalo (available online at http://1libertaire.free.fr/MFoucault319.html). There are significant differences between the two versions at the beginning and the end. The 1970 version omits the opening paragraphs of the 1969 address, and its final paragraphs have been substantially revised. I have not noticed any differences in the body of the argument. I cite the translation of the 1969 text by Donald F. Bouchard and Sherry Simon (cited in text parenthetically as Bouchard), and that of the 1970 text by Josué Harari (cited in text parenthetically as Harari). When neither Bouchard nor Harari is cited, translations are mine.

in Foucault's discussion of the use of "shifters" (often called "indexicals" in English) in certain works. There are certain special signs that the text "porte toujours en lui-meme [always bears within itself]," and which make texts more than mere "passive material" out of which the critic reconstructs the author function. These signs, called "shifters"—words like *I*, *here*, and *now*—"renvoyer a l'auteur [return us, send us back to, the author]" (*Littoral*, 16).

What are we to make, in the context of Foucault's whole argument, of the idea of a text *in itself* that can actively direct the critic's gaze outwards, toward the author? Neither of the standard translations of this essay has reproduced Foucault's phrase "texte [...] en lui-meme," thus occluding this logical dark spot for the English-only reader. Is Foucault admitting that one "function of discourse" is, precisely, to refer us to the author? But isn't this what psycho-biographical critics have always believed? More importantly, why would only shifters, of all a text's discursive properties, have such referential power, and why would such power be particularly linked to the author, that figure that Foucault had apparently promised to finally disappear for real?

Rather than addressing these questions, Foucault begins ambiguously to elide the author to whom shifters point. In novels with a first-person narrator shifters don't refer us *directly* to the actual writer, rather to an alter ego; but this other "I" might be closer or farther from the author ("un alter ego dont la distance à l'écrivain peut être plus ou moins grande"). In this remark the author function is ambiguously distinguished from the metaphysico-biographical figure who up to this point Foucault has fingered as the "author" in "author-function." The author function in such a narration, "is performed in the scission—in the division and distance" between the writer and the narrator. But if the scission is *very* small, then this alter ego is actually just our old friend the author/writer, and if it's *very large*, if the narrator is almost entirely a textual construct, then the formal markers point the critic to a feature of that "internal architecture" that Foucault says formalists can't analyze without covert reliance on the author function. Isn't the space of Foucault's scission, then, merely the familiar one between the author of Romantic-psychological-biographical criticism and that of the formalist's impersonal scriptor?

The distinction between narrator and author is, as Foucault recognizes, already in 1969 well-known. But, rather than adding new specification to this already-familiar notion, Foucault leaves his own implied author in the titillating obscurity of a metaphorically evoked "function" that is "performed" in a "scission," within which it rattles around between narrator and writer.

In the logic, such as it is, of Foucault's argument, this newly defined author function looks like an intermediate formation, one that has one leg in the old definition, the author as biographical absolute origin (let's call it *AF1*), and another leg in the new, strictly formal one (*AF2*) toward which the notion of the active text-in-itself might be thought to point. Let's call this intermediate formation *AF1α*: an author function that is not identical with the writer, yet is ambiguously still tethered to her.

This ambiguity persists into the following analysis of the "I" in a mathematical treatise, in which he finds three distinct "I"s pointing to three different "authors." At first sight it appears the author function here is purely the activity of the intra-textual shifters, thus *AF2*, a "complex and variable function of discourse" that takes the place of the subject. The first "I," however, points to "the empirical circumstances of composition" of the treatise, a slippery formulation that seems to refer us to the empirical author, but also suggests an empirical site with a void in the place of the author. Thus Foucault might, or might not, be popping the term "author-function" entirely free of the variable relation to the writer that was (ambiguously) still ballasting *AF1α*, and therefore entirely free of *AF1* (the author function that is his main target, and the only one that he ever defines as such).

In favor of the idea that he is here proposing a radically new, purely textual or formal, author function is the fact that, according to "What is an Author?" the primary methodological function of the critic's fantasized *AF1* is to serve as the principle of textual unity, and the author function that Foucault now identifies operates "so as to effect the simultaneous dispersion of [...] the three egos" (Bouchard, 130) in the mathematical text, and therefore the unity of the text. Apparently because unities are bad and pluralities good, Foucault does not notice that all his breakdown accomplishes is to define *three new well-defined formal unities*, corresponding to the three distinctly configured textual I's. That the boundaries of these unities do not coincide with those of the text as a whole adds nuance to the formalist analysis that Foucault here performs, but does not undermine the principle of formal coherence that underlies the question of textual unity. Thus, rather than extending the meaning of "author-function," this analysis suggests that author function as originally defined (*AF1*) can, indeed, be dispensed with by a rigorous formalism.

Whether Foucault is claiming that it's only in a non-fictional text that this is possible is something we are left to wonder about.

And there is an even more glaring, and more serious, problem with Foucault's critique of formalism, having to do with the concept of work. Formalist critics think that they can dispense with *AF1*, Foucault claims, because they simply project into the work itself the principle of unity that since Jerome has been located in the unity of an authorial self, whereas truly dispensing with the author means you can no longer identify a text or work as a bounded unity. "If some have found it convenient to bypass the individuality of the writer or his status as an author to concentrate on a work," he writes, "they have failed to appreciate the equally problematic nature of the word 'work' and the unity it designates" (Bouchard, 119). Formalism when it attempts to analyze only the "intrinsic and internal relationships" of the text presupposes this "strange unit" called a *work* within which these relationships are to be discerned, but which Foucault implies cannot be conceived as anything other than "something written by a person called an 'author'" (Bouchard, 118)—an author in the sense that, except for one section of the essay, where *AF1a* and *AF2* mysteriously emerge, Foucault defines as a *psychological individual*.

The explanation for why the concept of a work depends on that of the author emerges in the discussion of the name-of-the-author, which, Foucault claims, for the critic "is always present, marking off the edges of the text" (Harari, 147); "remains at the contours of texts—separating one from the other, defining their form" (Bouchard, 123).[10] A *work*, to be identified as that selfsame, unified entity that it is, requires the boundary of definition that only reference to the author, via the author's name, can provide. And if without the author function as *AF1* there is no such bounded entity as work or text, it seems we would be left with an unbounded flow of authorless discourse, the "anonymous murmur" that Foucault envisions at the end of this essay.

In itself this might sound like a plausible argument, but, in order to get it off the ground, Foucault has to define "work" in a startlingly tendentious way. He simply ignores works in the ordinary sense, things like poems and novels, in favor of the most marginal and problematic uses of the term "work" he can think of, uses related not to criticism but to

[10] In original: "court, en quelque sort, a la limite des textes, qu'il les decoupe, qu'il en suit les arretes" (*Littoral*, 12).

editing, and dealing not with individual bounded forms but with *collections* of such forms. To make his argument, he exploits the ambiguity in our use of the terms "work" and "oeuvre" to name both individual works and collections, asking, for example, whether the *Thousand and One Nights*, largely a compilation of tales from diverse sources and centuries, is a work, or whether the compiler of collected works of Nietzsche should consider Nietzsche's laundry bill a work. *Nietzsche's laundry bill*? His later discussion of Jerome's canons of interpretation likewise concerns editorial problems around disputed authorship of texts.

Obviously "work" and the "unit it designates" are problematic in such usages; Foucault has begged the entire question by using the term in the sense of a *collection* of works. But what if we went to the other extreme of the textual spectrum and considered something more properly called a work, like a sonnet or villanelle? Do we need to presuppose a biographical person as origin of a poem in order to "mark out its edges" as a sonnet, and to analyze it as such? We might interpret a sonnet very differently if we attribute it to one author or another, but we won't have any problem with its formal identity as a sonnet, and anyone familiar with the historical evolution of the sonnet form will find plenty of critical problems to explore that do not depend on knowledge of the author.[11]

All of this smoke-blowing of Foucault's matters because it dissimulates the question of the real-world origin of texts, of how, before they get to editors and critics, they get put down on paper in a way that matters sufficiently to others that they are willing to take so much trouble over them. This, and not how texts subsequently get managed—the question that Foucault wants explored—is the question of the author in which most of us are interested.[12] At some point, a text has been physically inscribed by an individual human body, or a group of such bodies, *for the first time*, or across an accumulating collection of such first times, and only afterwards do the questions of its circulation in which Foucault is primarily interested—and to which he made such indisputably important contributions—arise. He speaks as though the question of authorship, to the degree that "author" points to a worldly origin of well-formed texts, is

[11] See, for example, Booth, *Essay on Shakespeare's Sonnets*.

[12] Interestingly, in the 1969 version Foucault listed "Where does [the text] come from?" among the "new questions" he was proposing (Bouchard, 138); but in the 1970 revision this question is replaced by "How can it be used?" (Harari, 160).

bogus in its entirety.[13] To the degree that he is decrying the fetishization of authorship in modernity, or saying that we don't need to attach names to texts, one might agree with him; but his claim is far larger. He has argued that once we remove the author's name from the text, *we can no longer identify the text itself as a form with demarcated edges*. Yet three such forms are what he himself claims to detect in his reading of the intra-textual "I" in the mathematical treatise.

Strangely, what Foucault ignores in ignoring conventionally defined literary forms is the *historicity* that is deposited in them—an element of formal demarcation of edges that is independent of the form-imposing power of individual consciousness. It is assuredly not the case, as Foucault leads us to believe, that behind the positing of bounded textual wholes there must be the extra-textual author function (*AF1*), the fantasized figure of a bourgeois individual who created the text out of his boundless creativity, and which is now his legal property—that in its absence "all discourses [...] would develop in the anonymity of a murmur" (Harari, 160). Anonymity, perhaps, but definitely not that of a formless *murmure*. The poststructuralist polemic gave away too much to the "humanism" it criticized; in its rush to radicality it granted too readily what a certain form of humanism implies, that there can only be literary *form* where there is an author, with "author" conceived in the flatfooted, psychologistic, romanticized way that Foucault makes his main target. But it's a gross error to think that articulateness, the power to mark out the small and large edges of discourses, can only be conceived as the property of an individual author. Anonymous humanity does not produce an endless sausage of discourse that no one cuts into links; insofar as any individual or group of individuals or generations of individuals in any culture is capable of creating a coherent text or utterance of whatever sort, this capacity is a product of what today is known as *distributed agency*, a form-endowing agency that is, as such, anonymous, yet responsible for all the

[13] He apparently had doubts on this in 1970, when he replaced this sentence in the 1969 version, "We can easily imagine a culture where discourse would circulate without any need for an author" (Bouchard, 138), with a denial that he is calling for "a form of culture in which fiction would not be limited by the figure of the author." It would be "pure romanticism," he now says, to think that fiction could operate "in an absolutely pure state," without need of a "constraining figure" of some sort (Harari, 159). In his usual way, however, he remains vague regarding what sort of figure this would be, or even what sort of constraint he has in mind.

form-making of which humanity is capable.[14] The agency of the bourgeois writer equally with that of the collective agency that evolved folk tales like those collected in the *Thousand and One Nights* derives from the evolution of literary forms across innumerable generations, an action whose accumulated residue of effectivity is structured, and transmitted to new generations, in the form of the diversity of poetic *technai*—those that produce the morphology of the folk tale, or that of the sonnet—and which entail the predominance of what Lukács calls "social being" in the writer's or storyteller's labor process.[15]

Barthes's argument in "The Death of the Author" is similarly vitiated by his disregard of techne. He posits that "the modern scriptor is born at the same time as his text; he is not furnished with a being which precedes or exceeds his writing [...] there is no time other than that of the speech act, and every text is written eternally here and now."[16] The scriptor, the one who performs the physical act of inscribing words, is on this account the effect of that act, which is subjectless, something that surges spontaneously into being in the pure immediacy of each transient now (a vaguely Nietzschean account). The writer's hand, Barthes continues, "borne by a pure gesture of inscription [...] traces a field without origin"; but he apparently realizes that he has gotten a bit too rapturous, because he quickly adds, "or which at least, has no other origin than language itself."[17] What he means by language is, however, obscure. He has earlier said that "it is language which speaks, not the author,"[18] and then that language is "system,"[19] suggesting that it's language qua system that is the productive agent; but now he says a text is a "tissue of quotations" and the writer's only power the power to "mix writings" borrowed from elsewhere.[20] The notion of pre-existent writings is quite different from that of language as system, so if language itself is still speaking, it must be in the sense of language that has been formed by previous writers, not

[14] I have attempted to treat art-making in terms of distributed agency in Staten, *Techne Theory*.

[15] Lukács. *Ontology of Social Being*, 38–39.

[16] Barthes, "Death of the Author," 145.

[17] Barthes, 146.

[18] Barthes, 143.

[19] Barthes, 144.

[20] Barthes, 144.

in its sense as a pre-discursive combinatorial system, and in that case, this would be the place to mention the techne by means of which these writings have been formed, and which is embodied in them, and which the writer is learning by means of imitation. Imitation, of course, is how all educated people in Western culture learned the various *technai* of writing right up to the twentieth century, so here Barthes is on the edge of something very traditional indeed. But he then goes in the opposite direction; he says that writing is drawn from an "immense dictionary," the dictionary being the new "inner thing" in the soul of the writer that has taken the place of the passions and feelings that writers once expressed, or believed they expressed.[21] A dictionary, of course, is a list of isolated words, thus neither a language-system nor pre-existing writing. So it isn't clear at all what Barthes is saying. Unfortunately, the one notion his scattergun misses is the crucial one, the notion of the techne that shapes the words and the system of language into the writings that a scriptor can then mix and mingle using her own techne, itself formed under the influence of the pre-existing *technai*.

Despite its obscurity, however, Barthes's discussion does address the possible paths toward a rigorously impersonal conception of the author function. Barthes the literary critic recognizes, as Foucault the historian does not, that a text must be *made* by someone, and struggles with the question of how to neutralize the personal element in the making instance. The notion that a scriptor can only mix pre-existing writings comes close to identifying the nature of the agency involved. Techne, however, is something other than the pre-existing writings that it has made possible. The artist produces work, neither as spirit-that-imposes-form nor as a mere mixer and mingler of pre-existing writings, but as the skilled operator of an intentionality that originates elsewhere, in no punctual locale, an intentionality embodied in a techne of linguistic form-giving that is the historical precipitate of many previous acts of making of the same or related type, and which has the power to bring forth new texts because it encodes in its methods and devices the cunning of innumerable, immemorable previous acts of text-production by earlier practitioners who put this techne in its earlier forms into play—acts by which the techne was modified and revised in a historical dialectic of which the techne in its present form is the inheritor. Mere language, whether as lexicon,

[21] Barthes, 147.

system, or text, considered apart from the *technai* that are instantiated in the corpus of existing texts, and also in the skills possessed by those who have studied these *technai*, can generate only a subset of Borges's "library of Babel," the infinite set of all possible texts written in grammatical sentences, only a vanishingly small number of which would have any claim to be poems. Only language that has been yoked to a specific, historically evolved techne of poetry at a specific site of worldly production, always in essence collective, can produce poetry.

3 Part Three

The first step in understanding the kind of object a poem is, is to understand the poetry-making art that regulated its making. In common with practically every other art, craft, and social practice, the techne of poetry making—poetics in the original sense of the term—aims to produce an artifact or action that is a whole, with all its component parts in place. The vast majority of poems, like an immensity of other culturally constituted objects, rituals, speech acts, and actions (weddings, baseball games, jokes), are made to be whole and complete, with a beginning, middle, and end. Correspondingly, a rigorously conceived practice of reading poems would aim at reading the whole poem, not just parts of it. This would be true even of a poem that was intentionally made *not* to be a whole. We wouldn't be able to perceive its lack of completeness unless we read the whole thing. And, since the project of writing a poem that didn't adhere to the traditional protocol of wholeness would itself be conceived in a dialectical relation with that protocol, even if we read the whole (unwhole) thing we wouldn't be able to assess it as the kind of poem that it is if we as readers weren't ourselves familiar with that protocol.

The kind of whole in question, when optimally constructed, is made of parts that work smoothly together, or at least reasonably smoothly; or, if constructed to be jarring and dissonant in their interaction, then the parts must be optimally constructed according to some plan of dissonance that is decipherable by the reader. Otherwise, as J. L. Austin says of the speech act that misfires, it will be "infelicitous." Or, more plainly, it won't be a good poem. This functional conception of the unified whole was already set down by Aristotle in the *Poetics*. Aristotelian unity is not a product of magic, and isn't "organic" in the Romantic sense either, although it is organic in the original Greek sense of the term. *Organon* originally meant "tool" or "instrument," something useful for doing or making, and was only subsequently applied to living organs, which are themselves "organic" not because they participate in the mysterious life-essence that holds a living being in life but because of the interdependent functionality of their parts. This kind of organic unity is better conceived by analogy with a machine than with a living thing. Living things are just as much functional wholes as machines are, but living things can't be taken apart and put back together without loss, whereas poems can. In fact, like machines, they might well function *better* for the reader who has taken them apart and put them back together.

We should retire the concept of organic unity because of its misleading connotations, but there's no reason we shouldn't speak, more clearly and to the point, of *functional* unity. In a functional unity, such as a machine or a living organism, the parts are all adapted to function together because they have historically evolved together, and the functionality of the whole might well be impaired (depending on the individual case) if the functionality of one or more of the parts is impaired.

The formal dimension of a work of whatever kind, its functional unity, is not a product of the form-imposing power of individual consciousness but of sedimentation of earlier, often very partial and obscure, even accidental, acts of form-discovery and form-production that slowly evolve the cunning of any techne. To consider the *Iliad*, which was evidently created by such an evolutionary process, in relation to the problematic of authorship leads to conclusions very far from those Foucault draws on the basis of patristic commentary; nowhere is it clearer how little the author need matter to our sense of the form and identity of the text. Homer is the exemplary case of the name-of-the-author as pure textual function, pure back-formation from the text, the residue of pure anonymous historicity. Critics and editors read the *Iliad* on the basis of canons of consistency, coherence, unity, and so forth; but in the absence of any knowledge whatever of the living human being who put the *Iliad* together in its final form (*if* it was an individual human being, which is far from certain), these canons can only be determined in a purely formal way. As the great Hellenist Gregory Nagy says,

> the genius behind our *Iliad*'s artistic unity is in large part the Greek epic tradition itself. In order to accept this proposition, we may have to force ourselves to imagine the immensely creative process of this tradition, with all the many centuries of what must have been the most refined sort of

> elite performer/audience interaction that went into the evolution of the *Iliad* and the *Odyssey* as we know them.[22]

It's very curious that the question of Homer never rose to prominence in all the ballyhoo over the death of the author.

When one starts to think of aesthetic forms in these terms, one might even begin to wonder whether, rather than projecting unity on texts based on our notions of what a unified authorial intention is like, we project a unified authorial intention, and perhaps, in everyday life, also the unity of personal identity, on the basis of our experiences of well-formed stories and poems, originally anonymous forms like folktales and the *Iliad*. The notion that has increasingly taken hold in contemporary philosophy of mind, that personhood is essentially a narrative that we tell ourselves, would support such a notion.

However that may be, it's clear that the idea of coherent, well-formed texts does not depend on the projection of an individual authorial mind that would be the source of the text's form; certainly, neither Foucault nor Barthes has given us any reason to think that it does. And if it is still viable, it follows that criticism could, and in my view should, consistently submit itself to the discipline of the *whole* text, which we might judge to be much or little "unified" on a case by case basis, always subject to the test of functionality. Criticism that makes itself responsible to the whole stands on a larger expanse of textual ground than the kind that considers only snatches of the text. We might say that it has more interpretive "mass" in proportion as it responds to more of the interpreted text. Thus, it has, in a sense, more inertia of rest, and isn't as easy to push around, to counter with another of the limitless interpretations that critical cherry-picking makes so easy, even automatic, to generate. Because this principle of inertia makes it less easy to sprout new interpretations, it provides the beginning, at least, of an answer to the question we began with, of how the elasticity of the boundary between the poem's inside and outside finds a limit. The discipline of the whole would make the interpreter work harder and longer on the target text, and, among other things, restore some sense to the currently meaningless notion of close reading.

[22] Nagy, *Best of the Achaeans*, 79. This book is, by the way, the most impressive work of literary scholarship I have ever read.

References

Barthes, Roland. "The Death of the Author." In *Image, Music, Text*, edited and translated by Stephen Heath, 142–54. New York: Hill and Wang, 1977.

Brooks, Cleanth. *The Well-Wrought Urn: Studies in the Structure of Poetry*. New York: Harcourt Brace Jovanovich, 1947.

Booth, Stephen. *An Essay on Shakespeare's Sonnets*. New Haven: Yale University Press, 1969.

Eichenbaum, Boris. "Theory of the Formal Method." In *Russian Formalist Criticism: Four Essays,* edited by Lee T. Lemon and Marion J. Reis, 99–139. Lincoln Nebraska: University of Nebraska Press, 1965.

Foucault, Michel. "What Is an Author." In *Language, Counter-memory, Practice*, edited by Donald F. Bouchard, translated by Donald F. Bouchard and Sherry Simon, 113–38. Ithaca: Cornell University Press, 1977.

———. "What Is an Author." In *Textual Strategies*, edited and translated by Josué Harari, 141–60. Ithaca: Cornell University Press, 1979.

Greenblatt, Stephen. "Introduction." In *The Power of Forms in the English Renaissance*, edited by Stephen Greenblatt, 3–6. Norman: Pilgrim Books, 1982.

Lukács, Georg. *The Ontology of Social Being*. Translated by David Fernbach. London: Merlin Press, 1980.

Man, Paul de. *The Resistance to Theory*. Minneapolis: University of Minnesota Press, 1986.

McGann, Jerome. *The Beauty of Inflections*. Oxford: Oxford University Press, 1985.

Nagy, Gregory. *The Best of the Achaeans: Concepts of the Hero in Archaic Greek Poetry*. Baltimore: Johns Hopkins University Press, 1979.

Ransom, John Crowe. "Poetry 1: Formal Analysis." In *Selected Essays of John Crowe Ransom*, edited by Thomas Daniel Young and John Hindle, 436–56. Baton Rouge: Louisiana State University, 1984.

Staten, Henry. "How Not to Historicize a Poem: On McGann's 'Charge of the Light Brigade.'" *Victoriographies* 8, no. 1 (2018): 67–83.

Staten, Henry. *Techne Theory*. London: Bloomsbury Academic, 2019.

CHAPTER 3

Criticism and Attachment in the Neoliberal University

Mir Ali Hosseini

To rescue the work of reading from the bitter wars of method in which it is currently embroiled requires above all addressing the institutions which condition our day-to-day work.

In early 2017, when I was about to graduate from an MA program in English literature, which happened to have a heavily theory-oriented curriculum, I was frustrated with how, to borrow Derek Attridge's term, the "empirico-historicist" tendency in many of our graduate seminars overshadowed the work of literature. More fundamentally, however, as almost every other person enrolled in my program, I was disillusioned by the job prospects of a literature degree and disheartened by the world's indifference to what I had chosen to study. Thus, I had picked up Rita Felski's *The Limits of Critique* at the right moment. I found solace in her acknowledgment of the increasing irrelevance of the humanities and was somehow persuaded by her suggestion that the main share of the blame lies on the self-righteous persona of the critic. I am writing this

M. A. Hosseini (✉)
University of Freiburg, Freiburg, Germany
e-mail: mir.ali.hosseini@anglistik.uni-freiburg.de

A. Sridhar et al. (eds.), *The Work of Reading*,
https://doi.org/10.1007/978-3-030-71139-9_3

essay to explain that while I still share the concern about the public role of the humanities, I think Felski's diagnosis misleads us into taking critique itself—and not the way critics have approached literature—as the main source of our profession's declining status; but to understand the conditions in which the humanities operate, critique happens to be our best, if not the only, tool.

Is this essay then a critique of a critique of critique? Whatever this means, it is the postcritical mentality that needs to stay "hypervigilant" about remaining in an infinite regress of critique; my aim is to outline what is problematic about a "post-"critical mentality and thereby establish why reading closely and thinking critically about our institutions are not at odds, but complement one another.

According to Felski, critique as the dominant method of literary studies and more broadly of the humanities is characterized by a suspicious mentality. She argues that the dominance of this suspicion has turned literary studies into a dogmatic pursuit of debunking facts and truths, incapable of appreciating how literature and the arts cultivate our sensibility.[1] Felski's argument builds on Bruno Latour's popular idea that critique has "run out of steam"[2]: that debunking truths was once progress, because it helped us overcome the incontestable authority of tradition; as that authority has been effectively overcome, however, critique's debunking of truths has lost relevance; and thus, the academic humanities, the ivory towers in which critique dwells, have become dissociated from the ordinary and are no longer serviceable to the public. For Felski, literary studies and the humanities can become relevant once again if they overcome the suspicious mentality of critique and adopt a more generous, or, what I shall call, "postcritical attitude." In this way, post-critique can be understood as an academic campaign for positivity and efficiency, "mindfulness" and self-tracking.

Intriguingly, if we read Felski's *The Limits of Critique* itself as an embodiment of the postcritical ethos, we find key similarities between the critical and postcritical attitudes: a polemical or vanguard tone, a careful self-reflexivity, a promise for emancipation and progress, and a pose of detachment or neutrality. In this essay, I will argue that the

[1] Felski, *Limits of Critique*, 188.

[2] See Latour, "Critique."

similarities between critique and postcritique—which, given Felski's repudiation of these qualities as reprehensible characteristics of critique, are in effect postcritique's internal contradictions—show that the irrelevance of the humanities is not a matter of critical mentality, as she suggests, but of a mode of existence and a value system imposed on the humanities by the neoliberal university. As an academic campaign for "relevance" and "efficiency," postcritique fails not only to provide the radical vision needed for reimagining the work of the humanities but also participates in the neoliberal ethos of the modern university—and more broadly, postcritique fits all too neatly with the contemporary demand of experiential consumerism for forms of affective and immaterial labor. If we are frustrated with how irrelevant the humanities have become, I suggest we should start by addressing the limits of our discipline—that is, the administrative structures that govern our day-to-day practice of doing the humanities.

1 Part One

Is the crisis—if you are tired of the word "crisis," feel free to change it to "decline"—of literary studies and the humanities a crisis of methodology? The short answer is no. As I will argue, it is a crisis of higher education. Until the late twentieth century, liberal humanism was the governing ideology of higher education in the west. With the rise of neoliberalism, the old power structures of the university started to shift tectonically. The old liberal value system, it seemed, began to be replaced with market mechanisms. Since then, the future of the humanities has been negotiated according to these new rules. It is no surprise, in this setting, that debates about methodology have moved to the forefront of literary studies. The question of methodology is entangled with the question of what we read *for*—a question answering which assumes a vision for the humanities and higher education, whether made explicit or not. In evaluating local struggles about literary methodology, therefore, we must not lose sight of the larger battlefield. What follows is an attempt to portray that battlefield—a context in which we can locate and analyze postcritique.

In an event organized a few years ago by Homi Bhabha at the Mahindra Humanities Center at Harvard University, a panel of academics were asked to reflect on the future of higher education and the humanities. One of the panelists, Lawrence Bacow, at the time the recently retired President of Tufts University, responded:

> [...] as the real cost of education and the real cost of the scholarly enterprise has increased so dramatically, what happened is that we've taken a far more instrumental view of both what an education is all about and what a university is all about. And so, we tend to look only—or perhaps not "only," that's too strong, but "far more"—at the investment dimensions of what we do and far less at the others. That's not going to go away, because if we talk about the future of the university, I think we're talking about a future that probably includes less, not more in the way of public support [...]. We live in a world in which the university is going to have to partner with far more institutions in our society than we have traditionally done. We find ourselves working far more closely with industry, for example. We find our host communities demanding more of us [...]. So, what does that say though for the role of the humanities within this institution? Well, it means that like every function of the university, we are likely to have to do more with less. There will be more demands for accountability. There will be higher expectations of collaboration—more expected of all of us.[3]

Bacow's description captures perfectly what we can call the neoliberal ethos of the university, its motto being "do more with less." Bacow, who has a record of suppressing graduate student unionization at Tufts, was later appointed as the President of Harvard University—a testimony to how well he has understood the rules of the game (that is, the corporatization of the university).[4]

With the increasing corporatization of higher education and the triumph of neoliberalism, traditional roles in the university are being redefined: university as industry, researcher as entrepreneur, teacher as professional, student as consumer, and so forth. Profitability is now the gold standard according to which the managerial elite of the university decides about distributing material resources. Like business models, university administrators use self-tracking techniques to collect performance data at the end of each semester and plan accordingly to increase performance. Increasing performance is often sold as "positive thinking"—that is, in reality, a constant institutional pressure to adapt to precarious working conditions, to minimize expenses and maximize profitability. Hiring PR specialists and lawyers instead of teaching staff and

[3] "Future of the University"; transcribed from a video recording of the event available on YouTube.

[4] See "Grad Student Unionization."

relying on cheap labor by TAs and adjuncts are among other strategies of increasing productivity.

While these developments are clearly a departure from the liberal humanistic values that governed the university until recently, the administrators of the university (and the academics who support them) continue to sugarcoat their neoliberal policies in a vocabulary of liberal humanism. Lawrence Bacow's argument against unionization of graduate students at Tufts was not that unionization harms the corporate goal of extracting academic labor as cheaply as possible but that "The relationship between faculty member to graduate student is not one of employer to employee,"[5] implying that there is a sacred bond between the two. A similar argument was used a few years ago by a professor of political science at the University of Chicago against graduate students at his department who attempted to organize a union:

> Every year there are hundreds of applicants for a very small number of slots to study here. You are very lucky to be here, just as I am very lucky to teach here. When you were admitted to the university, you were not hired. You were offered a spot as a student [...]. To call yourself an employee and complain about an absence of cost-of-living adjustments, health insurance, or the burdens of being a graduate student [...] sounds both presumptuous and petulant.[6]

If universities are run like an industry, then university employees (academics as well as service workers) should be able to negotiate for their working conditions collectively. Yet, keeping up the liberal humanist façade allows the administrators to deny them that right on a supposedly moral basis. Similarly, academic publishers owned by big corporations profit from the free labor provided by academic workers. Writing without renumeration was once justified, because most academics used to receive a salary from public funding—or, in ideological terms, they had a "vocation"[7]; such gratis labor is nonetheless still expected at a time when academic labor is increasingly carried out by contractors.[8]

[5] Quoted in "Grad Student Unionization."

[6] Quoted in Robin, "When Professors Oppose."

[7] Elsewhere in this volume, William Rasch provides an intriguing genealogy of the term "vocation" and its relevance for the future of the humanities.

[8] Gusterson, "Change Academic Publishing."

The use of liberal humanistic discourse by the managerial elite of the university shows how the old liberal values are not completely replaced, but often blended with the emerging neoliberal values. Consider, for instance, the concept of "interdisciplinarity." On the one hand, interdisciplinarity gives the impression of free exploration of ideas across disciplinary boundaries, a truly creative work encouraged in liberal education. On the other hand, interdisciplinarity is about creating new marketable projects, fields, and degree programs, increasing performance, partnering with other institutions, and so forth—"to do more with less," to sum it up in Lawrence Bacow's words. The question is not whether "interdisciplinarity" or similar concepts and ideas are in themselves neoliberal values; what should be asked is: who uses these concepts and ideas, in what contexts, and to what ends. Ideas proposed in recent debates on methodology in literary studies are no exception, if we want to understand them in the larger picture.

A dominant tendency among recent interventions in methodology in literary studies has been a "turn" to aesthetics, form, and sensibility. Most proponents of the turn to aesthetics often defend themselves against the charges of conservatism and universalism, characteristic of mid-twentieth-century literary criticism. They emphasize that their proposed turn to the aesthetic is rather progressive but seem less concerned about defending themselves against potential complicity with the neoliberal university. To be sure, there is even an anti-neoliberal aspect to this turn. In insisting that literary studies claim an area of knowledge which is strictly their own (rather than, for instance, that of sociology or philosophy), a turn to sensibility seems to resist the neoliberal value of doing more with less[9]—for instance, the expectation that English departments should offer programs that appeal to a wider market by in fact pretending that enrolling in literature programs can help students become founders of successful startups by developing their "critical thinking" (another tricky term) and leadership skills. In inviting us to read more closely and slowly, to cultivate our sensibility, a renewed attention to the reading process can resist the "Move Fast and Break Things" of the age of social media. But like

[9] Ronan McDonald argues that "the renewed openness to the 'literary' is actually a sharpening of disciplinary focus and indeed social effect, not because it is a capitulation to a managerial university and neo-liberal ideology but rather because it affords the discipline better equipment to defend its province" ("Critique and Anti-Critique," 366).

"interdisciplinarity," a turn to form, aesthetics, and sensibility can be appropriated to radically different ends.

In the case of postcritique, a shift away from (or "beyond") critique in the name of sensibility is part of a larger project of depoliticization of the English department—and by depoliticization, I do not mean a total disappearance of discussions around issues of social injustice at the English department (capitalism's heart is big enough for "diversity trainers"); what I mean is the ongoing depoliticization of the institution of the university itself and the loss of freedom to think about justice in radical terms. As was the case with the neoliberal arguments about unionization of academic workers, the place to start is postcritique's rhetoric and mentality rather than the improved performance it promises to deliver.

2 Part Two

Rita Felski suggests that "critique," which she takes to be the dominant mood and method of literary studies and the humanities, is characterized by what Paul Ricoeur famously termed the "hermeneutics of suspicion": a "vigilant, wary, mistrustful" mentality that "blocks receptivity and inhibits generosity."[10] By drawing the limits of critique's mistrustful mentality, Felski hopes to help literary studies develop a more generous attitude. As a call to push beyond "the fault-finding mentality of critique,"[11] a call for finesse and generosity, *The Limits of Critique* is itself, however, far too bound in "a rhetoric of againstness."[12] Felski's work, in other words, is in chief part a deployment of critique's own weaponry against critique. As Felski herself acknowledges, roughly halfway through the book, it is not easy even for a sympathetic reader to go through the text without being somewhat frustrated by her incessant attacks on critique: "By now my more patient readers may be getting restive," writes Felski, adding in parentheses: "The rest will have long since tossed this book aside in a fit of exasperation."[13]

It is understandable that a critical assessment of critique will be to some extent caught up in "a performative contradiction": "in the act of

[10] Felski, *Limits of Critique*, 188.

[11] Felski, 172.

[12] Felski, 17.

[13] Felski, 117.

disagreeing with certain ways of thinking," Felski writes, "we cannot help being drawn into the negative or oppositional attitude we are trying to avoid."[14] The "critiquiness"[15] of Felski's work seems justifiable insofar as it serves only as a step to overcome critique—a ladder to be thrown away once we have climbed beyond our critical mentality. Indeed, her concluding remarks do make an early Wittgensteinian gesture:

> Having clarified, to the best of my ability, the reasons for my dissatisfaction with critique, I want to *move on*: to try out different vocabularies and experiment with alternative ways of writing [...]. The point, in the end, is not to redescribe or reinterpret critique but to change it.[16]

Felski, however, also insists that *The Limits of Critique* has *already* moved beyond the oppositional attitude of critique: "Let me specify at the start that this book is not conceived as a polemic against critique, a shouting from the rooftops about the obduracy or obtuseness of my fellow critics."[17]

Despite her denial, Felski's hostile tone and her reductive claims about critique (for instance, that critique assumes that "suspicion is an intrinsic good or a guarantee of rigorous or radical thought"[18]) make *The Limits of Critique* a textbook example of the genre of the polemic. Given postcritique's branding as an attempt to make us more generous readers, Felski's reservations about appearing polemical are not surprising. But to be sure, there is nothing wrong with polemicizing per se. Any call for radical change may be in one way or another polemical.[19] Reductive claims can help us build consensus, gather around a certain agenda, and direct our energy to change a current state of affairs. The problem is that by being polemical and insisting otherwise—by, as I will discuss, pretending to be emancipatory but conforming with larger socioeconomic forces that have

[14] Felski, 192.

[15] A word coined by Christopher Castiglia, used also by Anker and Felski, to refer to the "disposition" of critique as "a combination of suspicion, self-confidence, and indignation" (Castiglia, "Critiquiness," 79).

[16] Felski, *Limits of Critique*, 192–93. Emphasis mine.

[17] Felski, 5.

[18] Felski, 6.

[19] Although, as Doug Battersby argues elsewhere in this volume, polemicizing alone cannot transform literary studies.

made the work of the humanities irrelevant in the first place—postcritique turns the piled-up frustration of doing academic work in the humanities in the age of the neoliberal university into a futile mission of collective introspection, a campaign for "efficiency" and "mindfulness."

It is ironic that Felski's solution to suspicion is further introspection, since she and Elizabeth S. Anker condemn "self-reflexivity" as a "generic feature of critique": "Demanding a hypervigilance on the part of the critic," they insist, "critique [...] requires stringent self-critique and continued attempts to second-guess or 'problematize' one's own assumptions."[20] Felski's reservation over appearing polemical shows how postcritical mentality is itself no less self-reflexive than the critical mentality. In fact, it is not difficult to identify a larger pattern of self-reflexivity in Felski's work, of which the concern over being read as polemic is a part: that postcritique defines itself more as what it is not than what it is. Among the five chapters of *The Limits of Critique*, four are a series of attacks on critique; only the last chapter makes positive claims about what postcritical reading consists in. Similarly, in a two-page account of postcritique published in *American Book Review*, Felski devotes almost all her space to "clarify what postcritical reading is *not*," spending only a short paragraph or two on what it *is*.[21]

Postcritique's self-reflexivity is worth exploring in more depth. One of the ways in which Felski describes the suspicious mentality of critique is by comparing the critical reader to a detective, constantly looking for "agents who can be held to account for acts of wrongdoing."[22] To illustrate her point, she brings the most classic example of literary detectives. Better than Sherlock Holmes, however, I think, George Orwell's protagonist in *Keep the Aspidistra Flying*—whose favorite among all books happens to be *The Adventures of Sherlock Holmes*—captures the kind of suspicion at stake here. Gordon Comstock, who comes from an upper-middle-class family which has lost its wealth and status, is a well-educated young man but an unsuccessful poet. Having declared war on what he calls the "money-god," Gordon turns down a well-paid copywriting job and works instead in a bookshop. Gordon has an obsessive suspicion that everyone's behavior is motivated by money: every visitor to the bookshop, his friends,

[20] Anker and Felski, "Introduction," 8.

[21] Felski, "Postcritical Reading," 5–6.

[22] Felski, *Limits of Critique*, 83.

his relatives—behind every little gesture they make, Gordon sees money. Even at a climactic moment in the story, when Gordon is finally about to have sex with his girlfriend but is unable to, because she asks him to use a condom, it is the "money-god" which he blames: "Money, money, always money! Even in the bridal bed, the finger of the money-god intruding! In the heights or in the depths, he is there":

> "Money again, you see!" he said. "Even at a moment like this it's got the power to stand over us and bully us. Even when we're alone and miles from anywhere, with not a soul to see us."
>
> "What's *money* got to do with it?"
>
> "I tell you it'd never even enter your head to worry about a baby if it wasn't for the money. You'd *want* the baby if it wasn't for that. You say you 'can't' have a baby. What do you mean, you 'can't' have a baby? You mean you daren't; because you'd lose your job and I've got no money and all of us would starve. This birth-control business! It's just another way they've found out of bullying us. And you want to acquiesce in it, apparently."[23]

Gordon's reference to an unspecified "they," his inability to recognize any cause for what happens around him other than that which he customarily suspects, and his simultaneous senses of self-righteousness and victimhood typify a suspicious mentality. What makes Gordon a perfect example in the context of our discussion, however, is his blend of suspicion and self-consciousness. Orwell's ironic tone in the novel's free indirect discourse indicates how, even at his most hostile moments of suspicion, Gordon is aware of himself as the subject of suspicion. Postcritique's suspicion of critique's suspiciousness is not unsimilar to Gordon's ironic attitude toward himself: it surely complicates the picture, but it cannot solve the problem. Felski's reference to critique's "meta-suspicion" and "self-reflexive loop of spiraling distrust"[24] only reveals a quality of postcritique's own version of suspicion: it is a suspicion meant to be discarded once its purpose is served, but like the blood on Lady Macbeth's hands, there is something sticky about suspicion even when it is washed away.

[23] Orwell, *Keep the Aspidistra Flying*, 123.

[24] Felski, *Limits of Critique*, 106.

With these remarks, I do not intend to suggest that postcritique's self-reflexivity is a further step in Kant's "hell of self-knowledge," from which we are to emerge as godly.[25] My point is that postcritique promises to bring us back up to the ground, but is doomed to fail: when you wish to change a friend's mentality, you rarely succeed by *convincing* them that they should change their mindset because they are wrong (cracking a joke might help, reprimanding will probably not). It is hardly effective for individuals but arguably much less when it comes to entire institutions. Postcritique's project of attributing the decline of humanities to a collective mentality—or, one may say, almost a collective guilt—of the humanities scholars reduces the existential problems facing the humanities to a matter of our relationship with ourselves and implies that these could be solved by self-tracking and positive thinking—techniques which, as I discussed in the previous section, are characteristic of the neoliberal ethos of the university.

Another way in which Felski seeks to convince us to give up "critiquiness" is by drawing attention to how critique's suspicious mentality is motivated by an ideology of progress—a march toward an "ever-greater emancipation."[26] After Bruno Latour's injunction that "emancipation does not mean 'freed from bonds,' but *well*-attached,"[27] we have come to realize that the promised emancipation of critique is but an illusion. Ironically, however, what postcritique promises is precisely an emancipation: the goal of combatting suspicion, we are told, is "freeing up literary studies to embrace a wider range of affective styles and modes of argument."[28] And again somewhat ironically, "the progress narratives that drive the rhetoric of critique" are precisely what motivates postcritique. In inviting us to be less suspicious and more generous readers, Felski speaks from the position of "the adult in the room." Her occasional admission of guilt and expression of affection for critique work only to solidify the position from which she speaks—a position that maps almost perfectly to the Kohlbergian idea of moral development: while critique is stuck in

[25] Kant, *Metaphysics of Morals*, 236.

[26] Felski, *Limits of Critique*, 119.

[27] Quoted in Felski, 146.

[28] Felski, 3.

the conventional morality of its oath of allegiance to its family principles and expectations, postcritique recognizes the value of other forms of intellectual life.

As "progress" and "emancipation" are the backbone of the liberal humanist discourse, it is worth exploring postcritique's relationship with humanism in more detail. (It is a fair question to ask, given the vagueness of the term, why we should conceptualize postcritique in terms of "humanism." It is helpful because postcritique positions itself precisely in accordance with such vague concepts. An enterprise that sets itself up as antagonistic to the "spirit of modern thought" can be no less conceptually unspecific than its rival.) In his brilliant monograph on humanism, Tony Davies traces how the definition of "humanism" has been always bound up with the question of power:

> The important question, over and above what the word *means* in a particular context, is why and how that meaning *matters*, and for whom. On this at least, Humpty Dumpty's advice cannot be improved on by the cultural historian. When Alice wonders, innocently, "whether you *can* make words mean so many different things," the philosophical egg goes straight to the heart of the matter: "'The question is,' said Humpty Dumpty, 'which is to be master—that's all.'"[29]

Accordingly, there is no single humanism but various brands of humanism, which

> are not reducible to one, or even to a single line or pattern. Each has its distinctive historical curve, its particular discursive poetics, its own problematic scansion of the human. Each seeks, as all discourses must, to impose its own answer to the question of "which is to be master."[30]

In this conception, "humanism" does not simply refer to a fixed set of philosophical beliefs but signifies a discursive use of values and beliefs which happen to be deeply ingrained in our culture.

The humanistic component of Kant's thought is not only in the tenets of his transcendental idealism (which brought human perception front

[29] Davies, *Humanism*, 6.

[30] Davies, 130–31.

and center) and in his categorical imperative (which derived the principles of morality solely from human reason) but also in how the rhetoric of his essay on the Enlightenment and his famous injunction, "Sapere aude!" promoted an attitude of courage against what had been hitherto considered as incontrovertible truth. In a similar vein, there is a humanist component in the supposedly antihumanist ideas of post-Enlightenment "masters of suspicion" ("antihumanist" because Nietzsche, Freud, and Marx all argue for a subject that has less agency and is more conditioned compared to the freedom of the Kantian subject). Post-Enlightenment philosophies of Nietzsche, Freud, and Marx only take "Sapere aude!" to a higher level: a promise of emancipation could not be fulfilled, unless our deep epistemological, psychological, and social conditionedness are uncovered. Similarly, what postcritique takes on as its mission is to awaken us to our negligence of how we are conditioned by an oppositional mentality—negligence that has taken the form of self-deception, because we have come to be unquestionably convinced that this oppositional attitude is a "critical detachment" and "an absence of mood."[31] Thus, postcritique has a humanistic concern in common with critique: to emancipate us from the dogmas of the present and the past to make us masters of our future.

The humanism of critique is not the naïve humanism of the Enlightenment but more nuanced: what legitimizes critique's humanism is the authority of disinterested judgment—or an unacknowledged faith in critical detachment. There is a similar seemingly ideology-free, detached, and impersonal aspect in postcritique, which is—unsurprisingly—left unacknowledged. Felski's suggestion that the dominance of the critical mentality has made us dogmatic in our fight against dogma bears a close resemblance to T. E. Hulme's idea of the naturalization of the humanistic attitude in the Renaissance. According to Hulme, only after the "new attitude [of humanism] became firmly established [in the Renaissance], men sought to make it seem *objective* and *necessary* by giving it a philosophical setting, exactly as in the case of the religious attitude which had preceded it."[32] Setting out to separate this attitude or "Weltanschauung" from a "Pure Philosophy," Hulme developed a particular

[31] Felski, *Limits of Critique*, 21.

[32] Hulme, *Speculations*, 26.

fondness for Husserl's method of descriptive phenomenology. "Description," for Hulme, was the keyword for an impersonal, rigorous science and aesthetics that could sever from modern intellect the degenerate attitude of Renaissance humanism and its elevation of "man" to the center of the universe. Description had to be the objective of both philosophy and verse: "The great aim is accurate, precise and definite description," and "The first thing is to recognize how extraordinarily difficult this is."[33] A similar ideology of description underlies the postcritical mentality.

Frequently in *The Limits of Critique*, Felski stresses that she is describing rather than explaining the mood and method of critique. Even at a final moment of sincerity, she refuses to acknowledge that she, too, has offered *some* explanation:

> As a critic schooled in suspicious reading, I am hardly immune to its charms, yet I have tried, as much as possible, to avoid being drawn into a "critique of critique." That is to say, I have *described* widespread modes of argument *without* making imputations about hidden motives, diagnosing symptoms and anxieties, or attributing the rise of scholarly methods to larger social pressures or institutional forces that my fellow critics have failed to understand.[34]

Felski's preference for description over explanation is inspired by Latour's "actor-network theory":

> [...] Actor-network theory emphasizes both the necessity and the sheer difficulty of description, of attending to an empirical world that often resists or refutes our assumptions. Objectivity is not owned by the positivists, Latour remarks; that we are shaped by our situation does not prevent us from giving better or worse accounts of things at hand [...]. The task is to account for as many actors as possible, to be specific about forms of causation and connection (which are also forms of translation), instead of hitching a free ride on a preexisting theoretical vocabulary.[35]

Interestingly, for both Felski and Hulme, description is an "extraordinarily difficult" task. Hulme would probably also agree with Felski and Latour that while reality is not reducible to our descriptions, our task is

[33] Hulme, 132.

[34] Felski, *Limits of Critique*, 192. Emphasis mine.

[35] Felski, "Latour and Literary Studies," 740.

"to account for as many actors as possible" or "*all* that is given in experience."[36] In other words, although we can never fully describe reality, we must nonetheless be guided by a mystical epistemological totality. Thus, while critique is enchanted with disenchantment, postcritique seeks to enchant us with enchantment: in every painstaking act of description, we celebrate that which cannot be fully described—a task which has more of an ethos of data science ("account for as *many* actors as possible") than of humanistic work.

In suggesting that postcritique's mentality is guided by a Hulmean ideology of description, I do not want to imply that the kind of antihumanism conceptualized by Hulme is the same as that which postcritique proposes. Neither do I want to imply that Hulme's writings exemplify the kind of disposition that characterizes postcritical writing. I intend the comparison only to flesh out what is antihumanistic, "scientific," and impersonal about postcritique. Hulme's belief in the superiority of description was motivated by "a desire for austerity and bareness, a striving toward structure and away from the messiness and confusion of nature"[37]—a return from "an attitude of acceptance to life" back to "an attitude of renunciation."[38] Postcritique's antihumanism, on the contrary, is motivated by a desire to reverse the nay-saying attitude of the humanities scholar to an embrace of attachment and a yay-saying attitude to life[39]: literary scholars, like the modernist artists which some of them study, have become "estranged from, or at odds with, the mainstream of social life"[40]—a curse which postcritique promises to break. It is this embracement of life, attachment, and positive thinking combined with introspection and self-tracking dressed up in a garment of emancipatory polemic (not unsimilar to the rhetoric of Kant's "What Is Enlightenment?") that makes postcritique a prime example of how values of the neoliberal university can be blended and disguised in old liberal

[36] Latour, "Critique," 232. Emphasis mine. Latour suggests that the humanities need to cultivate a "realist attitude" and a new empiricism which deals not only with matters of facts, as did the (now) insufficient empiricism of the Enlightenment, but with "all that is given in experience."

[37] Hulme, *Speculations*, 96.

[38] Hulme, 25.

[39] Felski, *Limits of Critique*, 9.

[40] Felski, 16.

humanist values—or how market mechanisms of the neoliberal university appropriate our desire for shaping the future of the humanities.

3 Part Three

Anglophone literary and cultural studies often celebrate themselves as the most "progressive" of academic disciplines. Joseph North's *Literary Criticism* challenges this assumption. According to North, literary studies in the mid-twentieth century witnessed a struggle between "critics" and "scholars." At a point in the late 1970s and early 1980s, the critical paradigm was effectively defeated by the scholarly—or what North calls "the historicist/contextualist"—paradigm.[41] This moment, argues North, transformed literary studies "into a discipline of observation, tracking developments in the culture without any broader mandate to intervene in it."[42] Literary studies, thus, lost its capacity to be the site of cultural warfare against capitalism—a capacity to cultivate deeper forms of subjectivities and collectivities.[43]

As dissenting voices against the historicist or scholarly paradigm fall on more sympathetic ears, or so North believes, opportunities are afforded for a return to criticism—not in its mid-century liberal form, but with a more radical purpose.[44] As North points out, however, attempts to restore the lost capacity of literary studies to intervene in culture and cultivate new forms of subjectivities must be able to "outmaneuver the institution's default strategy for defusing dissent: first to ignore, second to incorporate by creating a new 'field,' and lastly, once the fuss has died down, quietly to let the new field go."[45] As a call for criticism (away from historicism and theory)—a call which professedly wants to, at the

[41] North, *Literary Criticism*, 1–3.

[42] North, 11–12.

[43] North, 20.

[44] North, 211.

[45] North, 211.

same time, stay clear of the ills of liberal mid-century criticism[46]—post-critique provides us with an example of what North calls "dissent."[47] It is also an example of how such "dissent" is entangled with the logic from which it seeks—or seems to seek—to break free.

In their introduction to *Critique and Postcritique*, Elizabeth Anker and Rita Felski chastise critique for always desiring "the new": critique's tendency to "transmute into self-critique has often lead to a penchant for the 'new,' as theory has revised and reinvented itself through a series of frequently exuberant movements and 'turns.'"[48] Although Felski states that she, too, is "a little weary of 'post' words,"[49] we may wonder: what the "post" in "postcritique" does if not satisfy a desire for the "new?" The "penchant for the 'new'" is not as much a problem of critique, as it is a problem of an institution which is increasingly governed by market mechanisms. Our styles of presentation, of critique and postcritique alike, are reflective of how material resources in the discipline are distributed: there are seldom funds available for proposals that do not promise to in some way "break grounds" or "revolutionize" our understanding of a particular subject. Each revolutionary "turn," often imported from another field, creates new opportunities for research. And, if that turn is powerful enough, it affords to create a cluster of publications which justify their existence, at least partly, by virtue of referencing one another.

For instance, Latour's 2004 piece on critique's loss of relevance (note that Latour is a sociologist and not a literary scholar), which calls for a turn to empiricism, is fueled mainly by a belief that we are in a new historical epoch—and that we must "address with the equipment of an older period the challenges of the present one."[50] To convince us of this belief, Latour poses a series of seemingly eye-opening questions:

> What has critique become when a French general, no, a marshal of critique, namely, Jean Baudrillard, claims in a published book that the Twin Towers destroyed themselves under their own weight, so to speak, undermined

[46] Felski, "Postcritical Reading," 5.

[47] "Criticism," for North, is "a programmatic commitment to using works of literature for the cultivation of aesthetic sensibility, with the goal of more general cultural and political change" (North, *Literary Criticism*, 3).

[48] Anker and Felski, "Introduction," 9.

[49] Felski, *Limits of Critique*, 12.

[50] Latour, "Critique," 231.

> by the utter nihilism inherent in capitalism itself—as if the terrorist planes were pulled to suicide by the powerful attraction of this black hole of nothingness? [...] What has become of critique when my neighbor in the little Bourbonnais village where I live looks down on me as someone hopelessly naïve because I believe that the United States had been attacked by terrorists?[51]

Latour's rhetoric here derives its energy from the same sentiment that after the 9/11 attacks dominated politics in the United States (and much of the Northern world): a sentiment that saw world history as divided into "pre-" and "post-9/11" eras to mark the moment when our innocent eyes were opened to the Evil creeping all around. Latour's confession of his own guilt in "debunking facts," therefore, seems bold only insofar as it blocks from view the ways in which his invitation to sanity amid "critical barbarity"[52] is a gesture of conformism, pledging allegiance to larger social forces. To be sure, any systematic reform of the humanities should be in some way connected to a larger social movement if it is going to create meaningful and lasting change.[53] But we may want to think about a reform proposal twice when it rides the wave of sensationalism. It is one thing that the humanities must stay in touch with ambient social and political happenings, but it is another that they should legitimize stories and sentiments pushed by the manufacturers of public opinion in order to promote their own work, or to stay "relevant."

In its use of political sensationalism as entrepreneurial opportunity and its inability to think in structural terms, postcritique exemplifies the mainstream of the neoliberal humanities, though appearing to be an alternative. Consider, for example, the all too well-worn case of Donald Trump. In approaching Trump, to what extent have the mainstream of the humanities been able to stay sober from the frenzy of rage and excitement in which TV pundits dwell and away from the collective project of distracting attentions away from structural problems and into a twitter account, pursued by big media corporations? We cannot expect

[51] Latour, 228.

[52] Latour, 240.

[53] I agree with North that "making broader alliances with the left outside the discipline" is a vital for reforming the literary studies, because a movement for reform within literary studies will ultimately depend on "a more general forward movement" (North, *Literary Criticism*, 211).

the humanities to agitate change, within or outside university, if our reaction to socio-political issues is on a par with media sensationalism. The inability of the university to have a voice distinct from its louder counterparts in society shows how the lost capacity of literary studies to intervene in culture is less a matter of this or that critical paradigm than of its wholesale conversion to an "economy" of ideas—let us accept it, the neoliberal university is truly a "marketplace of ideas"—whose production cycles are becoming shorter and shorter.

The idea that literary studies should return to "the literary" or pursue an "aesthetic education" may be favorable insofar as it puts literary studies on the track of sensibility—an area that falls exactly in the purview of literature and culture and not of philosophy, history, or sociology. However, we should be suspicious—and hopefully not be overcome by our fear of suspicion—of how a program of "aesthetic education" fits so well with the anarchic individualism characteristic of neoliberalism.[54] Any proposal to reform literary studies and the humanities should be scrutinized against the backdrop of not only the university's lack of intellectual autonomy from other institutions of capitalism but also the increasing adjustment of academic curricula to the needs of the job market. In the grand scheme of our neoliberal economies, literary and cultural studies are increasingly becoming a part of experiential consumerism. "Digital copywriter," "social media manager," and "web content editor" are among the most frequently cited jobs for future literary studies graduates. The more students learn about how "attachment" and "affect" work, the better they can produce and evaluate content that can attach and affect us. As much as a "cultivation of sensibility" can encourage deeper engagement with the experience of reading, it may help disseminate more rapidly consumed literature-related content on the web, produced by once aspiring poets and critics who, like Gordon Comstock, must sell their souls to be able to keep their aspidistras in shape. More tragic than Gordon's case, however, they will not become permanent employees but contractors, freelancers, gig and seasonal workers who cannot enjoy social benefits or join a union.

If, as I have argued, Felski and Latour are false prophets of change, and if postcritique is—to borrow Bruce Robbins's phrase—"a project of academic self-advertising"[55] which makes use of very legitimate concerns,

[54] See Harvey, "Neoliberalism Is a Political Project."

[55] Robbins, "Fashion Conscious Phenomenon," 5.

then where should literary studies invest its newly found energy that has built up from decades of frustration? I would like to venture a direction: organizing against the neoliberal university. As David Harvey reminds us, "The reorganization of the production process and turn to flexible accumulation during neoliberal times has produced a Left that is also, in many ways, its mirror: networking, decentralized, non-hierarchical."[56] Neoliberalism, in other words, has impaired our ability to fight systematically. This means that, just like in politics, organization is a key challenge for academic labor, if we care to change the current state of affairs. What affects our ability to organize most is not necessarily some abstract concept but the increasing demands of the professional academic life. We cannot think systematically and organize collectively when we must constantly run after submission deadlines and dream of tenure-track positions. The amount of work expected from a "junior researcher" in the humanities, given the nature of our field, is extremely disproportionate. The life of the humanities scholar seems to be perpetually governed by a value system which set "polished" CVs as the end goal of existence, even when what one criticizes is that very value system. But here we can learn from our recent political memory. Even in the lack of the traditional workplace and strong unions, people can still be mobilized around a certain agenda by the power of grassroots organization—as, for instance, the experience of Bernie Sanders's presidential campaigns show.[57] If academic workers gather around a set of concrete bureaucratic reforms and policy demands, then it would be possible to fight for the future of the humanities. We can shape the future of our discipline only when we address the basic worldly conditions in which we work and live. This—and not pyrrhic victories in the "method wars"—seems to be the place in which we should invest our frustration.

[56] Harvey, "Neoliberalism Is a Political Project."

[57] In the times of COVID-19, the faculty union at Rutgers University has set an example of how the true communities around higher education—teachers, researchers, service workers, students, and the host cities—can come together and effectively organize themselves to fight the managerial class for a more democratic administration of the university. See Wolfson, "Beyond the Neoliberal University."

4 Coda

Richard Feynman allegedly said once: "Physics is like sex: sure, it may give some practical results, but that's not why we do it." The same could be said about literature. People seldom read literature to learn about a historical era or to acquire critical skills. While a return to the aesthetic and the literary is welcome in that it invites us to read more closely and slowly—and any sensibility awakened thereby, we can only hope, will render contemporary states of affairs rebarbative to imagination—the refinement of mind will not in itself transform the institutions of higher education. We may devise curricula that pay attention to affect and attachment, but the market mechanisms of the neoliberal university will continue to extract from our work the practical results it desires—and there is surely high demand in the age of experiential consumerism for technicians of affect and attachment.

The humanities have long been in crisis, but now they find themselves in good company: theoretical physics and pure mathematics are also in a crisis for not yielding (to) the kind of practical results their distant "tech-savvy" cousins like data science produce.[58] As much as we talk about the "knowledge industry," the neoliberal university threatens the very pursuit of knowledge. In the long run, literary studies may end up retaining its name but in effect turn into something like communication studies—and postcritique, if not deliberately help facilitate this transformation, does nothing to prevent it. If we want to make a change, it is not our collective mentality but our institution that we need to transform. The limits of postcritique, like that of critique, are determined by the limits of the neoliberal university.

Many beautiful and eloquent "defenses of the humanities" have been written—who does not want to carry the prestigious title of "Savior of the Humanities?" But the humanities need no defense. The humanities will be part of the modern university as long as there is demand, be it for training technicians of affect or for educating leaders of developing countries in the tradition of western liberal humanism. If we want to reclaim the humanities, instead of adding to the long list of publications that defend the humanities by justifying, directly or indirectly, our

[58] A simple search on the web with "theoretical physics" or "pure mathematics" in combination with "crisis" will pull up numerous articles.

ability to produce "practical results," we should start to think and organize ourselves in larger timespans than does the elite neoliberal class. To be radical is not just to "defend" but to actively do something about the humanities.

Acknowledgements This essay is dedicated to H. Gustav Klaus (1944–2020), former Chair of Literature of the British Isles at the University of Rostock and a devoted scholar of working-class literature. Gustav was a true humanist in that he acted on the values which he studied and believed in, even when what could be achieved was as small as a fair treatment of an assistant or a cost-free interlibrary loan service for students.

I am very grateful to Derek Attridge, Anjali Katta, Benjamin Kohlmann, and Anirudh Sridhar for their insightful suggestions and comments on the text.

References

Anker, Elizabeth S., and Rita Felski. "Introduction." In *Critique and Postcritique*, edited by Elizabeth S. Anker and Rita Felski, 1–28. Durham: Duke University Press, 2017.

"Bacow Opposed to Grad Student Unionization." *The Tufts Daily*, April 1, 2002. https://tuftsdaily.com/archives/2002/04/01/bacow-opposed-to-grad-student-unionization.

Castiglia, Christopher. "Critiquiness." *English Language Notes* 51, no. 2 (September 1, 2013): 79–85.

Davies, Tony. *Humanism*. 1st ed. New York: Routledge, 1996.

Felski, Rita. "Latour and Literary Studies." *PMLA* 130, no. 3 (2015): 737–42.

———. "Postcritical Reading." *American Book Review* 38, no. 5 (2017): 4–5.

———. *The Limits of Critique*. Chicago: The University of Chicago Press, 2015.

Gusterson, Hugh. "Want to Change Academic Publishing? Just Say No." *The Chronicle of Higher Education*, September 23, 2012. https://www.chronicle.com/article/Want-to-Change-Academic/134546.

Harvey, David. "Neoliberalism Is a Political Project: An Interview with David Harvey." *Jacobin*, July 23, 2016. https://jacobinmag.com/2016/07/david-harvey-neoliberalism-capitalism-labor-crisis-resistance.

Hulme, T. E. *Speculations: Essays on Humanism and the Philosophy of Art*. Edited by Herbert Read. 2nd ed. London: Routledge & Kegan Paul, 1936.

Kant, Immanuel. *The Metaphysics of Morals*. Texts in German Philosophy. Cambridge: University Press, 1991.

Latour, Bruno. "Why Has Critique Run Out of Steam? From Matters of Fact to Matters of Concern." *Critical Inquiry* 30, no. 2 (2004): 225–48.

McDonald, Ronan. "Critique and Anti-Critique." *Textual Practice* 32, no. 3 (2018): 365–74.

North, Joseph. *Literary Criticism: A Concise Political History*. Cambridge: Harvard University Press, 2017.

Orwell, George. *Keep the Aspidistra Flying*. Oxford World's Classics. Edited by Benjamin Kohlmann. Oxford: Oxford University Press, 2021.

Robbins, Bruce. "Fashion Conscious Phenomenon." *American Book Review* 38, no. 5 (2017): 5–6.

Robin, Corey. "When Professors Oppose Grad Student Unions." *Jacobin*, May 12, 2013. https://www.jacobinmag.com/2013/12/when-professors-oppose-students-unions.

"The Humanities and the Future of the University | Mahindra Humanities Center." YouTube, May 17, 2013. https://www.youtube.com/watch?v=0q5kcFl27ic.

Wolfson, Todd. "Beyond the Neoliberal University." Interview with Astra Taylor. *Boston Review*, July 30, 2020. http://bostonreview.net/class-inequality/todd-wolfson-astra-taylor-beyond-neoliberal-university.

CHAPTER 4

Darkness Visible: The Contingency of Critique

Ellen Rooney

Reading remains an intractable theoretical problem for interpretation because it cannot be thought in a way to assuage our desires for continuity, predictability, and stable protocols while assuming ever-changing forms. The reading effect of the work of critique is an unexpected one: surprise.

1 In Lieu of a Preface: A Reading Effect

In "Lesbian Spectacles: Reading *Sula*, *Passing*, *Thelma and Louise* and *The Accused*," Barbara Johnson writes: "It is hard to pin down the origins of a reading-effect."[1] Johnson offers her quiet observation about the "reading-effect's" resistance to origin stories, precise mapping, or fixity, that is, to being pinned down, in the context of an experiment. Donning "lesbian spectacles," she seeks to read "explicitly as a lesbian,"[2] something

[1] Johnson, "Lesbian Spectacles," 162.
[2] Johnson, 157.

E. Rooney (✉)
Brown University, Providence, RI, USA
e-mail: ellen_rooney@brown.edu

A. Sridhar et al. (eds.), *The Work of Reading*,
https://doi.org/10.1007/978-3-030-71139-9_4

she had not undertaken in her career as a celebrated reader. Johnson notes that this project disputes the "fiction of universality,"[3] but she is exquisitely attuned to its risks. She fears reproducing either "media induced images" (that is, stereotypes) or "idealizations" (political clichés) of "what a lesbian is [...] or what a lesbian *should* be."[4] Neither outcome would count as reading in Johnson's understanding of the term.

Spectacles are an aid to vision, an instrument to bring things into focus and make them legible, that in this case makes a kind of spectacle of both (a) lesbian desire and reading as such. The ambivalent figure underscores the conventional yet real, felt yet ideological, unconscious yet political quality of even such a deliberately "personal" or "particular" undertaking. (Johnson references her "particular desire structure."[5]) Acknowledging the contending forces at work, Johnson stresses the unstable, divided character of her carefully reflexive reading: "I needed a way of catching myself in the act of reading as a lesbian without having intended to."[6] The "I" and the "act of reading" are under scrutiny (and pressure) here. As an interpretative strategy, reading beyond intention, sans intention, challenges not only a certain privileging of method, by which I think Johnson means reading as the application of method, but, more specifically, the reading subject as such, her sovereignty and her transparency, even to herself. In this process, the reader as existential ground or learned authority is eclipsed by the curious yet compelling emergence of the reader as an effect.

Johnson evokes similar challenges elsewhere in her work. In "Nothing Fails Like Success," she argues that "the impossible but necessary task of the reader is to set herself up to be surprised."[7] In "Lesbian Spectacles," the unexpected results of this oxymoronic "set up" are quite disappointing: Johnson discovers her erotic attraction to a powerful yet phallocentric femininity, the phallic mother seductively wielding authority in a patriarchal scene (for example, the legal system in *The Accused*). She ruefully concludes, "so much for reading with the unconscious," conceding that her effort, "far from guaranteeing some sort of radical

[3] Johnson, 157.

[4] Johnson, 157.

[5] Johnson, 157.

[6] Johnson, 157.

[7] Johnson, "Nothing Fails Like Success," 15.

or liberating breakthrough, brings me face to face with the political incorrectness of my own fantasy life."[8] As she tries to face down or face up to her libidinal investments, to explain her own responses to her increasingly unfamiliar self, surprising herself in the act of reading and succeeding all too well, Johnson encounters a "real disjunction"[9] between politics and the unconscious. This dislocation is realized, that is, made real, in and by the reading subject reading. What "remains" is the haunting question of "what the unconscious changes and what politics repeat."[10] If the unconscious is here palpably the site of reinscription and repetition, of continuity with patriarchal structures she programmatically refuses, Johnson avoids the conclusion that this result is inevitable. Rather, she insists that the unconscious may also, if unevenly or surprisingly, nurture change even as politics fails to constitute the emphatic break with hegemony to which we aspire.

Such uncertainty means that what initially reads as success may ultimately achieve little more than comfortably camouflaged defeat. But if the institutional power of a reading practice can render it "more simplistic, more dogmatic, and increasingly more conservative,"[11] the antidote Johnson proposes entails returning to reading to rethink its warrant: "the one imperative a reading must obey is that it follow, with rigor, what puts in question the kind of reading it thought it was going to be. A reading is strong, I would therefore submit, to the extent that it encounters and propagates the surprise of otherness. The impossible but necessary task of the reader is to set herself up to be surprised."[12]

I underline this oxymoronic imperative to highlight its articulation of the reader, the setup, and their necessary encounter. Johnson envisions an open-ended theoretical practice, subject-effects formed by volatile reading relations, and a break with origins and (a certain concept of) history; she embraces the generative putting into question of reading as such. I will argue that "symptomatic reading" in its Althusserian iteration enacts just such forms of contingency, surprise, and interrogation. No fixed determination for reading results. Rather, surprise is the disclosure of the forms

[8] Johnson, "Lesbian Spectacles," 163.

[9] Johnson, 164.

[10] Johnson, 164.

[11] Johnson, "Nothing Fails Like Success," 11.

[12] Johnson, "Nothing Fails Like Success," 15.

of contingency in history, in reading, and in politics. Surprise marks the moment when critique takes form.

2 Darkness Visible

> Not only in their answers but in their very questions there was a mystification.
>
> —Karl Marx, *The German Ideology*

Darkness visible is an oxymoron. Like other true oxymorons—such as bittersweet, fiend angelical, seductive reasoning, and far-right critique—darkness visible figures by conjoining contradictory terms, conjuring an apparent "impossibility" into being in a way that is "more pointedly witty for seeming absurd," as the Greek *oxy* (sharp) and *moros* (dull) suggest.[13] Oxymoron is a canny fool who speaks a pointed truth to make possible the impossible.

Darkness visible figures at the outset of Milton's *Paradise Lost*. A few lines into Book I, Satan and his "horrid crew / Lay vanquished, rolling in the fiery gulf, / Confounded though immortal."[14] The rebellious angels have been "Hurled headlong flaming from the ethereal sky" and rest now in "bottomless perdition" (ll. 45, 47). Satan glances about:

> At once as far as angel's ken he views
> The dismal situation waste and wild,
> A dungeon horrible, on all sides round
> As one great furnace flamed, yet from those flames
> No light, but rather darkness visible
> Served only to discover sights of woe [...] (ll. 59–64)

Paradise Lost offers a complex reading of the angels' rebellion: the weightiest questions of free will and the soul, solidarity and action, are already at stake as the poem begins, well before the calamity of the fortunate fall (another oxymoron). One of the animating flaws Milton

[13] A contradiction in terms (a logical error) is not an oxymoron, and oxymoron is not a comically contradictory locution such as "giant shrimp," which depends not on the disjunction between the gigantic and the shrimpy but on the pun on shrimp. The shrimp of the giant shrimp is not the sweet of the bittersweet.

[14] Milton, *Paradise Lost*, ll. 51–53. Hereafter cited parenthetically in text.

attributes to Satan is compelling for the way in which it entangles epistemology, formations of subjectivity, and agency or determination. In Book V, busy fomenting rebellion, Satan parries a counterargument offered by the angel Abdiel, who contends that heaven's angels owe obedience to the God who created them. Satan challenges not the logic that one's Creator should be one's master but the prior claim, the "strange," "new Doctrine," he calls it, that he in fact was "formed [...] and the work of secondary hands." He demands to know "whence Learnt" this thesis: "who saw / When this creation was? Remember'st thou / Thy making, while the Maker gave thee being?" Ultimately, he dismisses the notion as unfounded and absurd: "We know no time where we were not as now; / Know none before us, self-begot, self-raised / By our own quick'ning power" (ll. 853–61). "Quick'ning" is the moment in pregnancy when the fetus moves, gives (literally) palpable signs of its life. The defiant angel here insists that no power or being preceded him or gave him existence, sired, birthed, or authored him. Self-authored, self-begotten, self-raised, and even self-quickened, Satan furiously asserts his autonomy, self-identity, and untrammeled freedom to act, even as he cites these qualities as the evidence, fruits, and instrumentalities of his unconditioned origin. He is in no respect a despised "work of secondary hands." "Our puissance is our own, our own right hand / Shall teach us highest deeds, by proof to try / Who is our equal" (ll. 864–66).

Of course, Satan is wrong. He is not self-authored, neither self-begotten nor self-raised. He is a compelling rhetorician, and he may speak in pure bad faith. His questions mystify in every sense; truly rhetorical, they paint opposition as impossible. He feigns interest in evidence of this making, perhaps hoping to ensnare Abdiel in his doubts, and demands corroboration of his "formed" nature: where exactly did you pick up this Doctrine? Do you remember this alleged creation? Did you see it yourself? he wonders, sarcastically invoking the possibility that one might witness one's own birth. For myself, I have no memory of it, he insists; my memory is that the past was no different from the present, and we are as we have ever been and ever will be, ourselves. These boasts, queries, and arguments paradoxically demonstrate the limits of Satan's consciousness, its real dependence on what it does not and cannot know, the derived or mediated nature of its nonetheless equally real puissance and power. *Paradise Lost* assures us that there is no such thing as self-authorship, and one meaning of darkness visible—or one of the sorrowful consequences of being hurled headlong from Heaven—may be to become extravagantly, permanently, stubbornly blind to the unremembered past—a canon, lineage, fall—to the event of one's making that was not of one's making, to the formal conditions (and so the limits and contradictions) of one's puissance, which nonetheless enable one's highest deeds. This is a mistake.

3 Surprise, Surprise

> Because the reader has room to realize that the future may be different from the present, it is also possible for her to entertain such profoundly painful, profoundly relieving, ethically crucial possibilities as that the past, in turn, could have happened differently from the way it actually did.
>
> —Eve Sedgwick, "Reparative Reading"

Surprise is one of the more consistently cited values of the so-called "postcritical turn."

On the postcritical account of reading, critique is the opponent of surprise: indeed, critique's resistance to surprise is a defining trait and grave flaw. Dauntingly predictable, if not rote, critique monotonously indicts literature and culture more broadly. Suspicious and ventriloquizing, disenchanting and patronizing, it is trapped in repetitive, dogmatic, stale gestures. Critique banishes surprise, which can only derail its party line, undermining its suffocating authority. I propose the (almost) diametrically opposed view: that surprise, in the specific form of contingency, is fundamental to "symptomatic reading" as critique.[15] Indeed, contingency is indispensable—"necessary," Louis Althusser argues—to the problematic of symptomatic reading. In his formulation of the necessity of contingency, we glimpse terms that displace the descriptive rhetoric, theoretical evasion, and empiricisms at work across postcritical polemics.

But what is the so-called "postcritical turn"? And why nominate it with the epithet, "so-called"? Critique is a highly contested term, and the vehement debates it sponsors have predictable consequences for its derivative,

[15] These terms are not synonymous; symptomatic reading is one form of critique.

postcritique. I will attempt below what will certainly fail as a "description" of some features of critique and the postcritical.[16] Indeed, when I propose a "description," its scare quotes signal the very basic disagreements in play. To cite just one: I take the postcritical to be a critique of critique. That is not its self-description.

On the other hand, there is some consensus that postcritique's literary avatars sustain a quarrel that is literally about reading.[17] Arguably, the entire history of literary studies as a modern discipline is the history of writing about the problem of reading. That said, by any measure, literary studies has debated the problem of reading with marked intensity in recent years. These efforts have generated numerous distinctive programs: reparative reading, reading for form, distant reading, as well as symptomatic, surface, suspicious, and susceptible reading, to name a handful. Such discussions are a permanent feature of critical discourse, even in relatively unpolemical periods. This traffic in theory is not simply exported from literary and cultural studies into other scenes. Writing on reading is omnipresent.[18] The Althusserian question, "what is it to read?" is interminable.

Nirvana Tanoukhi, in her revelatory "Surprise Me If You Can," tracks the valorization of the unexpected by theorists of reading from J. Hillis Miller and Bruno Latour to Eve Sedgwick. Naming it a signature of what she calls "the new objectivism," she discloses a peculiar circularity in its form, whereby these theorists proffer only "neutrality as motive" for their methodological and ethical injunctions to "trust in appearances" and

[16] I touch upon the argument about description, its possibilities and/or impossibility, politics and ethical import, below.

[17] This may be true in some respect across disciplines but is explicit for literary critics.

[18] Reading debates resonate across the academy and beyond: arguments about alternative facts, confirmation bias, and fake news raise the question that dogs popular culture, music and cinema, political theory, philosophy, and cognitive science: what is it to read? These more-than-disciplinary debates are heterogeneous; their terms contentious and unfixed; they are political, intellectual, academic, popular, aesthetic, and personal. Questions of reading shape new formalism and science studies, genre and affect theory, flat ontologies, new materialisms, and speculative realism, along with traditions that draw on (or refuse) the idiom of critique, whether in a Kantian frame or critical race, feminist, Marxist, queer or postcolonial theories, canons, and vernaculars.

"dutifully read without reading."[19] Tanoukhi seeks some "epistemological framework"[20] or justification that might "mak[e] it worth giving up the challenges, pleasures, and adventures of interpretation"[21] for a flattened and strangely passive consumption but finds a closed circle where the question of motive is mooted: "What do we want? Surprise. Why do we want it? Because we want to be surprised."[22]

It is puzzling that the postcritical overlooks the surprising effects of critique.[23] This lapse is particularly striking in light of another observation Tanoukhi makes. As she ponders the "absent framework" that she intuits must be at work underwriting postcritical imperatives, she revisits Sylvan Tomkins's oeuvre (a touchstone for Sedgwick's thinking on surprise). Tanoukhi notes that Tomkins "regarded surprises as neither good nor bad"; rather, he defined surprise as "the perpetually unwelcome competitor to any ongoing central assembly; it does not favor anything and it is against peaceful coexistence with any visitor to consciousness who has outstayed his welcome."[24] She then makes the startling observation that "in Tomkins's conception of surprise, its necessary but double-edged clearing function gives it an uncanny resemblance to critique."[25] This uncanny kinship has several strands; the essential one for my purposes is the way in which surprise undoes, the "clearing function" it serves in relation to the given, the obvious, and the (apparently) self-same, one definition of the origin.

[19] Tanoukhi, "Surprise Me," 1428–29.

[20] Tanoukhi, 1426.

[21] Tanoukhi, 1427.

[22] Tanoukhi, 1429.

[23] The reasons for this are not easily untangled. They may have more to do with the history of particular instantiations of critique, both as insistent thematizations of critical thought in academic arenas that were deeply familiar and in the reiteration of urgent critical interpretations, whose gestures were also widely disseminated, than with critique. Unresolved tensions between humanities research and its pedagogy may also be in play, which could illuminate prominent references to students in postcritique. I consider avatars of surprise in Rooney, "Symptomatic," 141–44.

[24] Quoted in Tanoukhi, "Surprise Me," 1432.

[25] Tanoukhi, 1432. I cannot do justice to Tanoukhi's rich argument here. Johnson's concern that strong theory may fall victim to institutionalization echoes Tomkins's warning about the "ongoing central assembly."

4 The Critique of the Critique of Critique

> ...the contingency of necessity...the necessity of contingency, an unsettling pair of concepts that must nevertheless be taken into account.
>
> —Louis Althusser, "Underground Current"

To offer the most minimal terms: critique in its narrowest form is the revelation of the conditions that enable any text whatsoever to come into being, the tracing of the practice, history, or semiosis by which the text was formed by that which is other than itself, and the marking of a "break" with those enabling origins, a break that gives to every critical discourse a certain singularity, a quickening power, a power willy nilly aligned with a new politics of reading.

Critique is a kind of Abdiel, turning up to dispel our illusions of self-authorship and self-making, of tautological or solipsistic lineages, and of continuous historical developments, and so of absolute autonomy, indeed, of any autonomy that is not the paradoxical fruit of tangled, heteronomous branches and secondary hands. As such, critique may seek to discredit, deflate, or dismiss a text, to "cancel" it, if it inhabits a canon or historical tradition or a field of popular celebration (on its way to canonicity).[26] But critique is also, as Wendy Brown argues, "a practice of affirming the text it contests [insofar as it] passionately reengages the text, rereads and reconsiders the text's truth claims [...] It does not, it cannot, reject or demean its object."[27] As many have observed, Althusser's practice of symptomatic reading enacts critique in this mode: he insists we reread *Capital* to the letter, "in black and white,"[28] even as we rewrite for the present conjuncture.

I cannot do justice here to the heterogeneity of postcritical interventions. But several crucial features announce the problematic of surprise: (1) a theory of description that claims "modesty" for reading and so disavows its will to power; (2) a reductive account of the reading subject

[26] This is a topic for a lengthier analysis examining the disciplinary differences among postcritical interventions. Disciplines grounded in canons that bear ideological weight (and what canon does not?) have a more complicated relation to postcritique than disciplines—or other fields—where "progress" is understood as moving beyond outdated (historical) formulations, replacing them with new materials.

[27] Brown, "Untimeliness and Punctuality," 16.

[28] Althusser and Balibar, *Reading Capital*, 192.

on the grounds that her mood is "critiquey" and resists textual intimacies or is too knowing and eager for mastery, or contemptuous of enchantment and pleasure and too frankly theoretical to admit to aesthetic pleasures; (3) a disavowal of theoretical/political "translations" of texts as foreclosing attention to affects, attachment, and sometimes material bodies; and (4) the (astonishing) political miscalculation whereby scholars warn that critique has "run out of steam": it has now apparently been hijacked by those who once seemed its "proper" targets.

Of course, critique has no proper targets. No one is self-begotten; no text "arrives unaccompanied: it is a figure against a background of other formations."[29] When Bruno Latour tropes his analysis as a rhetorical question ("why has critique run out of steam?"), he may hope to hurry readers past any interrogation of his query. He quickly turns to what he jokingly (I think) calls the "virus of critique"[30] as it is disturbingly wielded by his paranoid neighbors, who believe the CIA and Mossad plotted the 9-11 attacks on the United States.[31] Latour forgets that conspiracists neither adopt nor aspire to the forms of critique, which do not converge on claims that public discourse masks global conspiracies. Fervent criticism and denunciation are not synonyms for critique. The indifference of conspiracy propagandists to the intricacies and insights of Actor–Network Theory (or deconstruction or psychoanalysis or …) is clear from their long history, predating any dissemination of late twentieth-century critique.

This alleged untimeliness of critique is twofold: the claim that critique is ineffectual, especially politically, joins a commonsensical judgment on the obvious fitness of new tools for new times. "The Way We Read Now" is not the way we once read. Generational change is natural, while critique has grown both tedious and dysfunctional. But the new and the now can be variously intertwined. Some proponents of critique's exhaustion simply argue that it has won. Sedgwick observes that its favorite target, the liberal subject, is a historical relic, dispatched by neoliberalism: "graduate students who are dab hands at unveiling the hidden historical violences that underlie secular, universalist liberal humanism" battle ghosts.[32] By

[29] Macherey, *Theory of Literary Production*, 53.

[30] Latour, "Critique," 231.

[31] Latour, 228.

[32] Sedgwick, "Reparative Reading," 139–40.

now, everyone recognizes the ruses of power, Stephen Best and Sharon Marcus conclude. For his part, we've seen Latour worry that critique has fallen into the wrong hands; but he also champions the new.

> Military experts constantly revise their strategic doctrines, their contingency plans, the size, direction, and technology of their projectiles, their smart bombs [...] I wonder why we, we alone would be saved from those sorts of revisions. It does not seem to me that we have been quick, in academia, to prepare ourselves for new threats, new dangers, new tasks, new targets.[33]

We should secure the latest, historically appropriate arms, not train "recruits" and "cadets" to fight the last war, still toeing the Maginot line. Leaving the (ironic?) martial imagery aside for now, it is striking that Latour anticipates no difficulty in characterizing the now, the new threat profile. The dangers, tasks, and targets of the current conjuncture are obvious: no need for critique to dispatch its weary, worn-out force.

Arguments citing critique's victory and the absolute quality attributed to the new seem curiously optimistic at best. The obviousness of exploitation, violence, and inequality remains something of which critique has yet to convince significant populations, no matter how thoroughly we (whoever we are?) have persuaded ourselves. The tenacity of these systems and their adaptable ideological problematics must strike every observer. Critique has not run out of steam.

To be sure, diverse postcritical interventions (which Bruno Penteado simply names "anti-critique") do not recommend identical responses to critique's pointless or impotent tactics. Best and Marcus celebrate a literal, sometimes machine-like (or algorithmic) descriptivism, "digital modes of reading" that would "correct for our critical subjectivity by using machines to bypass it."[34] Refusing to "translate" texts into metalanguage, they propose to take visible "surfaces" at face value. By contrast, Sedgwick's "reparative" reading eschews *purely* paranoid positions, strong theory, and the logic of exposure; but it seeks "good surprises" by "extracting sustenance from the objects of a culture—even of a culture whose avowed desire has often been not to sustain them,"[35] refusing the

[33] Latour, "Critique," 225.

[34] Best and Marcus, "Surface Reading," 17.

[35] Sedgwick, "Reparative Reading," 150.

lures of description and fidelity. Heather Love champions a method of thin description, a patient, minimalist practice, while Rita Felski chastises suspicion's arrogance and disdain, prodding literary studies toward something less corrosive and more ambitious to "articulate a positive vision for humanistic thought."[36]

These differences matter. But these interventions have been recruited in the service of the proposition, most explicit in the privileging of description and the (nominal) retreat from theory (and perhaps politics), that criticism ought to attend assiduously to what the text announces, to what it speaks, and so renounce our obsessive attention to its unspoken, not said, or excluded. Best and Marcus argue, under the rubric of

> *Attention to surface as a practice of critical description*: This focus assumes that texts can reveal their own truths because texts mediate themselves; what we think theory brings to texts (form, structure, meaning) is already present in them. Description sees no need to translate the text into a theoretical or historical metalanguage in order to make the text meaningful. The purpose of criticism is thus a relatively modest one: to indicate what the text says about itself.[37]

The commitment to "indicate what the text says about itself" disavows mediation to celebrate modesty: to "translate" a text's revelations into another (theoretical, political, or historical) language distorts and disrespects its "own truths," its plain sense. Its fascination with the concealed or mystified, silences, and gaps, condemns critique, not least because these absences appear to be known in advance, determined elsewhere, only to be transported to the scene of reading in which the text is outflanked, exposed, and defeated.

Best and Marcus concede: "this may sound like a desire to be free from having a political agenda that determines in advance how we interpret texts, and in some respects it is exactly that."[38] Descriptivism promises to purify reading, freeing it of commitments and debts to a certain "outside" (this is a complicated term; I use it provisionally) of the text, especially commitments and debts to problematics that "determine in advance" the

[36] Felski, *Limits of Critique*, 186–88.

[37] Best and Marcus, "Surface Reading," 11.

[38] Best and Marcus, 16.

trajectory of reading—and have become all but useless from a political point of view.

This spawns its curious anti-theory impulse and a parallel reluctance to acknowledge political and even certain historical claims. Emptying reading of its specificities shields the text from unwelcome, unwarranted, and unthinkable contaminations, that is, protects it from contingency.

5 Reading Remains Writing

> Although there is no Meaning to history (an End which transcends it, from its origins to its term), there can be meaning in history, since this meaning emerges from an encounter that was real, and really felicitous—or catastrophic, which is also a meaning.
>
> —Louis Althusser, "Underground Current"

Is anti-critique thus unwittingly engineered to contain surprise? Does surprise answer a question with "just one failing: it was never posed"?[39] The ambition only-to-describe wagers that humility can rein in critique's intellectual and political pretensions, suspicions, and consequent projections and distortions. "Modest" reading hopes to equip us for the now, to face its specificity and difference. But the longing for surprise seems the last desire postcritique will satisfy. If readings could be fastidiously cleansed of the contingencies of their theories, histories, and politics, they would ironically forestall unexpected departures and so neutralize difference(s), rendering reading as unmediated and familiar, self-same, rather than unsettlingly new. Whether seeking "surprise," intimacy with the text, or a politically astute analysis alive to change, anti-critique's disavowal of the productivity of reading obscures the genuine source of surprise. Rather than risk a reading that embraces its contingent condition as writing, productive but immodest and unpredictable, anti-critique enacts reading as repetition, resisting the disruptive effects of its (potentially dubious) political or theoretical investments, and throwing no shade on the text's claim to be itself, know itself, make itself.

I have argued elsewhere that postcritique obscures symptomatic reading's theorization of contingency to condemn critique as the already known and that this misreading tracks an odd indifference to the work of

[39] Althusser and Balibar, *Reading Capital*, 22.

form in symptomatic reading.[40] The valorization of surprise in the idioms of critique suggests a possible convergence, a continuity yet to be calculated, reconnecting critique and the postcritical, despite their apparent incongruences.[41] That is a possibility I must pursue elsewhere. In the space that remains, I want to examine the specificity of contingency and necessity as they appear in Althusser's later work and their distinctive formal character.

To begin with the latter: in *Reading Capital*, Althusser writes:

> we are thereby obliged to renounce every teleology of reason and to conceive the historical relations between a result and its conditions of existence as a relation of *production* and not *expression*, and therefore as what, in a phrase that clashes with the classical system of categories and demands the replacement of those categories themselves, we can call the necessity of its contingency.[42]

In this formulation, the "phrase" "the necessity of its contingency" articulates Althusser's renunciation of teleological concepts of history and of reading. These concepts misconstrue reading, either as instantaneous insight, advancing "an idea of reading which makes a written discourse the immediate transparency of the true and the real discourse of a voice,"[43] or as empiricism, the innocent, almost unintentional exposure of the kernel of the real secreted in its shell. Expressive totalities fantasize history as the progressive unfolding of an "'abstract' essence in the transparency of its 'concrete' existence,"[44] mystifying historical processes and relations that are in practice productive and so ineluctably contingent. To recall Tanoukhi's terms, contingency doesn't motivate symptomatic reading or reward its refusal of interpretation.[45] The "necessity of contingency" theorizes the repudiation of the historicisms and empiricisms that remain potent ideologies across our interpretative frameworks. The concept of

[40] See Rooney, "Symptomatic Reading," 137–40.

[41] These might be traced to responses to period specific developments or even unique critical histories in literary studies.

[42] Althusser and Balibar, *Reading Capital*, 45.

[43] Althusser and Balibar, 16.

[44] Althusser and Balibar, 16.

[45] Tanoukhi, "Surprise Me," 1428.

the necessity of contingency shifts the problematic, the terrain on which our thinking of reading and history formally unfolds.

On this new terrain, contingencies take form historically but lack singular origins, essences, or ends (whether nominated as intention or context or spirit), fostering reading that is incomplete and so interminable. This reading subject cannot be self-authored or begotten. While reading generates forms determined in the encounter of reader and text, the reader herself is recast, an effect of textual events that cannot be determined in advance, at once cause and effect of reading, determined and determining, a "condition modified by what it conditions."[46] As Althusser argues in "The Underground Current of the Materialism of the Encounter," every such "encounter is aleatory, not only in its origins (nothing ever guarantees an encounter), but also in its effects…every encounter might not have taken place."[47] These are true reading experiments, their outcomes uncertain, their results provisional. Surprise, surprise.

This symptomatic reading deconstructs the question of whether form is just there, present "in the text," or somehow (inevitably scandalously) "projected" onto it by a reader, is "given" or "not given." This ideological misdirection installs a false problem (and Althusser reminds us, "it is never possible to solve *a problem that does not exist*"[48]). Confounding logics of continuous development and repetition as pure return, symptomatic reading is the material trace of a material encounter, politically and formally open-ended. Its formations are always the belated effect of the work of reading and so of secondary hands. The contingency of the encounter is constitutive of history, politics, science, and reading, not a rare or exceptional event: indeed, intense ideological effort struggles to disguise and obscure it, to protect the thought of "origin as Reason or End."[49] Symptomatic readings repeat the question "what is it to read?" to disconcert narratives of development and escape historicism's attachment to prefiguration and continuity, and their soothing fables of identity. Its effects are real, determined and determining, but without guarantees.[50]

[46] Quoted in Pippa, "The Necessity of Contingency," 17.

[47] Althusser, "Underground Current," 193.

[48] Althusser and Balibar, *Reading Capital*, 115.

[49] Althusser, "Underground Current," 188.

[50] See Hall, "Problem of Ideology."

Althusser theorizes the reckoning with radical contingencies and their becoming necessary as a problem of form, and this formal engagement distinguishes symptomatic reading from other avatars of critique. Symptomatic reading is neither a purely conceptual critique nor a suspicious hermeneutics exposing the lies of priest and despots. Formal questions appear in various guises across Althusser's work, but in his thinking of the necessity of contingency, figural language, what in *Reading Capital* he calls the play on words, is critical. There, he describes history and political struggle, and the particular histories of science and philosophical thought (and, I would add, literature), as marked by "radical discontinuities [and] [...] profound reorganizations" that "inaugurate with their rupture the reign of a new logic,"[51] a new conjuncture whose emergence was not (and could not be) predicted. This new logic is not an unfolding or "mere development," neither "the 'truth' or 'inversion' of the old one."[52] Rather, it displaces the old logic and "*literally takes its place*,"[53] that is to say, metaphorically takes its place, as the root of the concept of metaphor in the Greek to "transfer" or "carry over" reminds us.

In the "Underground Current," the contours of these ruptural displacements deepen. Displacement is aleatory; it is itself provisional, "haunted by a radical instability;"[54] it must "take hold" materially and that taking hold depends on its "taking form." Althusser is adamant: no encounter escapes the mediation of form, which signals its potential by the very unexpectedness of its arrival, its failure to develop from the old logic according to its laws. "This is where th[e] *surprise* lies (*there can be no taking hold without surprise*)."[55] The form that would take hold must surprise; the very possibility of contingencies taking hold, disrupting the conjuncture, becoming necessary, depends on their aleatory and unforeseeable emergence. The work of reading is oxymoronic.

[51] Althusser and Balibar, *Reading Capital*, 44.

[52] Althusser and Balibar, 44.

[53] Althusser and Balibar, 44.

[54] Althusser, "Underground Current," 195.

[55] Althusser, 188.

6 The Conjuncture Cannot Be Televised

Better, of course, meant worse.

—Paul Auster, *The Invention of Solitude*

Times change.

Advocates and opponents of critique have both given a great deal of thought to how changing times impact intellectual work and how that work finds its place in the present conjuncture. Wendy Brown argues that critique "is essential in dark times [...] to contest the very senses of time invoked to declare critique untimely [...] [and] settled accounts of what time is, what the times are, and what political [...] temporality we should hew to in political life."[56] The times are never simply present, imperviously obvious, legible at a glance. Even "settled accounts" of the times may be unsettled. Critique contests not just a particular description of the times, but concepts of time, of the times, and of the historical as such.

This interrogation of "what time is" pervades Marx's and Althusser's rethinking of history and reading. "Not only in what [Marx] says but in what he does we can grasp the transition from an earlier idea and practice of reading to a new practice of reading and to a new theory of history capable of providing us with a new theory of reading."[57] The "conjuncture" is neither a historical context nor a ground but a concept that interrogates historicist ideologies of transformation. Conjunctures articulate multiple, autonomous histories whose heterogeneity blocks any effort to "make an 'essential section' in history" in the hope that we might capture the core or essence of a "homogeneous-continuous/self-contemporaneous time."[58] This displacement is not only or even primarily a theoretical matter, a "radical rejection of all philosophies of essence," but a "means with which to think not only the *reality* of history, but, the reality of *politics*, not only the essence of reality, but the essence of *practice* and the link between these two realities in their *encounter*, in *struggle*."[59] Necessity survives. But we now "think necessity

[56] Brown, "Untimeliness and Punctuality," 4.

[57] Althusser and Balibar, *Reading Capital*, 18.

[58] Althusser, "Underground Current," 115.

[59] Althusser, 188.

as the becoming-necessary of the encounter of contingencies,"[60] and this becoming is a matter of struggle.

Althusser writes:

> The encounter, one that is not brief, but lasts, never guarantees that it will continue to last tomorrow rather than come undone. Just as it might not have taken place, it may no longer take place: "fortune comes and changes," affirms Borgia, who succeeded at everything until the famous day he was stricken with fever. In other words, nothing guarantees that the reality of the accomplished fact is the guarantee of its durability. Quite the opposite is true: every accomplished fact, even an election, like all the necessity and reason we can derive from it, is only a provisional encounter, and since every encounter is provisional even when it lasts, there is no eternity in the laws of any world or any state.[61]

Our concept of the necessity that characterizes the conjuncture is revised; provisionality or the "contingency of necessity" follows from "the necessity of contingency at its root."[62] The provisional form of every conjuncture is the field of politics, one that instantiates precarity along with radical possibility and leaves us the problem of how to think or act historically, in time, in our times. Of course, it is obvious that a conjuncture—even a context—may be read otherwise and practically re-formed, but this only licenses a happy plurality of perspectives. The contingency of necessity announces the radical possibility of undoing of the conjuncture.[63] To confront the necessity of contingency is to rethink reversibility, the irreversible and the confounding form(s) of the present political conjuncture.

In "The Infinite Contradiction," Etienne Balibar argues:

> Philosophy is never independent of specific conjunctures […] I use this word in a qualitative rather than a quantitative sense, stressing by it the very brief or prolonged event of a crisis, a transition, a suspense, a bifurcation.

[60] Althusser, 194.

[61] Althusser, 174.

[62] Althusser, 187.

[63] I consider how the historical possibility of reversal is caught up in the figure of antiphrasis and the notion of the "opposition" in another essay, "The Opposite of Theory."

> Which manifests itself by irreversibility, i.e., in the impossibility of acting and thinking as before.[64]

"Irreversibility" announces a particular kind of impossibility, the impossibility of retreat. The conjuncture is a "qualitative" shift in the problematic that cannot be ignored: it has taken form. It designates a "before" on the far side of a "bifurcation"; hegemony is its signature. The conjuncture is impossible to evade in the sense that every way forward encounters it: no reading is self-begotten. This captures its necessity. The conjuncture forms us and our acting, reading, and thinking: it works upon us and we work through it: it installs a limit and so (in)forms our path forward.

But irreversibility suffers a kind of reversal in Balibar's account, not unlike the stricken Borgia. Balibar defines *antithesis* as the central task of philosophical reading and aporia as the trope that antithetical reading systematically displaces. The conjuncture cannot be ignored, but it may be rewritten, in unanticipated forms, even antithetically. Paradoxical figures of reversal proliferate, and Balibar aligns writing itself with the problem of the conjuncture: "not only do philosophers always write within a conjuncture, but conversely, within a conjuncture, they write. They think, no doubt, [...] but only through writing and in constant confrontation with problems writing poses for them."[65] No unfolding of the Idea here—rather, a material encounter with and through the figure.

This figuration is fundamental to thinking both the conjuncture as a contingent encounter taking form as necessity and its necessity as itself to-be-displaced, rendered contingent in its turn. Balibar theorizes this process with the fabulous "verb 'to incomplete' [inachever] in the active form." To incomplete is his oxymoronic neologism for the reversals that give chase in the wake of the irreversible. To find a way to act and think not "as before," we incomplete, rewrite, and so undo the conjuncture, though in a surprising way that will not lead to a return. The determination of an encounter, of its form, its historicality, that is, its future, can only be assigned as material consequence "by *working backwards*, from the result to its becoming, in its retroaction,"[66] rather than as the

[64] Balibar, "Infinite Contradiction," 144.

[65] Balibar, 145–46.

[66] Althusser, "Underground Current," 193.

unveiling of an immanent order, prefigured in its origins and so quite easily pinned down.

Crucially, Balibar's argument, ostensibly and literally about "writing," is not "purely" linguistic: "all these aporetic undertakings [mean], if not to 'transform,' probably to incomplete the world, or the representation of the world as 'a world.'"[67] To incomplete the representation of the world as a world in the present conjuncture seems terribly risky. But no conjuncture is inert, a static achievement: it is materiality in motion and opportunistic. Balibar concludes, "philosophy constantly endeavors to untie and retie from inside the knot between the conjuncture and writing,"[68] for better or worse.

The conjuncture, appearing in a bifurcating transition, an intersection in our time, is the form of our everyday. We are always falling into a new conjuncture that goes all the way down, a multilayered, "specific," internally contradictory, moving target. But it cannot simply reveal itself to us, rising into visibility while uncannily casting fresh light on new realities and speaking for itself; it tumbles or stumbles across the apparent path, always impeding our action or setting the terms by which even the questions it *fails* to thematize are disclosed and made workable, by which I mean available for work, which is also to say, for another contingent encounter that is reading in its true sense, as social practice and struggle. The conjuncture is irreducible to context, ground, or base: these are the concepts of postcritical description, bound to surfaces, expression, continuity, and historicism. The conjuncture does not manifest itself: it cannot itself think itself; its origin is hard to pin down. The conjuncture is made manifest, necessary, and undone by the contingent work of politics and of reading and so too of tropes. Reading in the conjuncture, reading as a contingent encounter that may take hold in a necessary form, is an oxymoron.

7 Coda: Angel's Ken

> To philosophize with open eyes is to philosophize in the dark. Only the blind can look straight at the sun.
>
> —Louis Althusser, *The Spectre of Hegel*

[67] Balibar, "Infinite Contradiction," 146.

[68] Balibar, 144.

The capacious concept of form is itself oxymoronic. Raymond Williams tells us that in English, the word "form" "embraces two conflicting meanings: a visible or outward shape, with a strong sense of the physical body and an essential shaping principle, making into a determinate of specific being or thing, for example, 'the body was only matter of which the soul were the form.'"[69] This division characterizes some contemporary work, in the emphasis on the shape matter takes, in work like Sandra MacPherson's "A Little Formalism," and in the account of abstract form, as shaping principle, in a text like Caroline Levine's *Forms: Whole, Rhythm, Hierarchy, Network.*

In the arguments Althusser advances, oxymorons insist across a range of materialities and principles: not only conceptually, as the necessity of contingency and the contingency of necessity, but in a rich collection of theoretical objects at work in the problematic of symptomatic reading: "the non-vision and vision within vision itself," the "silent voice," "the unuttered *question*," "the invisible…defined by the visible as *its* invisible," and the "*classical text itself which tells us that it is silent: its* silence *is its own words.*"[70] In practices, as well: the process of symptomatic reading produces its particular surprise by rendering an answer, a solution, as a question: the confounding structure of oxymoron.

Oxymoron is thus not a *metaphor* of the "taking form" in the encounter that Althusser theorizes with the concepts the necessity of contingency and the contingency of such necessity. The chiasmus he forms of this double conceptual imperative is directly theoretical and argumentative, not an ornament or illustration. His own reading reveals the way in which oxymoron is a trope of reading itself, as a material practice, in multiple registers: as the relation of reader to text and the form forged by their encounter; as the structure of the conjuncture and our time; and in the concept of form.

Oxymoron conjures an apparent "impossibility" into being in a way that is "more pointedly witty for seeming absurd." It is a naked trope: if its figural operation is to succeed, it cannot dissemble its contradiction. Its juxtaposition must remain "impossible." This trope shows its work;

[69] Williams, *Keywords*, 113.

[70] Althusser and Balibar, *Reading Capital*, 21, 143, 23, 26, 22.

the antithesis of tautology, it flaunts its disdain for the self-same. But oxymoron is never merely a contradiction in terms. Seductive reasoning, fiend angelical, and the bittersweet are surprising new forms, products of the work of reading. Self-contradictory but not self-falsifying: the bittersweet and the deafening silence are real.

Oxymoron's powerful displacement of logical binaries stalls paraphrase. All resistance to paraphrase entails a theory of form and so interrupts paraphrase by translation into the language of its own analysis, whatever that may be. Form is silent—Hamlet/*Hamlet* does not say "Iambic pentameter, that is the question." Unparaphrasable, it must be read. The encounter, like strong reading in Johnson's sense, is productive insofar as it discloses a necessary form, surprising because it fulfills no promise, ensures no future, expresses no preexisting idea.

Althusser theorizes form, subjectivity, and the conjuncture as products of an aleatory encounter and their "becoming necessary" as entailing their contingency. This analysis resonates with postcritical objections to reading that is "determined in advance" by a prior agenda. But the oxymoron of the encounter of reader and text refuses to shift determination toward a text that mediates itself. Oxymoronic reading tracks overdetermined relations, each element determined and determining, their mutually conditioning encounter neither inevitable nor knowable in advance.

The form that takes hold in this negotiation is also temporally oxymoronic, as is the reading subject. "Incompletion," which disrupts and revises the conjuncture, does not overthrow it any more than the sweetness of bittersweet banishes the bitter or causes it; the new form, should it take hold, reorients conjunctural effects. The conjuncture conjoins past and present, indifferent to their antithetical sitings and mutual antagonisms. The reading subject similarly takes form in symptomatic reading as a surprise, in a newly divided form, neither self-begotten nor a faithful avatar. Althusser describes the aleatory and contingent materialism of the encounter as a "materialism of the rain, the swerve, the encounter, the take,"[71] terms of relationality and/as movement. Oxymoronic form cannot be traced to the unfolding of an essence, the unveiling of a truth, or the exposure of the kernel of the real: it

[71] Althusser, "Underground Current," 167.

takes material shape without origin or end to foster reading that is in its necessity interminable, provisional, and incomplete.

Readers of Milton's epic know "the God of *Paradise Lost* is a puzzlingly unsympathetic figure."[72] You may not have encountered this view in quite these terms. The more familiar formulation doesn't feature God's limited appeal but celebrates Satan: Milton was of the Devil's party. These readings cite the greatness of the fallen angel's poetry, as well as the pathos of his doubt and struggle. I began with Satan misreading himself as self-begotten and consequently free from any obligation of obedience to the Father, a false claimant to his creation. Nothing I have argued redeems that error. But Adbiel's analysis is also flawed, not in its account of the origins of angels and heaven and earth, but in the assumption the loyal angel shares with Satan: that to identify an origin is to pin down a reading effect and thus to make theory and politics, agency and determination cohere. Satan and his band act in radical defiance of their origins, yet the rebel misses his chance to refuse the origin its primacy. God is unsurprised, as if such catastrophic incompletion were in the script, the conjuncture impervious to reversal. Nothing fails like success. Satan's attachment to self-sameness and originality tempts him from the better argument, the encounter that produces the unforeseen, a surprise that overthrows expectation, and illuminates darkness or rather makes our relation to the darkness visible. Obedience is not a debt owed to an origin; darkness visible is not a void. Darkness made visible reveals: what appears as absence of vision, mere oversight, the failure or affliction of the viewer, is itself another mode of insight. What seems to eclipse the visible, thinkable, readable world may be made vivid, palpable, and revelatory in the contingent encounter of reading.

References

Althusser, Louis. "The Underground Current of the Materialism of the Encounter." In *Philosophy of the Encounter: Later Writings, 1978–1987*, 163–207. New York: Verso, 2006.

Althusser, Louis, and Etienne Balibar. *Reading Capital*. Translated by Ben Brewster. London: New Left Book, 1970.

Balibar, Etienne. "The Infinite Contradiction." *Yale French Studies* 88 (1995): 142–64.

[72] Fish, "Why Milton Matters," 3.

Best, Stephen, and Sharon Marcus, "Surface Reading," Introduction to "The Way We Read Now." Special issue of *Representations* 108 (2009):1–21.

Brown, Wendy. "Untimeliness and Punctuality: Critical Theory in Dark Times." In *Edgework: Critical Essays on Knowledge and Politics*, 1–16. Princeton: Princeton University Press, 2005.

Felski, Rita. *The Limits of Critique*. Chicago: The University of Chicago Press, 2015.

Fish, Stanley. "Why Milton Matters; Or, Against Historicism." *Milton Studies* 44 (2005): 1–12.

Hall, Stuart. "The Problem of Ideology: Marxism Without Guarantees." *Journal of Communication Inquiry* 10, no. 2 (1986): 28–44.

Johnson, Barbara. "Lesbian Spectacles: Reading *Sula*, *Passing*, *Thelma and Louise* and *The Accused*." In *The Feminist Difference: Literature, Psychoanalysis, Race, and Gender*, 157–64. Cambridge: Harvard University Press, 1998.

———. "Nothing Fails Like Success." In *A World of Difference*, 11–16. Baltimore: Johns Hopkins University Press, 1987.

Latour, Bruno. "Why Has Critique Run Out of Steam? From Matters of Fact to Matters of Concern." *Critical Inquiry* 30, no. 2 (2004): 225–48.

Love, Heather. "Close Reading and Thin Description." *Public Culture* 25 (2013): 401–34.

Macherey, Pierre. *A Theory of Literary Production*. London: Routledge, 1978.

Milton, John. *Paradise Lost*. 1667.

Penteado, Bruno. "Against Surface Reading: Just Literality and the Politics of Reading." *Mosaic* 52, no. 3 (2019): 85–100.

Pippa, Stefano. "The Necessity of Contingency: Rereading Althusser on Structural Causality." *Radical Philosophy* 199 (September/October 2016): 15–25.

Rooney, Ellen. "Form and Contentment." *MLQ* 61, no. 1 (2000): 17–40.

———. "Symptomatic Reading Is a Problem of Form." In *Critique and Postcritique*, edited by Elizabeth Anker and Rita Felski, 127–51. Durham: Duke University Press, 2017.

Sedgwick, Eve. "Paranoid Reading and Reparative Reading, or, You're So Paranoid, You Probably Think This Essay Is About You." In *Touching Feeling: Affect, Pedagogy, Performativity*, 123–51. Durham: Duke University Press, 2003.

Tanoukhi, Nirvana. "Surprise Me If You Can." *PMLA* 131, no. 5 (2016): 1423–34.

Williams, Raymond. *Keywords: A Vocabulary of Culture and Society*. New York: Oxford University Press, 1976.

CHAPTER 5

Reading by Example: Disciplinary History for a Polemical Age

Doug Battersby

In this essay, I argue that the self-consciously polemical tenor of recent conversations about critical method has hindered, rather than catalyzed, efforts to diversify our repertoire of approaches to literary form and aesthetics.[1] Critics disenchanted with and seeking alternatives to what Derek Attridge, in the introduction to this volume, characterizes as the "empirico-historical" mode dominant in literary studies today have been greeted by any number of self-styled interventions—most prominently, surface reading, postcritique, and the new formalism—which proclaim the discipline's current practices inadequate or outmoded. My response to these polemics, in the first section of this essay, is to suggest that those who seek to challenge the purported dominance of a given method need to refocus their efforts away from telling others that their preferred

[1] I am grateful to Oxford University Press for permission to reprint material from my more wide-ranging essay on the same theme, "Reading Against Polemic: Disciplinary Histories, Critical Futures," *The Cambridge Quarterly* 49, no. 2 (2020): 103–23.

D. Battersby (✉)
University of Bristol, Bristol, UK
e-mail: doug.battersby@bristol.ac.uk

A. Sridhar et al. (eds.), *The Work of Reading*,
https://doi.org/10.1007/978-3-030-71139-9_5

approaches have "run out of steam," and toward giving readings which demonstrate, rather than merely assert, their novelty and value—as several essays collected here endeavor to do.[2] In the second section, I offer an ecumenical disciplinary history which illustrates that the movements which succeeded in transforming the field did so, not by publishing polemical manifestos (though they often did that too), but through exemplary readings which illuminated literary texts in ways critics had never seen before—whether discussing their rhetorical effects with unprecedented detail and elaboration, parsing their philosophical implications, placing them in surprising new historical contexts, or drawing our attention to attributes that had formerly been overlooked. If this essay seems unduly skeptical of recent developments in the field, that is principally because it aims to model a mode of engagement with methodological discourse that refuses to be diverted from the disarmingly basic question of what a "new" approach can tell us about a literary work that prior approaches couldn't. My argument therefore has implications not only for the discipline's would-be reformers but also for readers searching for an evaluative procedure by which to appraise the validity and potential efficacy of polemical treatises claiming to introduce new approaches to form and aesthetics.

1 Part One

Rita Felski's *The Limits of Critique* is an obvious place to start. Where other critics have (quite rightly) focused on the book's global characterization of the discipline as being in the hegemonic grip of critique, I want to focus on the rhetorical positioning of its argument.[3] Throughout *The Limits of Critique*, Felski states her intention to "expand our repertoire of critical moods while embracing a richer array of critical methods."[4] Who could object to such an apparently benign project? And yet vying with this rhetoric of supplementarity is a rather different posture, dimly felt in the reductive, slightly condescending, characterizations of "critique" in the abstract (as opposed to an actual critic practicing critique), present

[2] I allude to Bruno Latour's widely-read essay "Why Has Critique Run Out of Steam? From Matters of Fact to Matters of Concern."

[3] In a fashion not dissimilar to Mir Ali Hosseini's analysis of postcritical sensibility in his essay for this volume.

[4] Felski, *Limits of Critique*, 13.

from the opening page: "The task of the social critic is now to expose hidden truths and draw out unflattering and counterintuitive meanings that others fail to see."[5] I suspect that most self-identifying "social critics" would find this picture deeply uncharitable in its suggestion that their only interest is in unflattering and counterintuitive meanings. This is nevertheless all rather subdued compared with the more caustic rhetoric of Felski's earlier book, *Uses of Literature*: "Ideas that seemed revelatory thirty years ago—the decentered subject! the social construction of reality!—have dwindled into shopworn slogans; defamiliarizing has lapsed into doxa, no less dogged and often as dogmatic as the certainties it sought to disrupt."[6] In his forthright response to *The Limits of Critique*, Bruce Robbins takes aim at the implications of this tonal evasiveness:

> Faultfinding is the fault that Rita Felski's *The Limits of Critique* attributes to literary criticism. Faultfinding is also, of course, what Felski's book spends most of its time doing. Had it not abandoned itself so completely to faultfinding, its central insight might have led it to do more interesting things. [...] [Felski's argument] puffs itself up by expanding its range of targets so as to take in nearly the whole profession and then, sensing a challenge, steps back in mock horror so as to suggest, 'No, of course, I didn't mean that!'[7]

Without wishing to defend this pugnacious response in its entirety, it is hardly surprising that Robbins is quite so defensive; after all, Felski is attacking the kind of scholarship Robbins has produced, with great distinction, for much of his career, while simultaneously implying that her aims are merely pluralist. For all the caveats about not wishing to outlaw or supplant critique, the title of Felski's book is an accurate reflection of its prevailing stance: *The Limits of Critique*, not *Beyond* or *Other Than Critique*.

That the book's recursive attention to the pitfalls of critique crowds out any sustained argument for doing things differently is apparent from how brief and abstract its positive vision for an alternative critical future proves to be. As Susan Stanford Friedman notes, "Four and a half of the five chapters of *The Limits of Critique* focus on Felski's critique of

[5] Felski, 1.

[6] Felski, *Uses of Literature*, 1.

[7] Robbins, "Not So Well Attached," 371.

critique."[8] After promising in the introduction that the book will eventually "sketch out an alternative model" of "postcritical reading,"[9] Felski acknowledges the frustration readers may feel at the negativity of the preceding pages at the beginning of her final chapter,[10] and once again at the beginning of its final section: "The question of reading can no longer be deferred. It is time to connect these comments on the mobility and agency of texts to current debates about interpretation."[11] The "question of reading," then, turns out to be a matter of connecting Felski's theoretical contentions with the contentions of other critics, rather than involving any actual readings of literary works.

Best, one of Felski's more sympathetic responders, is right that "*The Limits of Critique* reads more like literary sociology than literary theory, more like a statement of literary ethics than a working out of method; and to the extent that the book calls for *return* without providing a clear map for how to get there, it remains weakly committed to that goal."[12] Felski accepts this charge, suggesting that "postcritical approaches" were not her primary focus, and instead directs us to *Uses of Literature*.[13] But while this earlier study offers compelling intellectual histories and phenomenologies of recognition, enchantment, knowledge, and shock, the readings of particular works, persuasive and eloquent as they are, are neither close nor sustained enough for something genuinely novel to emerge—and indeed it is far from clear that that is the book's aim. Insofar as its stated ambition is "to capture something of the grain and texture of everyday aesthetic experience,"[14] *Uses of Literature* is primarily about *recovering* ways of thinking and feeling that have apparently been diminished in contemporary criticism; its strategies of reading are more *ante-* than *post-* critique. It is conspicuous that the chapter on enchantment ends in the conditional mode: "Once we face up to the limits of demystification as a critical method and theoretical ideal, once we relinquish the modern dogma that our lives should become thoroughly disenchanted, we can truly begin

[8] Friedman, "Both/And," 345.

[9] Felski, *Limits of Critique*, 12.

[10] Felski, 151.

[11] Felski, 172.

[12] Best, "*La Foi Postcritique*," 388.

[13] Felski, "Response," 389.

[14] Felski, *Uses of Literature*, 132.

to engage the affective and absorptive, the sensuous and somatic qualities of aesthetic experience."[15] What this accurately suggests is that *Uses of Literature* has not yet begun to "truly" engage with the affective and absorptive; this is a promise of a criticism to come, not an inauguration or exemplification of that criticism. As another sympathetic responder, Diana Fuss, points out: "New ways of reading remain for [Felski] largely in the future and will only emerge when we stop assuming that critique is the only or best way to read."[16] But what are we to do in the meantime? It is unreasonable to suggest that those drawn to critique simply stop writing criticism; most of us are not engaged with methodological innovation for its own sake, but rather experiment with available approaches when exemplary readings demonstrate the intellectual and affective value of doing so. Critics will be converted when they are shown exciting alternatives, not when with a weary sigh they read—or hear about and decline to read—the latest methodological critique of the field. None of this is to diminish the vital service Felski has performed in shedding light on the intellectual and affective investments of a critical sensibility that undoubtedly has significantly shaped the history of the discipline.

Perhaps the best demonstration of why novel critical methods have struggled to gain ground is the most widely cited intervention of the last decade or so: "surface reading." Where Felski's book declines to offer a practical demonstration of "postcritical reading," Best and Marcus's proposal suffers from the opposite problem. In its original context, as the introduction to a special issue of *Representations*, "The Way We Read Now," "surface reading" is used to describe an exceedingly diverse range of critical projects: Margaret Cohen's advocacy of narratology over close reading amidst literature's forgotten archive; Mary Thomas Crane's cognitive, rather than Freudian, understanding of the unconscious; Leah Price's histories of the book; Anna Cheng's erotics of immersion; and Christopher Nealon's politically motivated, non-symptomatic reading.[17] The most explicit elaboration as to the connection between these projects, other than their shared weariness with symptomatic interpretation, is the suggestion that "[a]ll seem to be relatively neutral about their objects

[15] Felski, 76.

[16] Fuss, "But What About Love?," 355, n. 1.

[17] Best and Marcus, "Surface Reading"; Cohen, "Narratology," 51–75; Crane, "Spatial Imaginary," 76–97; Price, "'History of the Book,'" 120–38; Cheng, "Skins, Tattoos, and Susceptibility," 98–119; Nealon, "Reading on the Left," 22–50.

of study, which they tend less to evaluate than to describe."[18] But even this tentative claim sits uncomfortably with, say, Cheng's description of a "mutual pedagogy of erotics,"[19] or indeed Best and Marcus's own assertion, on the very same page, that "surface reading [...] want[s] to reclaim [...] the accent on immersion in texts"[20]; eroticism and immersion may be many things, but neutral is not one of them. Despite the salutary effect of bringing questions about interpretative priority to the fore, the very multiplicity of methodological possibilities makes it difficult to imagine an exemplary surface reading in the way that we can point to paradigmatic works of New Criticism or New Historicism—which has in turn made it difficult for detractors to frame their objections other than on the level of metaphor. Thus, James Simpson and Garrett Stewart invoke their own metaphors, of masks and depth charges, to counter Best and Marcus's claims for surface reading—and the critical discourse continues to slide further away from actual readings of literary works.[21]

The most discerning piece of critical analysis explicitly allied with Best and Marcus's aims is Love's reading of Toni Morrison's *Beloved* in "Close but Not Deep." Wary of the humanistic assumptions that have often accompanied the practice of close reading, Love turns to two social scientists, Latour and Erving Goffman, whose analyses provide a model for "modes of reading that are close but not deep" insofar as they "rely on description rather than interpretation."[22] To illustrate such an approach, Love turns to the coolly dispassionate first description of Sethe's attempt to kill her children to prevent them from being re-enslaved, rather than the more lyrical and resolutely subjective narration later in the novel which has elicited so much attention from readers and critics. Where James Phelan takes the racist epithets in the passage ("nigger woman" and "old nigger boy") as a sign that the prose holistically focalizes the dehumanizing perspective of the slave catcher, Love perceptively shows how an interpolating phrase—"in the ticking time the men spent staring at what there was to stare at"—more problematically suggests the presence of a non-characterized narrator whose "perspective cannot be cleanly

[18] Best and Marcus, "Surface Reading," 16.

[19] Cheng, "Skins, Tattoos, and Susceptibility," 102.

[20] Best and Marcus, "Surface Reading," 16.

[21] Simpson, "Interrogation Over," 378–79; Stewart, *Deed of Reading*, 16.

[22] Love, "Close but Not Deep," 375.

extracted" from the slave catcher's.[23] Where for Phelan, the scene pedagogically provides a negative ethical example of how it should never have been interpreted, for Love, its "flatness, objectivity, and literalism" demonstrate "how reading *Beloved* at the surface allows us to see Morrison's project as registering the losses of history rather than repairing them."[24]

My only criticism of Love's daring response is her characterization of the narrator's perspective as "neutral" and "purely descriptive,"[25] a characterization seemingly necessitated by the essay's prior methodological commitments; the rhythmic elegance, subtly evocative metaphor, and lilting alliteration of the phrase she foregrounds are surely more troubling than the neutrality she describes, presenting us with a narration which is simultaneously aestheticizing and affectively detached, unencumbered by the queasiness and horror that this scene arouses in so many of its readers. More consequentially, the great insight that Love brings to this passage emerges precisely from her exquisite attentiveness to novelistic form—specifically, to how different registers suggest the presence and absence of focalization (even within distinct phrases of the same sentence)—that is, insofar as she ignores her own methodological injunctions and traverses from description into interpretation. After all, shifts in perspective enacted through manipulations of style have been a cardinal concern for the close reading of modern novels at least since Percy Lubbock's *The Craft of Fiction*.[26] This is not to deny the subtlety and brilliance of Love's reading, only to say that it doesn't herald the methodological break announced in the essay's preceding pages. It is no surprise that other studies allied with surface reading have been no more effective at spelling out what distinguishes their approaches from conventional close reading.[27] A decade later, it remains unclear what an "orthodox" surface

[23] Love, 385.

[24] Love, 386.

[25] Love, 385.

[26] Lubbock, *Craft of Fiction*.

[27] The modesty of the modifiers critics use to describe their approaches—"mere reading," "just reading," and "minimal interpretation"—is a telling indication that such practices are characterised more by the critical manoeuvres they refuse to perform than any novel strategies for the interpretation of texts (Mitchell, *Mere Reading*; Marcus, *Between Women*; Attridge and Staten, *Craft of Poetry*).

reading might look like, and what it might contribute to literary studies by way of methodological innovation.

My claim that, though individually compelling, the range of methods Best and Marcus classify as "surface reading" are too disparate to amount to a cogent critical approach has also been made with respect to the New Formalism. In her widely read survey essay, Marjorie Levinson notes that, "despite the advocacy rhetoric, New Formalism does not advocate for a particular method."[28] Like postcritique, New Formalism knows more about what it is against than what it is for, other than formalism. In her introduction to *Reading for Form*, Susan J. Wolfson takes this as a point of pride, quoting the criticism of an anonymous reviewer that "it's hard to see a new program for formalist literary studies emerging from this volume" as a "positive advertisement" for the movement, and proclaiming that "the essays within demonstrate, again and again, the vitality of reading for form is freedom from program and manifesto, from any uniform discipline."[29] The refusal of programmatic thinking, as well as tenuous claims for an essential commonality among disparate enquiries, is welcome; but such methodological permissiveness makes it very difficult to discern any positive, alternative path to be taken by the discipline, or even individual critics. "What," Levinson asks, "is a shared commitment minus articulated agreement about the object to which one commits?"[30]

Or, to put the question differently, what is *new* about the New Formalism? Most new formalist work in fact closely resembles New Historicism with a "renewed" or restored commitment to form. Verena Theile, in the introduction to *New Formalisms and Literary Theory*, argues that the volume is "interested in the political motivations of a return to formalism, but, together with our contributors, we also, and perhaps simultaneously, want to propose and challenge the conception of New Formalism as an extension of contextual readings or a 'mere' return to aesthetic readings."[31] What exactly *is* being proposed gets lost in the syntax of this sentence. Apparently moving from theory to practice, Theile proposes to differentiate New Formalism from New

[28] Levinson, "What Is New Formalism?," 562. See also Otter, "Aesthetics in All Things," 116–17.

[29] Wolfson, "Introduction: Reading for Form," 5.

[30] Levinson, "What Is New Formalism?" 562.

[31] Theile, "New Formalism(s)," 6.

Historicism by discussing a Reuters article about the discovery of a trove of seventeenth-century decorative bowls.[32] Stressing the way that the interviewed archaeologist "initially gives a nod to form" but "soon moves on to cultural context," Theile concludes:

> Obviously, this is a crude example of New Historicist methodology, but the template fits. The New Formalism that this volume is proposing here would not have fit this template, however, and that is despite the fact that it likely would have provided similar historical context and would have likewise thought to link the earthenware to the seventeenth century culturally. But it would not have let go of the patterns; in none of the chapters below would such abandonment have been tolerated.[33]

Does the template fit? No one could accuse Stephen Greenblatt of abandoning the aesthetic particulars of *Othello* in his compelling reading at the end of *Renaissance Self-Fashioning*, arguably the paradigmatic New Historicist study. If there are important New Historicist readings which are inattentive to form, why conjure up a straw man? It is difficult to see why Theile resorts to a hypothetical, if literary criticism really does need the New Formalism. Also note that, once again, emphasis falls on the putative errors or omissions of other critics rather than any genuinely new mode of interpretation, something reflected in the prevalence of past-oriented prefixes ("recover," "rediscover," etc.).

It's worth asking why so many literary critical movements in the twenty-first century seems to be labelled and put into circulation before their (often tantalizing) interpretative potential has been realized; by contrast, in the previous century, critical innovations tended to be demarcated and classified years and sometimes decades after the fact. An ideologically suspicious reader might correlate the packaging up of new methods with the neoliberalization of the American universities in which they came to life and the increased prevalence of the marketized idiom of intellectual competition and personal branding.[34] In the absence of exemplary readings that concretely demonstrate, or even provide the

[32] Theile, 8–11.

[33] Theile, 10.

[34] The very pervasiveness of this idiom in the academy today reflects the shift in cultural expectations of the function of universities that Simon Grimble describes elsewhere in this volume.

basic building blocks for, a distinct critical approach, postcritical reading, surface reading, the new formalism, and other such interventions have little prospect of catalyzing disciplinary transformation—an absence that gives readers a good reason to arrive at a more modest assessment of the significance of these interventions to everyday literary critical practice than their extremely wide circulation might suggest.

2 Part Two

Disenchantment has of course been a powerful motivator for methodological innovation over the years, but merely expressing one's disenchantment has rarely been enabling for other critics. Moreover, allowing disaffection to play too prominent a role in our disciplinary histories risks making them more dry, anxious, and oppositional than they need be. In *Modernism and the New Criticism* (volume seven of *The Cambridge History of Literary Criticism*), Louis Menand and Lawrence Rainey describe the appeal of T. S. Eliot's critical style for the New Critics: "it had the look of being theoretical rather than journalistic or belletristic [...] [it] seemed a deliberate departure from the sort of appreciatory criticism the turn-of-the-century man and woman of letters produced, and thus an ideal model for an academic literary criticism."[35] Menand and Rainey go on to point out that the New Critics' own disciplinary histories almost entirely ignored any inheritances from the journalistic tradition—indifference being the ultimate expression of disparagement—and instead fashioned a new tradition, for which various poet-critics and philosophers from across the centuries (including Aristotle, Coleridge, and Kant) were recruited as allies and forebears.[36]

The unique role played by the New Critics in the institutionalization of literary studies is largely due to their insistence that the merits of the theories they promoted be measured by the practice. In their influential textbook, *Understanding Poetry*, Cleanth Brooks and Robert Penn Warren outline their paradigmatically New Critical "principles" for the analysis of poetry: "Emphasis should be kept on the poem as a poem"; "The treatment should be concrete and inductive"; "A Poem should

[35] Menand and Rainey, "Introduction," 10.

[36] Menand and Rainey, 11–12.

always be treated as an organic system of relationships."[37] But just as crucially, Brooks and Warren insist that their "book must stand or fall by the analyses of individual poems which it contains."[38] These analyses were unprecedented in their combination of formal attentiveness and self-reflexive theorization. Brooks later claimed that the anthology's subordination of historical context to formal analysis was primarily a product of the limited number of pages available for explication, and thus an effort "to apply the grease to the wheel that squeaked the loudest": "We believed that [the typical college instructor] could be counted on to supply historical and biographical material. We were concerned to provide help of another sort."[39] This fortuitous exigency facilitated a kind of interpretative ingenuity that—partly because of its replicability—swept the Anglo-American academy.

This practice of close reading was most directly inherited by American deconstruction, as indeed was the ethos of readerly exemplification. As Henry Staten details in this volume, deconstruction precipitated the creative destruction of the New Critical effort to demonstrate that literary works possess an aesthetic unity or coherence of the sort implied by Brooks's over-interpreted metaphor of the text as a self-enclosed object.[40] The extraordinary influence of Paul de Man, for instance, was due less to his philosophically sophisticated engagement with the theories of Jacques Derrida than his ability to mobilize that engagement so as to present texts as radically more unstable and contradictory than they had previously appeared. This is no more apparent than in the opening essay of *Allegories of Reading*, which moves from the mischievously overelaborated allegory of Archie Bunker's bowling shoes to the celebrated final lines of W. B. Yeats's "Among School Children" ("How can we know the dancer from the dance?").[41] Barbara Johnson's use of the allegory as an epigraph to *The Critical Difference* is a good indication of the nature of de Man's catalyzing appeal for his students and contemporaries, including Johnson, Geoffrey Hartman, and J. Hillis Miller. In

[37] Brooks and Warren, *Understanding Poetry*, ix. On the influence of New Critical textbooks, see Mark Jancovich, *New Criticism*, 87.

[38] Brooks and Warren, ix.

[39] Brooks, "New Criticism," 593.

[40] Brooks, *Well-Wrought Urn*.

[41] De Man, *Allegories of Reading*, 9–13.

turn, Johnson's canonical reading of *Billy Budd* (reprinted in *The Critical Difference*), which refused to privilege the implications of either plot or character as previous critics had and instead explored their fundamental incommensurability, exemplifies the kind of energetically inventive readings of previously familiar works that made deconstruction so successful in enthusing young scholars—Caroline Levine, for instance: "Deconstruction had encouraged a kind of intellectual pyrotechnics: my teachers had performed readings so dazzling that a physical thrill would run through me."[42]

Subsequent critical movements that pivoted away from the rhetorical focus of deconstruction largely concentrated their attention on the kinds of questions about identity that had previously been marginalized. But the complaint that such movements were motivated primarily by political rather than aesthetic matters—encapsulated by Harold Bloom's derisive allusions to the "School of Resentment"—misses much of the readerly force of, say, queer theory and postcolonial criticism at their best.[43] The theoretical tools that Sedgwick fashions in the introduction to *Between Men* are utilized in the book's first sustained close reading, which argues that the peculiar semantic and syntactic demarcations of gender difference in Shakespeare's "breathtaking" Sonnet 140 are central to what "makes the poem so disconcerted [*sic*] and moving."[44] In *Epistemology of the Closet*, Sedgwick goes toe-to-toe with deconstruction, showing how the problematics of signification Johnson identifies in her seminal reading of *Billy Budd* are closely bound up with the semantic field of homosexual/homophobic knowledge.[45] But perhaps most (in)famous of all was Sedgwick's reading of *Sense and Sensibility* alongside nineteenth-century medical accounts of female onanism, in "Jane Austen and the Masturbating Girl," which, as Susan Fraiman points out, played upon the "oxymoronic scandal of such a pairing."[46]

Around the same time, Jane Austen was the subject of another endeavor to bring to light hitherto overlooked or unrecognized facets of literary works—Edward Said's influential reading of *Mansfield Park* in

[42] Levine, *Forms*, ix.

[43] Bloom, *Western Canon*.

[44] Sedgwick, *Between Men*, 30–33, 31.

[45] Sedgwick, *Epistemology of the Closet*, 94–97.

[46] Sedgwick, "Masturbating Girl," 818–37; Fraiman, "Austen and Edward Said," 807.

Culture and Imperialism, which focuses on the way the novel at once divulges and conceals the fact that the Bertrams' country estate is financed by the slave labor of Antiguan sugar plantations.[47] Said argues that, though the novel undeniably belongs to "the canon of 'great literary masterpieces,'" "we must not say that [...] its affiliations with a sordid history are irrelevant or transcended, not only because it is irresponsible to do so, but because we know too much to say so in good faith"—suggesting, in effect, that there is no recovering from the knowledge his reading conveys.[48] For good measure, Said adds that he has "read *Mansfield Park* as part of the structure of an expanding imperialist venture [...] to illustrate a type of analysis infrequently encountered" in criticism of the time, underlining the replicable nature of his approach.[49] Fraiman notes that although the chapter on "*Mansfield Park* takes up relatively little space in the vastness of [...] *Culture and Imperialism*," it has been central to the reception of Said's thought in literary studies.[50] This is in fact not particularly surprising; at the risk of sounding obtuse, what literary critics mostly share is a fascination with literature and its study, and an imitable reading that transfigures our understanding of a major canonical novel naturally steals much of the show.

There is a very real sense in which each of these critical projects arose from a dissatisfaction with the New Criticism; the principal outlet of that dissatisfaction was not, however, methodological critique, but energetic efforts to demonstrate other ways of approaching literary works.[51] This is no more true than of the movement that has arguably shaped the contemporary critical scene more than any other: the New Historicism. In his provocative, revisionist account, *Literary Criticism: A Concise Political History*, Joseph North argues that since the 1980s literary studies has operated within a "historicist/contextualist paradigm" and places Stephen Greenblatt and Catherine Gallagher's *Practicing New Historicism*, "the closest thing to a manifesto the movement produced," at the heart of his description of the emergence and consolidation of that paradigm.[52]

[47] Said, *Culture and Imperialism*, 80–97.

[48] Said, 95.

[49] Said, 95.

[50] Fraiman, "Austen and Edward Said," 805.

[51] See Love, "Close but Not Deep," 372.

[52] North, *Literary Criticism*, 86.

Yet North's failure to find anything "radically new, exciting, and transgressive"[53] is precisely a *consequence* of this decision to concentrate on a quasi-manifesto which as he, Gallagher, and Greenblatt all recognize, trails the pioneering studies of the movement by nearly two decades—a decision which appears particularly ungenerous in light of North's own passionate commitment to the practice of close reading.[54] Like the disciplinary narratives of postcritique, a tendency to under-appreciate the *allure* of certain styles of reading and writing that have captivated other critics is in evidence here. In the introduction to *Learning to Curse*, Greenblatt elaborates on the narrative appeal of the anecdote, as the characteristic essayistic move of the New Historicism, in the context of his "will to tell stories, critical stories or stories told as a form of criticism."[55] The conversation Greenblatt stages between religious discourses about excessive intra-marital desire and the scene of Desdemona's murder in *Renaissance Self-Fashioning*, or his graceful movement in *Shakespearean Negotiations* from a police report about Christopher Marlowe, to Thomas Harriot's colonial account, to the history plays—these are not simply elegant forms of writing, but offer a new perspective on some of the most well-known works of English literature.[56] The New Historicist practice of reading across "literary" and "non-literary" works was not merely an unsettling of the canon, but represented a genuine expansion of what critics could do with texts, opening up new possibilities for surprising juxtapositions or the introduction of previously unrecognized or illegitimate contexts that naturally proved appealing to a great number of scholars. It is no accident that New Historicism remains most entrenched in the study of the early modern period, and especially Shakespeare. Though the circulation of a privileged set of theoretical terms—particularly relating to notions of subversion and containment—has largely fallen out of favor, across literary studies, many of the interpretative maneuvers that the New Historicism introduced (and in which Greenblatt excelled) have retained their currency.

[53] North, 87.

[54] Gallagher and Greenblatt, *Practicing New Historicism*, 1.

[55] Greenblatt, *Learning to Curse*, 6.

[56] Greenblatt, *Renaissance Self-Fashioning*, 246–52; *Shakespearean Negotiations*, 21–65.

3 Part Three

Though the sketch above, for reasons of concision, is necessarily partial, it is a fair representation of those critics who have most dramatically modified or added to the discipline's repertoire of critical approaches. One assumption that has governed the preceding argument is, however, worth briefly registering: the notion that the value of a critical method lies principally in the innovative readings it makes possible. This is an assumption that Attridge, for instance, does not share, instead describing the role of the critic as that of doing "justice" to works of literature.[57] Outlining his and Staten's theory of minimal interpretation, Attridge warns that critics "need to stop congratulating each other on producing ever more ingenious interpretations, as if originality and out-of-the-wayness were guarantees of rightness."[58] Yet even the discipline's most iconoclastic innovators have, like Attridge, invariably voiced their concern that "the most basic norms of careful reading are sometimes ignored in the rush to say something ingenious or different," indicating just how deep the critical desire to shed light on texts runs, which is the principle reason that readings which are gratuitously or merely clever have tended not to ignite sustained or widespread enthusiasm and have rarely stood the test of time.[59] Which is to say that a desire to do justice to the distinctiveness of particular literary works is baked into this essay's understanding of critical excitement, and the allure of novel interpretative methods. None of this is to deny that many (though far from all) of the most influential works of criticism also combine readerly insight with considerable writerly flair.

In a different but related way, though comparatively uncommon, there are some schools of criticism which purportedly *don't* strive to produce new readings of texts. In *Structuralist Poetics*, Jonathan Culler argued for the importance of structuralism in such terms:

> The type of literary study which structuralism helps one to envisage would not be primarily interpretive; it would not offer a method which, when applied to literary works, produced new and hitherto unexpected meanings. Rather than a criticism which discovers or assigns meanings, it would be a poetics which strives to define the conditions of meaning. Granting

[57] In Attridge, *Singularity of Literature* and *Work of Literature*.

[58] Attridge and Staten, *Craft of Poetry*, 13.

[59] Attridge and Staten, 5.

> new attention to the activity of reading, it would attempt to specify how we go about making sense of texts, what are the interpretive operations on which literature itself, as an institution, is based.[60]

Despite the emphatic denial here, it is difficult to see why paying attention to "the conditions of meaning" and "the activity of reading" should not also lead to a newly qualified understanding of the aesthetic qualities of particular texts—as the book's subsequent discussions of numerous quotations, from a wide range of literary works, eloquently attest.

But critical innovation need not and in fact rarely does take the form of fundamental methodological transformation. There is no shortage of critics producing new, sometimes profound, insights about particular genres, literary forms, modes of attention, authors, works, or specific passages from texts. To stick solely with, say, the study of the novel, examples include: Peter Brooks on the dramatization of ethical conflicts in *The Melodramatic Imagination*; Sianne Ngai on "minor" affects in *Ugly Feelings*; H. Porter Abbott on unknowable narratives in *Real Mysteries*; and John Frow's *Character and Person* and Alex Woloch's *The One vs. the Many* on the slippage between characters and persons. Woloch's virtuosic prologue on Homer's *Iliad*, which approaches Thersites as "the first truly minor character in Western literature," performatively demonstrates how the implications of the book's claims about character and narrative attention in the nineteenth-century novel far exceed that period and genre—an argumentative mode that has made it one of the most important and influential works of narrative theory of the last two decades.[61]

To ascribe real methodological value to these pursuits is to place oneself at odds with the current propensity for critics (including some contributors to this book) to declare that literary studies is in a state of crisis due to the hegemony of historicism, contextualism, or critique. North, for instance, sees only glimmers of hope for the discipline, mainly in the later work of Sedgwick and D. A. Miller. There is something to his claim that Sedgwick and Miller, in "Paranoid Reading and Reparative Reading" and *Jane Austen, or, The Secret of Style* respectively,[62]

[60] Culler, *Structuralist Poetics*, xiv.

[61] Woloch, *One vs. the Many*, 4.

[62] Sedgwick, *Touching Feeling*, 123–51.

in different ways and to different degrees, refuse to turn their experiments into injunctions for others to follow, and thus are in some sense working beyond or without a paradigm.[63] But then so were William Empson, Cleanth Brooks, and Stephen Greenblatt. Paradigms and manifestos can and often do come later—and sometimes much later—than the readings that make them possible. In *Seven Types of Ambiguity* and afterwards, Empson was deeply committed to studying authorial intention; that did not stop the mode of close reading he practiced being taken up by those, such as Brooks, who deployed it with a different, even antithetical, set of theoretical commitments and aims, and with great success.[64] North is right that Miller's bravura performance is utterly inimitable in its writerly charisma and flair, that it is "quite evidently not of such a kind as to be generally repeatable without massive adjustment, not only of the performance itself, but of the wider disciplinary context in which such efforts would have to take their place"[65]—and again, the same was true of Empson. At the risk of sounding like Bloom, it was precisely the provocative power of that readerly performance that caused massive changes to take place in the discipline. In much the same way, Miller's performative exhibition of the indelibly personal drives that impel critical writing, and his drawing out the entanglement of two related senses of the word 'style' (with all their affective investments) in his opening reading of *Sense and Sensibility*, has already inspired many scholars. Likewise, nearly every critic involved in debates about critical method passionately claims Sedgwick as a forebear. Much of the energy of her extraordinary essay comes from its incisive engagement with the argumentative and rhetorical mode of Miller's *The Novel and the Police*, with its jostling paranoid and reparative strains, its strong theory and local pleasures, the latter famously described by Sedgwick as "a wealth of tonal nuance, attitude, worldly observation, performative paradox, aggression, tenderness, wit, inventive reading, obiter dicta, and writerly panache"—a catalogue so often quoted partly because it enumerates the textual features that criticism both possesses

[63] North, *Literary Criticism*, 162, 168.

[64] As Staten elucidates in Chapter 2 of this volume, aspects of Brooks's own practice were in turn taken up by critics who did not share his convictions about the organic unity of literary texts.

[65] North, *Literary Criticism*, 168.

and obsessively peruses.[66] Which is to say that Sedgwick's essay is a readerly *tour de force* as much as a theoretical one, and that is central to its success.

In *Loving Literature*, Deidre Shauna Lynch tells the story of "how it has come to be that those of us for whom English is a line of *work* are also called upon to *love* literature and to ensure that others do so too."[67] The feeling that historicism and critique are inimical to such foundational passions has been at the heart of many recent methodological polemics (including some of those to be found in this book). But for those polemics to gain the ground they deserve, it is not enough to demand that other critics take up a more positive affective orientation toward texts. As Sedgwick has shown us, and Freud before her, love and aggression often work hand in hand: "it is sometimes the most paranoid-tending people who are able to, and need to, develop and disseminate the richest reparative practices."[68] In a sense, many of the protagonists in debates about critical method have forgotten the lesson that Greenblatt learnt so well—that, as scholars of literature, we are peculiarly susceptible to writerly strategies of persuasion, including suspense, exhilaration, suspicion, and, above all, fascination. Of course, most of us can't spin a critical tale like Greenblatt, or write in Miller's near-Jamesian style, with those lithe turns in tone, attitude, and affect—but we can explicitly demonstrate how our methods or lines of enquiry allow us to see or know things about literary works that we couldn't before.

"Whether or not a critic or theorist thematizes reading as a topic," Paul Armstrong argues, "the measure of what his or her argument signifies—not only its validity, but its very meaning—is how (or whether) a reader will read differently as a result."[69] The lesson of this essay's genealogy of critical method for the discipline's would-be innovators is to refocus their efforts away from packaged polemics and toward compelling readings that have the potential to persuade others of the analytic value of their intellectual insights. Meanwhile, a more granular historical sense of the forms of rhetorical argumentation that have succeeded in producing real changes to disciplinary practice should encourage us to compel critics pushing new

[66] Sedgwick, *Touching Feeling*, 135–36.

[67] Lynch, *Loving Literature*, 1.

[68] Sedgwick, *Touching Feeling*, 150.

[69] Armstrong, "In Defense of Reading," 89.

approaches to practically demonstrate the readerly payoff of their theoretical contentions in the elucidation of aesthetic form, and more generally to adopt a more pragmatic stance toward the methodological polemics that have dominated the field for the past two decades.

References

Abbott, H. Porter. *Real Mysteries: Narrative and the Unknowable*. Theory and Interpretation of Narrative Series. Columbus: Ohio State University Press, 2013.

Armstrong, Paul B. "In Defense of Reading: Or, Why Reading Still Matters in a Contextualist Age." *New Literary History* 42, no. 1 (2011): 87–113.

Attridge, Derek. *The Singularity of Literature*. New York: Routledge, 2004.

Attridge, Derek. *The Work of Literature*. Oxford: Oxford University Press, 2015.

Attridge, Derek, and Henry Staten. *The Craft of Poetry: Dialogues on Minimal Interpretation*. New York: Routledge, 2015.

Best, Stephen. "*La Foi Postcritique*, on Second Thought." *PMLA* 132, no. 2 (2017): 337–43.

Best, Stephen, and Sharon Marcus. "Surface Reading: An Introduction." *Representations* 108, no. 108 (2009): 1–21.

Bloom, Harold. *The Western Canon: The Books and School of the Ages*. New York: Harcourt Brace, 1994.

Brooks, Cleanth. "The New Criticism." *The Sewanee Review* 87, no. 4 (1979): 592–607.

———. *The Well-Wrought Urn: Studies in the Structure of Poetry*. Revised ed. London: Dobson, 1968.

Brooks, Cleanth, and Robert Penn Warren, eds. *Understanding Poetry: An Anthology for College Students*. New York: Holt, 1938.

Brooks, Peter. *The Melodramatic Imagination: Balzac, Henry James, Melodrama, and the Mode of Excess*. New Haven: Yale University Press, 1995.

Cheng, Anne Anlin. "Skins, Tattoos, and Susceptibility." *Representations* 108, no. 1 (2009): 98–119.

Cohen, Margaret. "Narratology in the Archive of Literature." *Representations* 108, no. 108 (2009): 51–75.

Crane, Mary Thomas. "Surface, Depth, and the Spatial Imaginary: A Cognitive Reading of The Political Unconscious." *Representations* 108, no. 1 (2009): 76–97.

Culler, Jonathan. *Structuralist Poetics: Structuralism, Linguistics and the Study of Literature*. New York: Routledge, 2002.

Empson, William. *Seven Types of Ambiguity*. 2nd ed. London: Chatto & Windus, 1949.

Felski, Rita. "Response." *PMLA* 132, no. 2 (March 2017): 384–91.

———. *The Limits of Critique*. Chicago: The University of Chicago Press, 2015.

———. *Uses of Literature*. Blackwell Manifestos. Oxford: Blackwell, 2008.

Fraiman, Susan. "Jane Austen and Edward Said: Gender, Culture, and Imperialism." *Critical Inquiry* 21, no. 4 (1995): 805–21.

Friedman, Susan Stanford. "Both/and: Critique and Discovery in the Humanities." *PMLA* 132, no. 2 (2017): 344–51.

Frow, John. *Character and Person*. Oxford: Oxford University Press, 2014.

Fuss, Diana. "But What About Love?" *PMLA* 132, no. 2 (March 2017): 352–55.

Gallagher, Catherine, and Stephen Greenblatt. *Practicing New Historicism*. Chicago: University of Chicago Press, 2000.

Greenblatt, Stephen. *Learning to Curse: Essays in Early Modern Culture*. Routledge Classics. New York, 2007.

———. *Renaissance Self-Fashioning: From More to Shakespeare*. Chicago: University of Chicago Press, 1980.

———. *Shakespearean Negotiations: The Circulation of Social Energy in Renaissance England*. Oxford: Clarendon Press, 1988.

Jancovich, Mark. *The Cultural Politics of the New Criticism*. Cambridge: Cambridge University Press, 1993.

Johnson, Barbara. *The Critical Difference: Essays in the Contemporary Rhetoric of Reading*. Baltimore: Johns Hopkins University Press, 1985.

Latour, Bruno. "Why Has Critique Run Out of Steam? From Matters of Fact to Matters of Concern." *Critical Inquiry* 30, no. 2 (2004): 225–48.

Levine, Caroline. *Forms: Whole, Rhythm, Hierarchy, Network*. Princeton: Princeton University Press, 2015.

Levinson, Marjorie. "What Is New Formalism?" *PMLA* 122, no. 2 (March 2007): 558–69.

Love, Heather. "Close but Not Deep: Literary Ethics and the Descriptive Turn." *New Literary History* 41, no. 2 (2010): 371–91.

Lubbock, Percy. *The Craft of Fiction*. London: Jonathan Cape, 1921.

Lynch, Deidre. *Loving Literature: A Cultural History*. Chicago: The University of Chicago Press, 2015.

Man, Paul de. *Allegories of Reading: Figural Language in Rousseau, Nietzsche, Rilke, and Proust*. New Haven: Yale University Press, 1979.

Marcus, Sharon. *Between Women: Friendship, Desire, and Marriage in Victorian England*. Princeton and Woodstock. Princeton: Princeton University Press, 2007.

Menand, Louis, and Lawrence Rainey. "Introduction." In *The Cambridge History of Literary Criticism*, vol. 7, *Modernism and the New Criticism*, edited by A. Walton Litz, Louis Menand, and Lawrence Rainey. Cambridge: Cambridge University Press, 2000.

Miller, D. A. *Jane Austen, or, The Secret of Style*. Princeton: Princeton University Press, 2003.

———. *The Novel and the Police*. Berkeley: University of California Press, 1988.

Mitchell, Lee Clark. *Mere Reading: The Poetics of Wonder in Modern American Novels*. Bloomsbury Collections. New York: Bloomsbury Academic, 2017.

Nealon, Christopher. "Reading on the Left." *Representations* 108, no. 1 (2009): 22–50.

Ngai, Sianne. *Ugly Feelings*. Cambridge, MA: Harvard University Press, 2007.

North, Joseph. *Literary Criticism: A Concise Political History*. Cambridge, MA: Harvard University Press, 2017.

Otter, Samuel. "An Aesthetics in All Things." *Representations*, no. 104 (2008): 116–25.

Price, Leah. "From *The History of a Book* to a 'History of the Book.'" *Representations* 108, no. 1 (November 2009): 120–38.

Robbins, Bruce. "Not So Well Attached." *PMLA* 132, no. 2 (2017): 371–76.

Said, Edward. *Culture and Imperialism*. New York: Knopf, 1993.

Sedgwick, Eve Kosofsky. *Between Men: English Literature and Male Homosocial Desire*. New York: Columbia University Press, 1985.

———. *Epistemology of the Closet*. Revised ed. Berkeley: University of California Press, 2008.

———. "Jane Austen and the Masturbating Girl." *Critical Inquiry* 17, no. 4 (1991): 818–37.

———. *Touching Feeling: Affect, Pedagogy, Performativity*. Durham: Duke University Press, 2003.

Simpson, James. "Interrogation over." *PMLA* 132, no. 2 (2017): 377–83.

Stewart, Garrett. *The Deed of Reading: Literature, Writing, Language, Philosophy*. Ithaca: Cornell University Press, 2015.

Theile, Verena. "New Formalism(s): A Prologue." In *New Formalisms and Literary Theory*, edited by Verena Theile and Linda Tredennick, 3–28. New York: Palgrave Macmillan, 2013.

Wolfson, Susan J. "Introduction: Reading for Form." In *Reading for Form*, edited by Susan J. Wolfson and Marshall Brown, 3–24. Seattle: University of Washington Press, 2006.

Woloch, Alex. *The One vs. the Many: Minor Characters and the Space of the Protagonist in the Novel*. Princeton: Princeton University Press, 2003.

Critical Styles

CHAPTER 6

Does Knowledge Still Have a Place in the Humanities?

William Rasch

About a decade ago, I was asked by Derek Attridge and Jane Elliott to contribute to a volume entitled *Theory after "Theory."* In the essay that I wrote for the volume—with the imitative title "Theory After Critical Theory"—I made a plea for a more exploratory mode of theoretical thinking to stand beside, if not in good measure replace, the type of hermeneutics of suspicion that has historically gone by the name Critical Theory and which is most often associated with the Frankfurt School in particular and Marxism in general. I in no way wished simply to dismiss Critical Theory and certainly had no intention of turning my back on "theory" altogether, no matter how defined; I have, after all, made a career, such as it is, out of "doing theory," as the phrase has it, and for the old dog that I am, it is too late now to learn new tricks. I merely pleaded for an unapologetic expansion of the field of theoretical inquiry. Because of this essay (I was led to believe), I was invited to present a keynote lecture at an English Department graduate student conference

W. Rasch (✉)
Indiana University, Bloomington, IN, USA
e-mail: wrasch@iu.edu

A. Sridhar et al. (eds.), *The Work of Reading*,
https://doi.org/10.1007/978-3-030-71139-9_6

at the University of Freiburg, which was dedicated to exploring post-Theory definitions of literary study and serves as the basis for this volume. Fearing I would disappoint the attendees and, at the same time, impishly attempting to demonstrate my English-literature chops (despite the fact that I am a Germanist by training) and thereby justify my inclusion in the conference, I declared at the outset:

I come to praise theory, not to bury it.

The declaration, with its ironic reversal, was admittedly a dramatic hyperbole, for it was not praise I meant to offer, but indispensability, that is, acknowledgment of the unavoidable participation of a theoretical component in all thoughtful deliberations on aesthetic matters. Nevertheless, I tried, as I put it then, to stay close to the bone while at the same time re-affirming what I take to be a truism, namely, that knowledge of theoretical narratives may enrich our understanding of literature and literary criticism. Given that I practice neither literature nor literary criticism, my declaration may be presumptuous. I ask, therefore, for a tolerant reader, but not one from whom I expect unqualified—or even qualified—affirmation.

I will make my case by revisiting one of the seminal critical essays of Anglo-American modernism, "The Metaphysical Poets," written by one of its major poets, T. S. Eliot, who was also one of the most important inspirations for US American New Criticism. The occasion of the essay, published first in October 1921, was a review of Herbert J. C. Grierson's edition of the so-called "metaphysical poets" of early seventeenth-century England.[1] In his review, Eliot famously articulated his influential thesis about a mid-seventeenth-century "dissociation of sensibility" evident in all English poetry subsequent to the metaphysicals up until his day, against which he wished to agitate. In embracing the task to talk about this old chestnut of a concept, I realize I am walking over the bodies of generations of scholars much more versed in the topic than I. Nevertheless, I wish to make two claims: (1) that Eliot's (in)famous "dissociation of sensibility" is a theoretical claim that speaks to questions concerning knowledge and the humanities that serves as the title to this chapter; and (2) that it, the dissociation of sensibility thesis, implies a well-charted historical narrative about the dissociation of reason, one developed and

[1] Grierson, *Metaphysical Lyrics*. The review was published in *The Times Literary Supplement*. I cite from the essay as it appears in Eliot, *Selected Essays*, published in 1951.

repeatedly lamented in the twentieth-century German philosophical tradition. I end with some ruminations about what we may still learn from Eliot's thesis.

1 The Theoretical Claim

In his review of the *seventeenth*-century poetry that Grierson had collected, Eliot begins with an *eighteenth*-century assessment, namely that penned by Samuel Johnson. Eliot writes, "Johnson, who employed the term 'metaphysical poets,' apparently having Donne, Cleveland, and Cowley chiefly in mind, remarks of them that 'the most heterogeneous ideas are yoked by violence together.'" Eliot then comments: "The force of this impeachment lies in the failure of the conjunction, the fact that often the ideas are yoked but not united."[2] I wish to linger a moment over Eliot's language: "The force of this impeachment lies in the failure of the conjunction"—a statement so pleasurably compressed it rings in my ear and flashes like the facets of a diamond to my eye, much like the poetry Johnson disparages and Eliot rehabilitates. Eliot follows this clause with a second, which explicates more prosaically: "the fact that often the ideas are yoked but not united." The yoking, Johnson asserts, is arbitrary and thus inhibits understanding—apparently like an ox cart that is unevenly propelled—but Eliot accuses him of judging the school by its failures, not its success. What follows, then, are example upon example of poetic accomplishments by Donne, King, Herbert, and the Elizabethan Chapman, finally contrasted—and Eliot wittily admits that the contrast is "perhaps somewhat less fair, though very tempting"[3]—with an abysmally risible passage from a poem by the Victorian Tennyson. Let me take one positive example, a famous passage—quite possibly made famous or more famous by Eliot's treatment—from Donne's "A Valediction," and then reveal the "less fair" comparison. Here is Donne:

> On a round ball
> A workeman that hath copies by, can lay
> An Europe, Afrique, and an Asia,
> And quickly make that, which was nothing, All,
> So doth each teare

[2] Eliot, *Selected Essays*, 283.

[3] Eliot, 287.

Which thee doth weare,
A globe, yea world by that impression grow,
Till thy tears mixt with mine doe overflow
This world, by waters sent from thee, my heaven dissolved so.[4]

Eliot comments that "instead of the mere explication of the content of a comparison," we have "a development by rapid association of thought which requires considerable agility on the part of the reader." The reader's agility, he continues, must follow "two connexions which are not implicit in the first figure, but are forced upon it by the poet: from the geographer's globe to the tear, and the tear to the deluge."[5] In contrast, little agility is required to follow Tennyson, and the leisurely stroll through the imagery is enlivened only by unintended levity.

One walked between his wife and child,
With measured footfall firm and mild,
And now and then he gravely smiled.
The prudent partner of his blood
Leaned on him, faithful, gentle, good,
Wearing the rose of womanhood.
And in their double love secure,
The little maiden walked demure,
Pacing with downward eyelids pure.
These three made unity so sweet,
My frozen heart began to beat,
Remembering its ancient heat.[6]

Ah yes, one has in one's life experienced the heart's ancient heat on occasion, as Sweeney, both Erect and Apeneck, knew more directly!

In examining the poems of Donne et al., Eliot operates less analytically than empirically, laying specimen upon specimen down on the lab bench, allowing each to advocate for itself—implying of course that each exceeds Johnson's reservations—and then comparing the healthy specimens with one that is aged and diseased (Tennyson's). It is by the force—and yes, I am deliberately repeating Eliot's word—it is by the force of his descriptions, coupled with the need to read each cited

[4] Quoted in Eliot, 282.

[5] Eliot, 282–83.

[6] Quoted in Eliot, 287.

passage repeatedly because of each's complexity, and capped by the utter banality of the counterexample, that he makes the case. But "empirical" may generate the wrong referent; perhaps Eliot operates more like a craftsman who admires features in the handiwork of others and does so by simply pointing to the exposed delicacies. But this too, though accurate enough, is also deceptive; for all along the way he gathers material to fashion an[7] historical conjecture by foreshadowing its terms. Of Herbert's ode "Beyond," he writes: "The effect, at its best, is far less artificial than that of an ode by Gray. And as this fidelity induces variety of thought and feeling, so it induces variety of music" (*SE*, 285). This, too, is a fascinating passage. The phrase "far less artificial" becomes "fidelity." Fidelity to what? Presumably the initial impulse—born of an experience?—that generated the need to resort to well-crafted language. Thought, feeling, and finally music form: if not a unity, then at least a trinity, the components of verbal intellect and pleasure. But let me continue the litany of phrases that are carefully being gathered together. Countering Johnson, Eliot wishes us to "consider whether" the "virtue" of the poets in question "was not something permanently valuable, which subsequently disappeared, but ought not to have disappeared" (*SE*, 285). Johnson did get one thing right, Eliot admits, "when he observes that 'their attempts were always analytic'; he would not agree that, after the dissociation, they put the material together again in a new unity" (*SE*, 286). Eliot finds that "dramatic verse of the later Elizabethan and early Jacobean poets expresses a degree of development of sensibility which is not found in any of the prose," for these poets "incorporated their erudition into their sensibility: their mode of feeling was directly and freshly altered by their reading and thought" (*SE*, 286). The comparison, then, between the Elizabethan and Jacobean poets, on the one hand, and those who followed is not dictated by a mere difference of taste. It registers a seismic shift.

> The difference is not a simple difference of degree between poets. It is something which had happened to the mind of England between the time of Donne or Lord Herbert of Cherbury and the time of Tennyson and Browning; it is the difference between the intellectual poet and the reflective poet. Tennyson and Browning are poets, and they think; but they do

[7] Yes, I am mimicking Donne. It is infectious.

> not feel their thought as immediately as the odour of a rose. A thought to Donne was an experience; it modified his sensibility.[8]

All these examples and this amassing of words and phrases—thought and feeling; something permanently valuable, which subsequently disappeared; analytic; dissociation; sensibility; erudition; mode of feeling directly and freshly altered by their reading and thought; mind of England; difference between intellectual poet and the reflective poet; feel their thought; a thought was an experience; it modified sensibility—all this then becomes summarized in a single phrase which he offers as a theory and a historical break, to wit: "In the seventeenth century a dissociation of sensibility set in, from which we have never recovered."[9]

What are we to make of this? I ask this in faux innocence, knowing full well that over many decades much, very much has been made of the claims contained in this modest package of a book review, not least that it served as a manifesto for the project of poetic modernism but also that it was politically reactionary, highlighting court poetry and diminishing the importance of Milton and the radical Romantics. I wish to highlight two points only marginally related to the two just mentioned. First, Eliot offers us an historical narrative. Modernism needs a past against which to push, and often, an even more distant past to reclaim and renew. More to the point, *modernity* is unthinkable without a past to overcome. It is therefore not in the least bit surprising that Eliot offers us an historical fable with a decisive break that serves as the moral of the story. And second, that break reveals a crack in reason. Eliot does not use the word reason, relying instead on "intellect" and "thought" in opposition to but also in companionship with emotion. Nevertheless, his parable shares features with a more general twentieth-century European or "Western" narrative about reason, knowledge, and *Wissenschaft*—that is, science in the more expansive sense that the German word conveys. As my use of the words "fable" and "parable" above was meant to indicate, historical narratives are fictions, contingently chosen possible variants of a general tale of human existence that serve explanatory purposes. The tale I will recap briefly is about the decline, splintering, and restriction of the power of reason.

[8] Eliot, *Selected Essays*, 287.

[9] Eliot, 288.

2 The Historical Narrative

Once upon a time, human reason, whether divinely inspired or endowed by nature, was thought to have the purpose and strength to understand the universe that the human being inhabited. With the help of logic and the mathematical sciences, reason and reason alone could explain the workings of physical nature. More significantly, with a more concentrated and universal exercise of all its powers, the form of reason that is embedded in language could discern the lineaments of *moral* nature with a view to understanding the place of the human creature in the cosmos. The rational revelation of purpose was said to be demonstrated in the purported unity of the True, the Good, and the Beautiful. What was true was also believed to be good and beautiful, what good was also true and beautiful, what beautiful also true and good. There was a coherence to the universe, represented by physical laws and moral meaning, and it was this totality that we were asked to understand.

There came a time when it was recognized that the claim of reason overstepped its limits and abilities. The mechanisms of the empirical universe could be discerned logically and confirmed by experiment, but what lay behind the cogs and wheels that made the physical world move remained unknown and unknowable. By scraping off the hubristic accretions that had attached themselves to reason over the centuries, Immanuel Kant devised a sleek, purified notion of our capacities. We could produce knowledge of the empirical universe, deduce moral obligations without reference to empirical reality, and make reflective judgments about beauty based on inklings of design in nature, but the simple unity of these three faculties could no longer be assumed or recreated. Knowledge of the mechanical world told us nothing about our moral obligations, and our intimations of beauty and design could be used as *signs* that the world was home to the otherwise lonely human creature, but most assuredly *not* as evidence, at least not as the same type of evidence that confirmed the machinations of physical nature. The aim of Kant's economy of reason was to make it serve the same *function* of the older version, but the old self-evidence of a substantial notion of reason had to be replaced by the fabrication of self-consciously fictional narratives that were deemed necessary if nihilism were to be kept at bay. The following surprisingly frank passage comes from Kant's famed essay, *Idea for a Universal History with a Cosmopolitan Purpose.*

> *A philosophical attempt to work out a universal history of the world in accordance with a plan of nature aimed at a perfect civil union of mankind must be regarded as possible and even as capable of furthering the purpose of nature itself*. It is admittedly a strange and at first sight absurd proposition to write a *history* according to an idea of how world events must develop if they are to conform to certain rational ends; it would seem that only a *novel* could result from such premises. Yet if it may be assumed that nature does not work without a plan and purposeful end, even amidst the arbitrary play of human freedom, this idea might nevertheless prove useful.[10]

Notice the choice of words: "it may be assumed," "might prove useful." Kant's historical narrative was knowingly hypothetical, an "as if" story designed to teach us how to act in accordance with a belief, an unsubstantiated but, he felt, *necessary* belief, in human progress.

Hegel took up Kant's challenge and wrote the novel Kant forecast, a classic comedy with happy ending, only he refused to acknowledge its fictional character. In what must be the most disarmingly, even enchantingly immodest statement ever uttered in a university lecture hall, Hegel, in his lectures on the philosophy of history, said the following.

> Those among you…who are not yet acquainted with philosophy could perhaps be asked to come to these lectures with the belief in Reason, with a desire, a thirst for its insight. It is indeed the desire for rational insight, for cognition, and not merely for a collection of facts, which ought to be presupposed as a subjective aspiration in the study of the sciences. For even though one were not approaching world history with the thought and knowledge of Reason, at least one ought to have the firm and invincible faith that there is Reason in history and to believe that the world of intelligence and of self-conscious willing is not abandoned to mere chance, but must manifest itself in the light of the rational Idea. Actually, however, I do not have to demand such belief in advance. What I have said here provisionally, and shall have to say later on, must, even in our branch of science, be taken as a summary view of the whole. It is not a presupposition of study; it is a *result* which happens to be known to me because I already know the whole.[11]

[10] Kant, *Political Writings*, 51–52. Italics in the original.

[11] Hegel, *Reason in History*, 12. Italics in the original.

By the end of the century, however, Friedrich Nietzsche, that great model of our trade—namely, criticism—exposed the literary devices of such a lullaby.

In the *Genealogy of Morality*, Nietzsche wrote: "Strictly speaking, there is no 'presuppositionless' knowledge, the thought of such a thing is unthinkable, paralogical: a philosophy, a 'faith' always has to be there first, for knowledge to win from it a direction, a meaning, a limit, a method, a *right* to exist."[12] In effect, Nietzsche made Kant's knowing wink of the eye the foundation of knowledge about knowledge by stating that knowledge is *enabled* by some fundamental presupposition. Contra Kant, however, he punctures rather than places counterfactual faith in the fiction; and contra Hegel, no supposition can be thought of arising from right reason acting like some pre-existing unmoved mover, for it too must be enabled, set in motion by some other presupposed agency, and such a regression is never-ending, even if we wish to give grandiose names to them, names like God or Nature or History. We may make the preconditions of our argument explicit (to the extent we are aware of them) or we may be driven by forces of which we have but the slightest notion—though what remains blind to us may be crystal clear to some other reader of our texts. But no matter, for what was once the pursuit of truth has now become the eternal hunt for latencies and what they enable. These latencies, when for instance labeled as ideology, *may* serve as grounds for a hermeneutics of suspicion, but need not. They simply are the starting blocks for our footloose race of reason.

Nietzsche, as filtered through Max Weber, sets off the twentieth-century discourse of modernity. Its components were summarized in Weber's justly famous Munich lecture "Wissenschaft als Beruf" ("Science as a Vocation"). The term translated as "vocation" is the German *Beruf*. Here, Weber knowingly channels Luther. In his *Protestant Ethic and the Spirit of Capitalism*, Weber had written:

> An audible echo from the religious realm unmistakably resonates in the German word "Beruf." Perhaps this connotation is even more apparent in the equivalent English term "calling:" one's *task* is given by God. The

[12] Nietzsche, *Genealogy of Morality*, 112.

more vigorously we place the accent on this term in actual usage, the more perceptible becomes the religious echo.[13]

However, had not Nietzsche already told us that God was dead? Indeed, he had, and Weber repeatedly admonished his listeners and readers that only "overgrown children" could believe the fables of old, whether religious or, presumably, Hegelian. We are therefore left with a *Beruf* without a *Ruf*, a calling without a call, or a call that comes from nowhere. Here is why.

In condensed form, Weber introduced his listeners to a radical critique of reason and meaning that would set the table at which many a subsequent theorist took nourishment, while others vehemently abstained. With reference to Nietzsche and Baudelaire, Weber gives us a powerful version of the True, the Good, and the Beautiful torn asunder in the resurrection of a multiplicity of warring gods, each in opposition to the others, an animated version of the incommensurability of what he called "value spheres" and what we now call language games (à la Wittgenstein and Lyotard) or (following Parsons and Luhmann) social systems. And perhaps most famously, in Weber's lecture, we also find a thumbnail sketch of rationalization—the belief that every mechanism of empirical reality is capable of being understood and explained rationally and naturalistically, leaving the world "disenchanted," devoid of inexplicable forces and power—God for instance—with which we once gave meaning to our existence.[14] *Wissenschaft*, in other words, can give us (now or eventually) answers to every technical question we ask of it, but none to the truly crucial ones: "What should we do? How shall we live?"—questions

[13] Weber, *Protestant Ethic*, 99. The term "calling" appears in bold in the English text for reasons that have to do with pedagogical aims of the volume. I have changed the bold to conform to the way *Beruf* was framed. In contemporary German, *Beruf* generally means "profession," "occupation," "career," and *Ruf*, among other things, "a call." Weber evokes Martin Luther's usage in the latter's translation of the Bible. Here, in addition to the secular meaning, it can also refer to a call from God to eternal salvation. The pathos of my sentence—*Beruf* without a *Ruf*—exploits both the secular and divine notions to evoke the loss of the divine, the loss of transcendent meaning. See Weber, *Protestant Ethic*, 99–105; see also the translator's note 3, pp. 306–310.

[14] See Weber, *Vocation Lectures*, 30: "Our age is characterized by rationalization and intellectualization, and above all, by the disenchantment of the world. Its resulting fate is that precisely the ultimate and most sublime values have withdrawn from public life. They have retreated either into the abstract realm of mystical life or into the fraternal feelings of personal relations between individuals."

Weber attributes to Tolstoy but could just as easily have been taken from Kant. We are left, then, with a notion of reason that grants no access to the question of the ends of human existence, but provides only the means of achieving aims that are determined elsewhere, outside the bounds of *Wissenschaft, Wissen, and Vernunft*. The evacuation of reasoned meaning from our lives is mirrored in the evacuation of meaning from *Wissenschaft* itself. Here we hear Weber's direct echo of Nietzsche.

> People are wont to speak nowadays of a science "without presuppositions." Does such a thing exist? It depends on what is meant by it. Every piece of scientific work presupposes the validity of the rules of logic and method. These are the fundamental ways by which we orient ourselves in the world. Now, there is little to object to in these presuppositions, at least for our particular question. But science further assumes that the knowledge produced by any particular piece of scientific research should be *important*, in the sense that it should be "worth knowing." And it is obvious that this is the source of all our difficulties. For this presupposition cannot be proved by scientific methods. It can only be *interpreted* with reference to its ultimate meaning, which we must accept or reject in accordance with our own attitude toward life.[15]

A few pages later he added an exclamation point to this observation.

> Science today is a profession practiced in specialist *disciplines* in the service of reflection on the self and the knowledge of relationships between facts and not a gift of grace on the part of seers and prophets dispensing sacred goods and revelations. Nor is it part of the meditations of sages and philosophers about the *meaning* of the world. This is of course an ineluctable fact of our historical situation, one from which there is no escape.[16]

Yet we still feel called, even as we know that the call to pursue a calling comes from us and us alone. Our calling—that is, the writing we write, the teachings we teach, the institutions we serve, and the way we serve them—is not self-evident. We must provide our own justifications, and these justifications seem to be internal to the systems we inhabit and the disciplines we exercise. To put this colloquially and thus crudely: There is

[15] Weber, *Vocation Lectures*, 17–18. Italics in the original.

[16] Weber, 27.

no pre-given presupposition, no meaning, no god, no spirit, no force in the universe that gives a good god damn about any single word, sentence, page, chapter, or book that I have ever written. The calling I follow has no author or authorization other than my own, and is in competition or collaboration with all other motherless callings, including yours. Yet, or rather, *therefore* we go on.

3 Our Task

I assert that with his "theory" of the dissociation of sensibilities, Eliot participates in the discourse of modernity described above, albeit more or less unwittingly and in modest fashion. The change in the "mind of England" that he charts is but the local rumbling of a continental shift. What nearly all the versions of the narrative of modernity share is the observation that the century of figures like Galileo and Francis Bacon, a century bridging the 1500s and 1600s, marks the construction of a fatefully novel "world picture," to use Heidegger's phrase,[17] inaugurated by Cartesian metaphysics and the new empirical and mathematically based natural sciences. You may recall the presence of Bacon in the opening pages of Horkheimer's and Adorno's *Dialectic of Enlightenment*. Noting Bacon's claim that the empirical sciences will now reinstate the "happy match between the mind of man and the nature of things,"[18] they characterize that claim not as liberation of the faculties but the enchainment of nature.

> Although not a mathematician, Bacon well understood the scientific temper which was to come after him. The 'happy match' between understanding and the nature of things that he envisioned is a patriarchal one: the mind, conquering superstition, is to rule over disenchanted nature. Knowledge, which is power, knows no limits, either in its enslavement of creation or in its deference to worldly masters...What human beings seek to learn from nature is how to use it to dominate wholly both it and human beings.[19]

[17] Heidegger, "Age of World Picture."

[18] Horkheimer and Adorno, *Dialectic of Enlightenment*, 1.

[19] Horkheimer and Adorno, 2.

This, I believe, is the dissociation of sensibility Eliot alluded to, though Horkheimer and Adorno articulated their account in a more brutal manner, one that consciously looks back to Weber ("disenchantment") and forecasts Foucault ("knowledge is power"). That is, thought dissociated from feeling leads to domination of nature, feeling dissociated from thought is but a weak and sentimental compensation, a mollification of a ruffled and rubbed soul that can only *recollect* its ancient and wondrous heat. Working without the trappings of the Nietzschean-Weberian discourse of modernity, we can articulate Eliot's account now in a way that may open up some possibilities for our present moment, without, however, falling for the fantasy of annulling the dissociation, the fallacy of reconciling instrumental and moral reason.[20]

To do so, let me remind you of the basic structure of the medieval university. Two faculties composed the curriculum. The Upper Faculty housed the disciplines of the three occupations that required a university education: Law, Medicine, and above all, Theology. These have become the contemporary professional schools, with Schools of Business, preaching the gospel of prosperity, now replacing the representatives of wine and wafer. The Lower Faculty comprised what in the Anglophone world we call the Liberal Arts, or, Colleges of Arts and Sciences. The disciplines that here found their home were further grouped: grammar, logic, and rhetoric were collectively known as the Trivium; mathematics, geometry, astronomy, and music comprised the Quadrivium. On the one hand, the sciences of language (logic still being Aristotelean, not symbolic); on the other, mathematics (music being also a discipline based on numerical

[20]What I call "fantasy" and "fallacy" was the project proposed by minds far greater than mine, including not least Heidegger, "Age of World Picture," Husserl, *Crisis of Sciences*, and Strauss, *What Is Political Philosophy*? (the title essay) and Strauss, *Natural Right and History*, so I acknowledge unwarranted hubris. Another, if surprising, advocate of substantial or objective reason, Horkheimer, *Eclipse of Reason* (originally published 1947), gives the most succinct definition of the type of reason to be reclaimed: "The philosophical systems of objective reason implied the conviction that an all-embracing or fundamental structure of being could be discovered and a conception of human destiny derived from it" (12). Ironically sounding like the putative conservative Strauss, the Marxist-trained Horkheimer identifies the champions and the enemies of what he called objective reason: "Catholicism and European rationalist philosophy were in complete agreement regarding the existence of a reality about which such insight could be gained…The two intellectual forces that were at odds with this particular presupposition were Calvinism, through its doctrine of *Deus absconditus*, and empiricism, through its notion…that metaphysics is concerned exclusively with pseudo-problems" (16–17).

proportion). Together they prepared students for advanced study in the professions.

Nominally, our universities still roughly follow this pattern, but the relationship between the Trivium and the Quadrivium is often no longer collegial. With the hegemony of quantity over quality in the sciences, reason underwent a fundamental change. Weber no longer used the term reason, preferring rationality, specifically *Zweckrationalität*, a term Horkheimer, in his *Eclipse of Reason*, translated as "instrumental reason," a phrase that has since become a prominent feature of the English language.[21] If classical reason pretended to communicate with nature using both the disciplines of the Trivium and the Quadrivium, instrumental reason—*Zweckrationalität*—increasingly knows only number. Quite literally, what counts now as truth can be enumerated; what can be alphabetized and only alphabetized, is regarded merely as opinion or worse, as entertainment. As the saying goes, "Someone without data is only a person with an opinion." The dissociation of sensibility that separates thought from feeling, thinking from experience, can also be seen as the dissociation of mathematical truth and linguistic fancy. Put in contemporary terms, only the quantitative research conducted in the STEM disciplines—science, technology, engineering, math—is said to produce knowledge. The arts (now including demoted music) and the qualitative, language-based research that investigates them, are relegated at best to the realm of leisure, the realm of *feeling*, of sentiment, of sweetness and light—and *not* work. In this regard, the distinction between theory and critical practice—close reading—has little relevance. We are all condemned as *ir*relevant. *This* is the dissociation of sensibility that not only affected the fibers of English poetry, as Eliot lamented; it is the hostile, ugly divorce that currently threatens our profession, or rather, our vocation, our calling, our *Beruf*.

Thus, the famous question: What is to be Done? I have no surefire answer. Let me, however, end this meander through time and language with a possibly plausible thesis. It will be up to you to decide whether it is adequate to the issue of this volume.

Was the "mind of England" altered on or about the time of the Glorious Revolution of 1688, as Eliot claimed? His thesis is in accord with the various narratives of modernity that dominated the twentieth

[21] See for instance Horkheimer, *Eclipse of Reason*, 6, fn. 1.

century. If one finds that narrative a productive presupposition with which to work, then Eliot should be added to the list of its proponents. The more interesting question to ponder, however, is whether the "mind of *English*," the English language, changed, not just for the worse in the post-seventeenth centuries, but *also* for the better in the first third of the twentieth. The proof would be in the reading. I think, or would like to think, that the latter, the twentieth-century change, *did* happen. The power and persuasiveness—if in fact you are persuaded—of Eliot's thesis lies not in his theory per se, not in any explicit or implicit philosophy of history that I or anyone else may wish to chart, but in the power of his prose.[22] Truth be told, Eliot found or had confirmed some of his ideas in Grierson's introduction to the volume of poetry that Eliot used to stage his assault. Take for instance Grierson's claim that the word "metaphysical" is the correct descriptor for the poetry of Donne et al., because it "lays stress on...above all the peculiar blend of passion and thought, feeling and ratiocination which is their greatest achievement. Passionate thinking is always apt to become metaphysical, probing and investigating the experience from which it takes its rise."[23] The conjunction Eliot elevates to a world-historical thesis Grierson blandly gives as a marker of a specific type of poetry written by a limited number of practitioners, the metaphysical poets, without further consequence. Nevertheless, the package Eliot designs for such observations, the concision of the phrase "dissociation of sensibility," indeed, of the word "dissociation" itself; the familial allusion to the "mind of England," eschewing a grander, more

[22] In repeatedly invoking the power of Eliot's prose, I feel the necessity of reminding the reader also of Eliot's irony, surely a complication (but not, I think, a refutation) of what I offer up for consideration. Here is Hugh Kenner's take on Eliot's literary-critical prose: "*The Egoist* reviews were often satiric in method. In a long sequence of reviews written for Middleton Murry's *Athenaeum*, Eliot extended and generalized his *Egoist* manner into what was to be, until fame overtook him, his fundamental critical strategy: a close and knowing mimicry of the respectable. So thoroughly did he master this technique that he was able to compose two of his most important and blandly subversive essays, 'Andrew Marvell' and 'The Metaphysical Poets,' within the confines of reviewing commissions from *The Times Literary Supplement* itself. The rhetorical layout of essay after essay can best be described as a parody of official British literary discussion: its asperities, its pontification, its distinctions that do not distinguish, its vacuous ritual of familiar quotations and bathetic solemnities. The texture of an Eliot review is almost indistinguishable from that of its neighbors; only the argument, and the tone derived from an extreme economy of phrase, are steadily subversive" (*Invisible Poet*, 99).

[23] Grierson, *Metaphysical Lyrics*, xvi.

distant and abstract term like "modern" or "modernity;" and the precision of an exact date—the politically portentous 1688—all this operates by way of seduction, flattery, and also a flagrant punch in the face. If we are convinced, we are convinced by his deceptively descriptive dissections of the poetry he admires laid against that which he loathes. In between the poetic diction of Donne and Tennyson lies Eliot's own command of language. We may recoil at the political implication of his thesis, the implied sense that with incipient parliamentary sovereignty comes a slackening of the collective intellect; we may recoil as so many over the past century have, but we have yet to demonstrate that with mass, state-sponsored education, of which the present author was a grateful beneficiary, comes mass elevation of intellect (which observation is not meant as a condemnation of what we call democracy, only an observation that it too has its limits). We may not like Eliot's politics, but if we find ourselves caressed and cajoled by his language, we are hard pressed to deny the terms of his argument. Do we not want, or why would we not want the coupling of thought and emotion into a complex whole? Why would we not want to grant poetry, or for that matter, prose, the power to utter truths that number cannot properly approach? Why would we want to have the one instrument that, barring rare disabilities, is universally shared—so-called natural language or human speech—why would we want to have *our* language be denied the capacity to utter truths that do not rely on ratification or verification by some other symbolic mechanism?

There is no way to *assert* the *right*—to use the abused lingo of the day—there is no way to assert the right to grant language this power. The only option is to *practice* it. If Eliot is convincing, it is not because of some philosophical discourse on which he relies (though he does mimic the language of a now forgotten English idealist, F. H. Bradley), but because of the writerly skill he possesses, and, admittedly, the authority that his poetry bestowed upon him, both the poetry he wrote before his review and the modernist landmark, *The Waste Land* (sleekly edited by Ezra Pound), published a year later.[24] Even if we lack the poetical skills, we should nevertheless attempt to hone our critical prose as our means of persuasion. For reasons I cannot explain, "The force of this impeachment lies in the failure of the conjunction" puts a smile on my face and reduces all the catchphrases coming from the past half century

[24] See Eliot, *Waste Land*.

of "theory," including those I have staked my career on, sound like so many commercial jingles. Whether we write *on* theory or work explicitly or implicitly *with* theory when we work on literary or any other kind of texts, or whether we feel we have emancipated ourselves clearly and cleanly from all theoretical presuppositions and stand naked before the texts we read, no matter—we should write with the passion and descriptive precision that triggers a similar concentrated passion in the reader, a similar precision of thought, a similar sensitiveness to detail, to the mechanisms of argumentation, to the evidence displayed, *and*, not least, a sheer joy in the act of reading. It is not without cause that rhetoric was taught in the Trivium—the tools and skills of argumentation, but also the tools and skills of manipulating language aesthetically to engage the reader's emotions and passions, coordinating them with the rigors of the intellect. For all the negative associations that have accrued to it, we may wish to eschew the term rhetoric and simply say we seek to persuade, or more graciously, to invite the reader to entertain the trajectory and aim of our claims. We have no mathematical proofs, no written in stone symbolic representations to anchor (correctly or incorrectly) our beliefs. We *do* have language, and we are trained to persuade. We should therefore write our prose to the best of our concentrated abilities in the same manner as Donne and Herbert wrote their poetry—not of course with the same diction and skill, but, per impossible, with the same power, the power that would provoke us and our readers to feel our thought. Only in this way can we hope to persuade those who have not yet divorced their relationship to us to take notice.

There is of course no assurance that we will ever be read or read wisely. There is often little or no external reward for our efforts. There is no one, no force finite or infinite, to call us to this project. We can only call upon ourselves, and that is the reason why we found ourselves gathered together in Freiburg, Germany, in the summer of 2017, and that is also the reason why we find ourselves gathered again in this volume.

References

Eliot, T. S. *Selected Essays*. 3rd ed. London: Faber and Faber, 1951.

———. *The Waste Land: A Facsimile and Transcript of the Original Drafts Including the Annotations of Ezra Pound*. Edited by Valerie Eliot. New York: Harcourt Brace, 1971.

Elliott, Jane, and Derek Attridge, eds. *Theory After 'Theory'*. London: Routledge, 2001.

Grierson, Herbert J. C., ed. *Metaphysical Lyrics and Poems of the Seventeenth Century*. Oxford: The Clarendon Press, 1921.

Hegel, G. W. F. *Reason in History*. Translated by Robert S. Hartman. Indianapolis: Bobbs-Merrill, 1953.

Heidegger, Martin. "The Age of the World Picture." In *Off the Beaten Track*, edited and translated by Julian Young and Kenneth Haynes. Cambridge: Cambridge University Press, 2002.

Horkheimer, Max. *Eclipse of Reason*. New York: Continuum, 1974.

Horkheimer, Max, and Theodor W. Adorno. *Dialectic of Enlightenment: Philosophical Fragments*. Edited by Gunzelin Schmid Noerr. Translated by Edmund Jephcott. Stanford: Stanford University Press, 2002.

Husserl, Edmund. *The Crisis of European Sciences and Transcendental Phenomenology: An Introduction into Phenomenological Philosophy*. Translated by David Carr. Evanston: Northwestern University Press, 1970.

Kant, Immanuel. *Political Writings*. 2nd ed. Edited by Hans Reis. Translated by H. B. Nisbet. Cambridge: Cambridge University Press, 1991.

Kenner, Hugh. *The Invisible Poet: T. S. Eliot*. New York: Harcourt, Brace and World, 1959.

Nietzsche, Friedrich. *On the Genealogy of Morality*. Edited by Keith Ansell-Pearson. Translated by Carol Diethe. Cambridge: Cambridge University Press, 2007.

Rasch, William. "Theory After Critical Theory." In Elliott and Attridge, *Theory After 'Theory'*, 47–61.

Strauss, Leo. *Natural Right and History*. Chicago: University of Chicago Press, 1953.

———. *What Is Political Philosophy? And Other Studies*. Chicago: University of Chicago Press, 1959.

Weber, Max. *The Protestant Ethic and the Spirit of Capitalism*. Translated by Stephen Kalberg. Oxford: Oxford University Press, 2011.

———. *The Vocation Lectures*. Edited by David Owen and Tracy B. Strong. Translated by Rodney Livingstone. Indianapolis: Hackett, 2004.

CHAPTER 7

"Our Beloved Codex": Frank Kermode's Modesty

Ronan McDonald

1 Part One

Frank Kermode (1919–2010) never founded a movement or fomented a revolution. It is not surprising if, ten years after his death, his star has dimmed a little or if he has fallen into comparative neglect. Yet at the time of his death, he was Britain's leading literary critic, one who anticipated, with remarkable foresight, some of the predicaments we now face around the precarity of our discipline and its institutions and the need to articulate its social and educational purpose. While he was instrumental in the rise of literary theory in Britain, he also sought a mode for positive literary evaluation and to identify how and why canons are formed. He recognized and affirmed the critic's role in the process of interpretation and meaning making, but also insisted on the immense and determining role of history, not only the social context from which a literary work emerges but also that in which it is received. He searchingly explored questions

R. McDonald (✉)
Gerry Higgins Chair of Irish Studies, University of Melbourne, Melbourne, VIC, Australia
e-mail: ronan.mcdonald@unimelb.edu.au

A. Sridhar et al. (eds.), *The Work of Reading*,
https://doi.org/10.1007/978-3-030-71139-9_7

which animate the discipline of literary studies today—not just how we read and why, but also *what* we read, how we select the works we deem enduring or worthy of notice. In his later career, he sought to articulate a function of criticism between the poles of history and value, where the critic has a role of active custodianship. His reflections on these themes, despite or perhaps *because of* the qualified, cautious register in which they are articulated, repay analysis by literary studies today.

The names of some critics, like some writers, become adjectives: Leavisite, Empsonian, Vendleresque. "There aren't many Kermodians in the world," Frank Kermode once remarked in an interview, without too much ruefulness.[1] Kermode, always modest and self-deprecating, is also hard to pin down, let alone caricature. If he has a signature style it is one of tact, caution, plurality of approach, attentiveness not just to the words on the page but to the contesting cries of historical context, the criticism that the text has already generated, and the reader's own position in the hermeneutic process. Michael Wood rightly cautions that "Frank Kermode is too multifarious a writer to have anything as dogged as a theme in his critical work; too sane and stealthy to boast of anything as limiting as an obsession."[2] What differentiates him from other leading critics like F. R. Leavis, William Empson, and T. S. Eliot is the mildness of his persona, an absence of fervor or mission. This is not to suggest a lack of faith in his own judgment: his is a diffidence born of a confident and capacious sensibility, a genial civility which always knows that there may be something it does not know. In person, according to Christopher Norris, Kermode conveyed the odd sense of "having thought longer and deeper than oneself about the topic in hand but not wishing to let that be known, or preferring to let the talk go on just in case some better idea came up."[3]

Should the word exist the connotation of "Kermodian" would, then, be of tone and approach rather than ideology or method. It would indicate cautious modesty, laced through with gently sardonic wit, acuity of perception, a capacity to tease out ambivalence and nuance, a style always ready to doubt and to qualify its own judgments. His hard-to-pin-downness is reinforced not only by these qualities but also by the

[1] Salusinsky, *Criticism and Society*, 111.

[2] Wood, "Introduction," 1.

[3] Norris, "Remembering Frank Kermode," 6.

size and range of his output over a long career that runs the gamut from the bible to the contemporary novel, from Botticelli to Barthes. His critical approach is permeable and receptive, open to new ideas and methods, such as deconstruction, and also eager to cross the borders between academia and higher journalism. He instigated the founding of the *London Review of Books* in 1979, for which he would write more than two hundred reviews right up to his final months. His early collection of essays *Puzzles and Epiphanies*, he claims, "has the unity imposed upon it by a limited mind of promiscuous habit."[4] The critical promiscuity would endure, not just in subject, but in methodological reflexivity.

While we certainly do not now think of Kermode as a pioneering literary theorist, he nonetheless has a fair claim to be the figure who more than anyone galvanized and enabled the reception and circulation of French post-structuralist theory in the United Kingdom. His legendary Critical Theory seminar conducted while he was the Lord Northcliffe Professor of English at UCL (1969–1974) was the incubator for just about every major British theorist of the coming generation. They were also where his more reflexive and meta-critical books were nurtured, *The Sense of an Ending: Studies in the Theory of Fiction* and *The Genesis of Secrecy: On the Interpretation of Narrative*. For the rest of his career, Kermode spoke about this period as the highlight of his career, and bemoaned giving up the University College London post, for the Edward VII Chair at Cambridge University. "To Cambridge then I came, where a cauldron of unholy hates hissed all around me," he recalls in his memoir.[5] There he became embroiled in the notorious Colin MacCabe affair, where a theoretically inclined young academic was denied a fellowship. Partly as a result of this episode, and what he regarded as a failure to reform a sclerotic and complacent department, he resigned from his Chair prematurely.

Kermode's whole self-image and self-presentation are those of an interloper. It is no accident that his 1995 memoir is called *Not Entitled*. Born in the Isle of Man, to a family of modest means, he was always partly outside the august institutions of higher education to which he ascended, even when he accepted a knighthood in 1991 (a rare laurel for

[4] Kermode, *Puzzles and Epiphanies*, 1.

[5] Kermode, *Not Entitled*, 248.

a literary academic). This inside-outside quality is one reason for his intellectual restlessness. He was not simply drawn to dissent and iconoclasm, but retained a suspicion of dissent itself, especially when it threatened to become a cult or a new orthodoxy. While Frank Lentricchia astutely observes that Kermode waits and watches "at the first moment of avant-garde thrust, when passions are most inflamed" and the "outrage seems to be normalized," the inverse is also true: he deploys new ideas and fresh concepts before they congeal into the charisma of iconoclasm.[6] Kermode was drawn to the intellectual excitement and emancipatory possibilities of post-structuralism and cultural theory but became wary of its fervor and radicalism, which threatened to usurp or flatten literary value itself. Literary theory, he recalls, was "another country in which I went to live without feeling truly at home, even when it still seemed exciting, even before it became drugged with self-regard."[7] It was because he felt like an outsider from the beginning that he was primed to question and criticize theory as its power and academic capital grew. The intellectual allure of theory, which Kermode felt and also wanted to share pedagogically, would lose out to a greater imperative: writing about literary art and communicating its richness to a wide audience. His urge to write with clarity, modesty, and circumspection, meant he was ill-at-ease in technical theoretical language. He was pressingly aware of the obligations of custodianship, the need to bequeath his artistic and literary heritage to future generations. How to preserve the tradition, or the very tenability of a canon, without resorting to reactionary retrenchment or moat-building? How can we open literary criticism to the forces of cultural history and the cleansing power of critique without dissolving the distinctions and discriminations which underpin the idea of the literary classic? How can we recognize the ideology of the aesthetic without debunking artistic quality? These are the questions which pervade his later career. They trouble us still.

Kermode begins his career by arguing, *pace* the new criticism, for the need for literary studies to reckon with history, by proclaiming the untenability of the isolated and self-identical literary artwork. Later in his career, he comes to see the opposite danger, in which literature is only historical and ideological, a cultural document or text of no more intrinsic

[6] Lentricchia, *Forms of Attention*, ix.

[7] Kermode, *Not Entitled*, 198.

interest than a shopping list, where the idea of literary value is disdained or eschewed. From the 1970s, a major preoccupation of his work is to think together questions of history and value, to understand the genesis of the canon and the constitutive role of the interpretative and critical tradition in its construction, without thereby debunking or cancelling the status of the classic or the value of literature itself. He explores these questions in his most famous meta-critical work *The Genesis of Secrecy*, but also the more neglected works with a theoretical aspect, including *The Classic: Literary Images of Permanence and Change*, *Forms of Attention*, and *Culture and Value*.

His solution, which he would admit is only partially successful, is to bring reception and reading into the mix, to think of the classic not as a timeless masterpiece, but rather as an artwork that lives through shifting commentaries and critical responses that animate and re-animate it across the generations. In a version of Pound's declaration that "Literature is news that STAYS news," he defines a classic not as the unchanging object outside history, but rather one that is brought to different lives at different times through acts of interpretation.[8] The variety of his methods and approaches means different levels of closeness to the text are needed to optimize responsiveness to the literary work, including an acknowledgment of history and the author's intention. This is why for Kermode a weak theory is necessary. The possibility of surprise must be maintained.

Many of these concerns are enduringly relevant. We are not likely to dispense with the question of value and canonicity and the role of history and reading any time soon. Yet some have also been given fresh significance by the recent turn to postcritique in literary studies, which also looks for ways to preserve a more reparative and affective mode of reading against suspicious and critical approaches.[9] Kermode's circumspection and diffidence arguably resonate with the "new modesty" in literary studies, one which seeks to counter the skeptical tone that pervaded the discipline in the final decades of the twentieth century.[10] Andrew Hadfield ruefully argues in *Textual Practice* in 2014, that the calls in the

[8] Pound, *ABC of Reading*, 13.

[9] See for instance Felski, *Limits of Critique*. The most famous essays articulating a weariness with the hermeneutic of suspicion include Latour, "Critique," and Sedgwick, "Paranoid Reading."

[10] Williams, "The New Modesty in Literary Criticism."

1980s for literary studies to expand into an all-embracing political criticism, "actually made subjects like English inchoate, unfocussed, arrogant, and over-ambitious in their aims and understanding of what they could achieve."[11] Writing precisely at this period, Kermode would have agreed and indeed was sounding the alarm. In this respect, Kermode was not so much out of place, as he always held, but rather before his time.

2 Part Two

The two critics who Kermode admired most throughout his life were I. A. Richards (1893–1979) and his student William Empson (1906–1984), both pioneers in sophisticated close reading and formal analysis. Yet Kermode's career began in dissatisfaction with the excesses of formalism and the new criticism that had dominated the discipline in the middle years of the twentieth century. His 1957 break-through book *Romantic Image* came out a year before Raymond Williams's *Culture and Society* and both these interventions emphatically re-inserted history into literary studies, revealing the limits of the formalist approaches that had dominated in the middle decades of the century. Yet Kermode was to steer away from the path to cultural studies that Williams inaugurated, just as later, he would resist the siren call of Paul de Man's deconstructive project. He seeks to mediate between historicism and deconstruction. Yet, even while he refuses the petrified literary object outside of history, Kermode holds fast to the notion of "literary" specialness. He seeks to understand literature within the historical forces which produce it without thereby rendering literary art as cultural document or linguistic discourse. Central to this mediation is the constitutive role of interpretation. He points at the irreducible fecundity of literary meaning, unlocked by acts of interpretation which open up the text but never exhaust it. The hermeneutic tactic was also a way of preserving a specifically literary inquiry from the scientific blandishments of semiotics, with its promise of firm and systemic knowledge acquisition. As early as 1969, Kermode could be found pushing against structuralist analysis, arguing that these tools could not replace the singularity of interpretative criticism:

[11] Hadfield, "Turning Point," 5.

> The structures of fiction are plural, inaccessible without severe instrumental interference, and possessing no validity or interest except in union with acts of idiomatic interpretation. The reason why it is wrong to distinguish as Barthes does between science of literature and criticism is that there is nothing of interest that the former can do without the intervention of the latter; the naked structure which we rush to clothe with meanings of our own is only a model, and a misleading one, since the only structures there are arise from those imported meanings and our attempts to hold them somehow in a single thought.[12]

There is no stable object, or naked structure, meaning emerges interactively, between the object and the reader whose relationship is never separable. So, even early in his career, Kermode perceives the danger in the search for a strong method that will allow literary studies to cohere around a procedure or theory. He recognizes a complexity in a textual reading that cannot be simply solved or flattened: interpretation will always generate superfluities beyond the strictures of method or ideology. Reading is not decoding, it is a process of open-ended hermeneutics, itself enmeshed in the collaborative history of reading. This compact with indeterminacy explains his attraction to post-structuralism, especially to Barthes.

His view of literary interpretation, and for that matter human life itself, is marked by tragic anomaly, rent as it is by an irreconcilable split between the human need for coherent narrative and a dumb and deaf world's inability to provide it. "My task," he says in *The Genesis of Secrecy*, "is not so much to offer interpretations as to speak of their modes, their possibilities, and their disappointments."[13] In literature, and in life, the human yearning for shape and legible form is thwarted by perpetual uncertainty, contingency, a babel of meanings, from which we can only extract provisional sense. In *The Sense of an Ending*, he famously traced the human urge to find narrative shapes and coherence within lives of accident and open-endedness. Ours is a fallen condition in that knowledge of the world, and the book, is only perceivable through a glass darkly. There is a theological comparison here and, though not a believer, Kermode's enduring interest in the bible is vital to any understanding of his criticism.

[12] Kermode, "Structures of Fiction," 915.

[13] Kermode, *Genesis of Secrecy*, 133.

We look, but do not perceive, we only see partially, in a world of differentiated and pullulating signs, turned into "narratives only because of our impudent intervention."[14] Speaking of Mark's Gospel in *The Genesis of Secrecy*, he writes:

> For the world is our beloved codex. We may not see it, as Dante did, in perfect order, gathered by love into one volume; but we do, living as reading, like to think of it as a place where we can travel back and forth at will, divining congruences, conjunctions, opposites; extracting secrets from its secrecy, making understood its relations, an appropriate algebra. This is the way we satisfy ourselves with explanations of the unfollowable world—as if it were a structured narrative, of which more might always be said by trained readers of it, by insiders. World and book, it may be, are hopelessly plural, endlessly disappointing.[15]

We are then "fallen" readers and critics, intuiting a unity of sense and meaning that we can grasp fleetingly but incompletely. There is a perennial tendency for Kermode to trace his finger around this breakage or cleft between fact and value, owning and acknowledging its scar. Yet there is always politics behind his epistemological humility, one that emerges from an awareness of how totalizing knowledge, the certainties of interpretation and value, can harden into myth and fanaticism. "Kermode hopes to halt the rush to the referent," argues Jonathan Arac, "that leads us to the insider's deluded hope for truth, on which are founded the murderous fictions of our history."[16] It is a history that Kermode witnessed first-hand during Royal Navy service in the war. Kermodian tact is not just donnish diffidence but also a hesitation before that "rush to the referent" that coarsens fictions into myths, in which hubristic interpreters presume to have unlocked the codex.

The humility also emerges in Kermode's attitude to the role of the critic. While many of the theorists of the 1970s and 1980s seek to demolish the hierarchy between critical and creative writing, Kermode is happy with the notion of the critic as interpreter of great literary works, rather than their producer. The critic is essential to the endurance of literature, but as an active custodian rather than an originator. Kermode

[14] Kermode, 145.

[15] Kermode, 145.

[16] Arac, "History and Mystery," 152.

realizes that holding on to literary value necessitates a canon of important works, and that this canon and the forms of value that it licenses, are institutional. At the same time, unlike Harold Bloom, Kermode does not position himself as a defender of a timeless western canon of hierarchically arranged great works. He moves the emphasis from the originating culture to the receiving one. For him, literary value is dynamic and historically contingent, but also renewable, refreshed not only in the readings of different individuals, but in the ever-shifting demands of sense-making to which individual critics, in tune with their own culture, respond. According to Jan Gorak, Kermode's canonical text has three attributes: "it is hospitable to interpretation; it has sufficient depth to support the multitude of interpretations it attracts and, as a direct result of these qualities, it becomes charged with mystery."[17] In a quotable phrase, Kermode identifies a "classic" not as an unchanging monument but rather as a literary work "patient of interpretation."[18] The critic's task is to germinate the interpretation relevant to each generation, and thereby bring the work to life across the decades. The importance of interpretation for Kermode rests, then, in its reanimation of an artwork in each new context. And this is why critics and scholars are *active* custodians: they do not simply preserve the exhibition behind glass, but rather coax it into new formations and meanings, which themselves encrust or harden onto the text's passage through history, moving from latent to manifest.

In his 1975 work, *The Classic*, Kermode elaborates his idea of the modern "classic" in these terms, a de-centering of the text toward its dispersal and reception across space and time. At this stage, still lured by the indeterminacies of French post-structuralism, he sees the death of the author as a mode of readerly liberation. Yet he maintains that this empowerment does not break "or sever our communications with the dead." There is a substance that endures, "however powerful the agents of change", claims Kermode, "*King Lear* underlying a thousand dispositions, subsists in change, prevails by being patient of interpretation."[19] But what is this substance, apart from a perennial stickiness, which may have as much to do with the rising bubbles of cultural capital, as any quality in the work itself? Eager to move away from an imperial idea

[17] Gorak, *Modern Canon*, 157.

[18] Kermode, *Classic*, 134.

[19] Kermode, 134.

that the author-creator generates and circulate value, Kermode locates the canonical text in the plurality of its readers. Properly practiced criticism can keep a work alive, by deriving ever fresh and relevant interpretations of it. But this process always falls short of truth and finality, it is always an approximation. Consistent with his early distinction between myth and fiction, Kermode is wholly distrustful of coercive interpretation, the one that purports to have the final word, a presumption he sees as incipiently totalitarian. The practice of divination that all interpreters deploy will never capture meaning, it will always be disappointed. Without mystery, there is no interpretation, without interpretation no mystery.

This reliance on a productive lack, an indeterminacy in the text where each generation of critics derives a newly relevant meaning, risks tautology. Kermode's explanation of the classic comes too close to saying that "the greatness of a text emerges from it being continually perceived as great." If so, how does Kermode justify a hierarchy of readings, from all those taken from the endlessly fecund hermeneutic text? Some must surely be truer and more faithful to an anterior meaning? Clearly, Kermode considers some readings better than others—he claims, for instance, that Q. D. Leavis's reading of *Wuthering Heights* "dwarfs all others." [20] According to what measure, if the objective meaning does not reside in the work? It is hard to be satisfied with this perpetual vacuity, hard to see how it vouchsafes a substance that subsists in change. What is left to ground the "patience" aside from structures of language and institutions? Craft, imagination, and intentionality have been swamped by an appeal to semantic superfluity.

Kermode attempts to have his literary cake and to interpret it too. As Ankhi Mukherjee astutely discerns in her recent account of the "classic," "Kermode seems to present the modern version of the classic as both plenitude and lack." She argues that Kermode's approach, which interestingly she finds echoed in the emphasis on transnational circulation in David Damrosch's world literature project, evades the

> *constitutive* depth and magnitude of the classic work that invites and organizes successive readings. It is as if the classic can only be determined retroactively and across a hermeneutic gap, the survival of the classic being the greatest proof of its ontic status.[21]

[20] Kermode, 131.

[21] Muhkerjee, *What is a Classic?*, 43.

In fairness to Kermode, he is aware of this objection, the implicit circularity in the claim that classic literature is that which endures through interpretation. Through the rest of his career, he circles around the problem. If he fails to ever answer it fully, he nonetheless joins an august group of thinkers from the eighteenth century who have sought to give a grounding to aesthetic value outside the vagaries of mere taste.

3 Part Three

He tries to answer it in *Forms of Attention*, the book he pinpointed in an interview as his own favorite, while also comparatively neglected.[22] In that book, accounting for Botticelli's neglect and then revival, he distinguishes between the role played by "opinion" (that of Swinburne and Pater), and by "knowledge," in the scholarly projects of Herbert Horne and Aby Warburg, which reinforce (but do not themselves establish) Botticelli's reputation. Kermode demands that we recognize the interdependence of knowledge and opinion, or scholarship and criticism. The final chapter of the book, "Disentangling Knowledge and Opinion" comes to the conclusion that the disentanglement cannot conceptually be done, no more than one can look at one's own eye. The endurance of a work depends on opinion, the "preservative" which is also a "destructive" force.[23] Opinion, supported importantly by chance, is that which leads to the survival of works of art, and produces the intensified forms of attention which canonical literature receives. New opinions prop up the currency and modernity of literature:

> The process of selecting the canon may be very long but, once it is concluded, the inside works will normally be provided with the kinds of reading they require if they are to keep their immediacy to any moment; that is to maintain their modernity. They quickly acquire virtual immunity to textual alteration, so necessary changes must be interpretative; and all interpretation is governed by prejudice.[24]

The interpretative patience of the great work, of which Kermode wrote in *The Classic*, is here supplanted by the prejudice that gives to one

[22] Birns, Boe, and Kermode, "'Creative Pulse,'" 18.

[23] Kermode, *Forms of Attention*, 72–73.

[24] Kermode, 75.

artwork the attention denied another. Kermode incipiently acknowledges the compelling frame afforded by sociology in any reckoning with literary value. There is no eschewing the ideological coloring of the age and to presume to do so is to be guilty of a sort of hubris. In other words, Kermode acknowledges the immanence of our judgments, our inseparability from networks of meaning. We are free to interpret, indeed we must in order to be custodians or curators of the literary past. It is a freedom which biblical scholars can only envy, confined as they have been by the strictures of canon law and firm institutional boundaries against heresy. Academic literary criticism, for all its resonance with the traditions of scriptural exegesis, polices its scribes and scholars with a much lighter touch. Literary mandarins in the university do not generally decree opinion which masquerades as knowledge heresy. The permeable borders of the literary canon mean "we are able to preserve the modernity of our choices without surrendering the right to add to them."[25] We add to them, in Kermode's vision, through continuing a conversation. The institution acts as a shock absorber, it turns the lack of canonical rigidity into strength: it endures not by resisting but by yielding. Kermode's canon is a plastic one, open to reform and the recovery of hitherto neglected works, such as those advanced by feminist or post-colonial scholars.

However, the price of this comparative freedom is epistemological humility, circumspection, and awareness that all interpretation is located:

> What we have to remember as a condition of this liberty of interpretation is that we enjoy no privileged view, that we proceed with our interpretations with no confidence that we are somehow definitively seeing matters in their right proportions and relations at last.[26]

There is a necessity of error built into the grammar of our judgments, or the systems upon which they rest. This is true for knowledge too, not because there is no knowledge or no truth but because what we deem to be true, what commands our notice and our narratives, is colored and shaped by our prejudices too. All observation "is dependent upon theoretical presupposition; for such presupposition must vary from age to age, from one community of interpretation to another, and even from one

[25] Kermode, 79.

[26] Kermode, 79.

individual to another."[27] In *Forms of Attention* this line of thought leads him to Paul Feyerabend, and the sociology of science, but also toward Richard Rorty and American pragmatism. If facts are shot through with value judgments, then from a cognate perspective, the truth value of a proposition becomes subordinated to its usefulness.

These factors make the quest for a solid system of knowledge undergirding and upholding the literary tradition a vain one. It also means that literary value and canonicity are vulnerable to suspicion and critique. Scrutiny will inevitably reveal or expose the sociological currents and prejudices that led to the elevation of some texts above others, currents that may be ideologically or ethically noxious from a contemporary perspective. The presumed preservative of interpretation, in which we grant the literary past active life in current institutions, can dissolve under the hermeneutic of suspicion. A porous canon, informed by the recognition of one's immersion in a prejudicial culture, does not escape the censure of radical opponents of literary hierarchy itself.

For Kermode, however, the pliable canon, like the endurance of literary periodization and genre, affords an institutional coherence that acts as a preservative, one that we should itself preserve, even as we mold and expand it. In his essay "The Institutional Control of Interpretation," Kermode claims that interpretations are constrained by institutional control, above all by the academic community, which accredits not just works but also approaches and modes of interpretation. The institution absorbs even those radical innovations which purport to unsettle or discredit it (Kermode's examples are Barthes, Lacan, Derrida and Foucault). There is, Kermode acknowledges, a "necessary conservatism" in learned institutions, because, he believes, it is by "recognizing the tacit authority of the institution that we achieve the measure of liberty we have in interpreting. It is a price to pay, but it purchases an incalculable boon."[28] The boon is that of continuity combined with liberty; we do not grip too tight to our convictions lest we break the institutional means by which we might promulgate them. We leave room for the unknown, doubting even our own habitual skepticism.

With the authority of literary criticism and university English, we can cultivate close reading, and the intensity of intention and interpretation

[27] Kermode, 82.

[28] Kermode, "Institutional Control of Interpretation," 86.

that follows. "What matters, so far as I can see," he concludes *Forms of Attention*,

> is that ways of inducing such forms of attention should continue to exist, even if they are all, in the end, dependent on opinion. The mere possibility that something of value will not fall under the rule of time—and here we need not raise the question of how that value originated, whether inherent or the creation of interpreters—is the real justification for our continuing the clamorous opinionated conversation.[29]

Unlike more conservative defenders of the canon, Kermode does not assert the timeless quality of great literature, nor does he swathe it in the rhetoric of civilizational flourishing, nor quasi-religious invocations of numinous aura. Because Kermode's instincts are liberal and reformist and his sense of the canon capacious and pliable, he lacks the defense of tradition and community that a more forthright conservative commentator would likely invoke. His "clamorous opinionated conversation" does not have the cohesive quality of Matthew Arnold's sense of culture or the simultaneous order that T. S. Eliot finds in the notion of tradition. Yet it does speak to a connectivity and inter-communication between realms of thought that looks forward to some branches of literary sociology. "Every verse is occultly linked, in ways to be researched, with all the others; the text is a world system," he concludes.[30]

Ultimately, the importance of the canon hinges on practical necessity. We have not got "enough memory to process everything," Kermode writes in his 1988 book *History and Value*, therefore

> canons are useful in that they enable us to handle otherwise unmanageable historical deposits. They do this by affirming that some works are more valuable than others, more worthy of minute attention.[31]

Those historical deposits have become all the more massive since the internet revolution of the intervening decades. They may be more manageable, because more searchable using digital technology, but the access to vast seams of writing from across history and the globe means

[29] Kermode, *Forms of Attention*, 91–92.

[30] Kermode, 75.

[31] Kermode, *History and Value*, 13. Hereafter cited parenthetically in text.

that there are only a tiny proportion to which we can give our "minute attention." The need for selection and curation is more pressing than ever and always will be so while time remains finite. In *History and Value,* Kermode explicitly dismisses the idea that time is the impartial judge of quality. But he also discards the idea that literature is merely a bourgeois category, which should be opened up to proletarian modes. By looking at 1930s novels which have been forgotten, even those he's fond of—such as Stephen Haggard's *Nya*—he puts them into comparison with canonical novels by E. M. Forster and Ford Madox Ford, to illustrate that they lack "resonance" (itself a resonant word in contemporary literary studies).[32] He suggests that one of the markers of endurance is a tendency to transgress. Considering *Nya* in contrast to Nabakov's *Lolita*, both dealing with sexual relations between adult men and underage girls, illustrates that this transgression goes much deeper than simply taboo subject matter: the latter, Kermode argues, resonates across the decades, gaining in "permanence," because it exceeds the frontiers that *Nya* only pretends to challenge. In doing so, it connects with a long tradition of aberrant love in literature. Unlike the hermeneutic plenitude that Kermode had earlier found in the classic, he here does seek to discern attributes in the text itself that help it endure. Not coincidentally, in this late book, he seeks to discriminate literary value in novels of the 1930s by focusing on the class injustice that some Marxist theorists deploy to bring down the very literary hierarchy that the canon affords. In order to understand that question, which has preoccupied him in his later career—why some literary works become classics—he focuses on a selection of those that have fallen into neglect and disrepair. Contrasting them with the successful novels allows a more productive and constitutive sense of the canon's capacity to refresh and renew. Although he is sympathetic to the Marxist project of revealing the historical conditions behind the aesthetic work, he is aware of the negative terms on which the hermeneutic of suspicion—or to use Kermode's equivalent handle, "the discrepancy theory"[33]—proceeds. Aesthetic value emerges historically not transcendentally. But allowing that fact does not negate the value. The problem remains as to how literary value can be of its time and yet endure.

[32] Dimmock, "Theory of Resonance," 1060–71.

[33] Kermode, *History and Value*, 99.

The second part of this book, itself called "History and Value," is based on Kermode's 1987 Northcliffe lectures (the first is based on the Clarendon lectures). It addresses the question of value more theoretically than the historical orientation of the first, mainly with a view to rebut discrepancy theory, to show how the question of value tends to recur and metastasize even when it is pushed aside most vigorously, and to put forward a case for the received categories, like periodization and institutions. He subjects leading works of Marxist symptomatic literary criticism, Terry Eagleton's *Criticism and Ideology* and Frederic Jameson's *The Political Unconscious*, to a taste of their own medicine, detecting how beneath their sophisticated historicism, both hold on to an "institutionalized version of history" and both "find political reasons for placing high valuations on work that is already highly valued, though evidently not for the right reasons."[34] The ideological fissures and discontinuities that Eagleton and Jameson unearth do not exempt them from the problem of value and, with it, that of judgment and inheritance.

Kermode concludes by reaffirming the importance of the institution. Even though literary institutions are "bound to be reactionary in some sense," they nonetheless percolate with dissent and discontent, including challenges to the canon or the development of sub-canons, "to suit say feminists and Afro-Americans or Derrideans."[35] However, Kermode continues cautiously, "What is certain is that revolutionary revisions would require transfers of powers, a reign of literary terror the prospect of which many of us enjoy less than the Professor of English and Human Relations."[36] The recoil from revolution and "terror," even if spiced with some wryness and irony here, nonetheless reveals Kermode's inclination toward the safety afforded by tradition, albeit without a fully elaborated idea of tradition that a conservative intellectual would advance. In retrospect, however, as the prestige of English as a discipline has fallen further in the last thirty years and as the humanities look increasingly vulnerable to the depredations of government financiers and policy makers, his wariness and sense of vulnerability seem prescient. The instruments by which we select favored texts may be contaminated by noxious ideology and "tainted with privilege and injustice." Yet they allow us to talk to

[34] Kermode, 103.

[35] Kermode, 126.

[36] Kermode, 126.

our predecessors, to qualify their judgments, to compare how we value and how they do. This "valuable inheritance" may yet be destroyed by "some catastrophe," but "the destruction should not be encouraged by members of the rather small community that cares about writing or about art in general."[37]

It is not a rousing or revolutionary call. It does not have the allure of a new movement or a charismatic leader. "Kermodism" points down a path not to utopia or to salvation, but rather to survival and continuity. For Kermode the role of the critic is to value and to bequeath, to create a context of cultural conservation. He recognized the need for the institution in the custodianship of the literary inheritance, a canon which can also be disrupted and remolded but which nonetheless has an organic coherence and continuity. He also realizes that no barriers to interpretation do not mean libidinous freedom but rather the closure of reading in the guise of its emancipation. While, like his hero I. A. Richards, he does much to encourage liberty of interpretation, he wants to prevent that liberty from becoming license.[38] If we embrace a purely postmodern indeterminacy or the (now routine) call for the dismantling of disciplinary boundaries, we lose the necessary conversation and innovation that is involved in the hermeneutic project.

Kermode's modest ambition is at odds with the hunger in academia for a more bracing and radical agenda, such as that which gripped the humanities precisely when Kermode articulated his defense of institutions, justified canons, and literary values, and advocated a curatorial role for literary criticism. As one who had been hospitable to theory in his UCL seminars, and who broke down barriers between the academy and high journalism, he could not be cast in the role of mandarin or reactionary. He was also too prominent and prolific to be ignored, though he was sometimes portrayed as a genial, liberal-minded don, too moderate, and humanist for the revolution. These epithets do not quite fit the wry and saturnine, yet capacious sensibility of Kermode. Ten years after his death, he seems less like a trembling defender of the status quo and more like one who rightly realized the fragility of his discipline and its institutional ecosystem. One of Kermode's less trumpeted qualities is his awareness of precarity and instinct for survival. "It seems, rereading

[37] Kermode, 127.

[38] Kermode, "Institutional Control of Interpretation," 74.

him now," observes Jacqueline Rose astutely, "that Frank Kermode was always, directly or indirectly, writing about survival. That the form of attention he conferred on literary objects was designed above all to allow them, and himself, to survive."[39]

References

Arac, Jonathan. "History and Mystery: The Criticism of Frank Kermode." *Salmagundi*, no. 55 (Winter 1982): 135–55.

Birns, Nicholas, John Boe, and Frank Kermode. "'Some Kind of Creative Pulse': An Interview with Frank Kermode." *Writing on the Edge* 16, no. 2 (Spring 2006): 8–19.

Dimmock, Wai Chee. "A Theory of Resonance." *PMLA* 112, no. 5 (October 1997): 1060–71.

Felski, Rita. *The Limits of Critique*. Chicago: University of Chicago Press, 2015.

Gorak, Jan. *The Making of the Modern Canon: Genesis and Crisis of a Literary Idea*. Atlantic Highlands: Athlone Press.

Hadfield, Andrew. "Turning Point: The Wheel has Come Full Circle." *Textual Practice* 28, no. 1 (2014): 1–8.

Kermode, Frank. *The Classic: Literary Images of Permanence and Change*. New York: Viking, 1975.

———. *Forms of Attention*. Chicago: University of Chicago Press, 1985.

———. *The Genesis of Secrecy: On the Interpretation of Narrative*. Cambridge, MA: Harvard University Press, 1979.

———. *History and Value: The Clarendon Lectures and the Northcliff Lectures, 1987*. Oxford: Clarendon Press, 1988.

———. "Institutional Control of Interpretation." *Salmagundi*, no. 43 (Winter 1979): 72–86.

———. "The Institutional Control of Interpretation." In *The Art of Telling: Essays on Fiction*, 168–84. Cambridge, MA: Harvard University Press, 1985.

———. *Not Entitled: A Memoir*. London: HarperCollins, 1995.

———. *Puzzles and Epiphanies*. London: Routledge and Kegan Paul, 1962.

———. "The Structures of Fiction." *MLN* 84, no. 6 (December 1969): 891–915.

Latour, Bruno. "Why Has Critique Run Out of Steam? From Matters of Fact to Matters of Concern." *Critical Inquiry* 30, no. 2 (2004): 225–48.

Lentricchia, Frank. *Forms of Attention*. Chicago: University of Chicago Press, 1985.

[39] Rose, "The Art of Survival."

Muhkerjee, Ankhi. *What is a Classic? Postcolonial Rewriting and Invention of the Canon*. Stanford: Stanford University Press, 2013.
Norris, Christopher. "Remembering Frank Kermode." *Textual Practice* 25, no. 1 (2011): 1–13.
Pound, Ezra. *The ABC of Reading*. London: G. Routledge and Sons, 1934.
Rose, Jacqueline. "The Art of Survival." *Critical Quarterly* 54, no. 1 (April 2001). https://onlinelibrary.wiley.com/doi/abs/10.1111/j.1467-8705.2012.02034.x.
Salusinsky, Irme. *Criticism and Society*. Abingdon, Oxon: Routledge, 1987.
Sedgwick, Eve Kosofsky. "Paranoid Reading and Reparative Reading, or, You're So Paranoid You Probably Think This Essay Is About You." In *Touching Feeling: Affect, Pedagogy and Performativity*, 123–51. Durham, NC: Duke University Press, 2003.
Williams, Jeffrey J. "The New Modesty in Literary Criticism." *The Chronicle of Higher Education*, Jan 5, 2015. https://www.chronicle.com/article/The-New-Modesty-in-Literary/150993.
Wood, Michael. "Introduction." In Frank Kermode, *Bury Place Papers: Essays from the London Review of Books*, 7–16. London: London Review of Books, 2009.

CHAPTER 8

Polonius as Anti-Close Reader: Toward a Poetics of the Putz

Rachel Eisendrath

It is well known that in *Hamlet*, William Shakespeare's arguably most self-reflective play, the brooding prince expresses a poetics and a theory of theater and of the arts. He talks, famously, about holding a mirror up to nature in order to present a reflection of the real and thereby to show the living what life is actually like. And he extols a method of acting that is naturalistic, matching the word to the action and the action to the word; too often, he says, the stage shows men strutting and bellowing and imitating men badly or, to use his word, *abominably* (3.2.34)—which, spelled "abhominably," looks like a terrific pun (*ab homine*, away from the human).[1] Less well known is that Polonius, the relentlessly busybody and bumbling father of Ophelia and Laertes, also expresses a poetics—albeit a poetics that the play, or at least Hamlet, constantly mocks. Polonius's poetics offers a negative example, one that is overly hasty, overly intrusive;

[1] The real etymology is different: *ab omen,* away from omen, as pointed out in Shakespeare, *Hamlet*, 298. Hereafter cited parenthetically in text.

R. Eisendrath (✉)
Barnard College, Columbia University, New York, NY, USA
e-mail: reisendr@barnard.edu

A. Sridhar et al. (eds.), *The Work of Reading*,
https://doi.org/10.1007/978-3-030-71139-9_8

one that actually disregards the particularity of the objects he claims to be studying. His mode of reading expresses, the play suggests, what the reception of art and literature and even the world should *not* be like.

In this chapter, I will look at two aspects of what I will call Polonius's poetics of the putz: the *speed* with which he reads the world and the *distance* he wants to claim from it. Both these aspects of his poetics are anti-close reading in that close reading is of course not just about (or even primarily about) closeness but also about slowness. In his desire for speed and for distance (a distance that turns out to be strangely intrusive), Polonius provides a warning case, an example of what a literary-critical practice might become in a world that is out of joint.

1 "This Is Too Long": Drive-Through Poetics for the Man on the Go

Polonius is a busy man. An advisor to the king, he exists in a culture of counsel, concerned with problems of advising royalty and of navigating the power struggles of the court.[2] Having little time for lingering or for mulling, he is impatient with the theater—as he is with almost everything else. The Player's speech, he says, is "too long" (2.2.436). Despite his experience in the theater during his youth, when he played Julius Caesar (3.2.99), Polonius now has no time for such frivolous activities. Given that *Hamlet* is Shakespeare's longest play, the claim that the Player's speech is too long almost jars with the spirit of the tragedy itself.

Polonius's impatience with the theater exemplifies his mode of reading not just art but reality in general. When, for instance, Ophelia reports to him her recent interchange with Hamlet, she makes in words a kind of picture of the prince. For twenty-one lines, she describes how he appeared in her room with his doublet open, his stockings dirty and fallen down, his knees knocking, and his face pitiful and pale:

> He took me by the wrist and held me hard,
> Then goes he to the length of all his arm
> And with his other hand thus o'er his brow
> He falls to such perusal of my face
> As 'a would draw it. (2.1.84–88)

[2] For recent work on early modern political counsel, see Kiséry, *Hamlet's Moment*; and Rose, *Politics of Counsel*.

Just as Hamlet, struggling to discern the secrets that reside in Ophelia's face, peers at her as intensely as though he were trying to draw her, we are made to stare at him or at this verbal representation of him. In both cases, the meaning is elusive: Ophelia's appearance is as mysterious to Hamlet as his appearance is to us (and to her). Yet if this ekphrasis highlights the difficulties of interpretation, Polonius does not hesitate both to assert his reading of the scene and to jump into action:

> Come, go with me: I will go seek the King.
> This is the very ecstasy of love. (2.1.98–99)

Polonius uses the deictic "this" to point at the scene that Ophelia has just represented and to affix it with a label that aims to end any hesitations about its meaning: "This is the very ecstasy of love." He decides almost instantaneously what the indexical but notoriously vague "this" means[3] and also, in the same instant, settles on a course of action—so quickly that he reverses the order of those two steps so that the articulation of the action ("Come, go with me") occurs before the interpretation ("This is the very ecstasy of love").[4]

Ironically, the reason that Polonius reads too hastily is that he is so busy seeking out the truth. He is, in this way, like the man that Erasmus described in 1511 who loses himself in words precisely because of his impatience with words. "We often find," Erasmus wrote, "that no one is so apt to lose himself in verbal arguments as the man who boasts that facts, not words, are the only things that interest him."[5] Consider the moment when Polonius reports to the king on Hamlet and Ophelia's relationship:

> If I had played the desk or table-book,
> Or given my heart a working mute and dumb,
> Or looked upon this love with idle sight,
> What might you think? No, I went round to work [...]. (2.2.133–36)

[3] "How abundant and how important is the doubt produced in the world of the meaning of this syllable, *hoc* [this]!" wrote Michel de Montaigne, referring to debates swirling around the words of Eucharistic benediction, "This is my body" [*Hoc est corpus meum*], Matthew 26:26; "Apologie de Raymond Sebond," (Montaigne, *Essais*, 2:192).

[4] On Polonius's pompous (and misplaced) confidence that he can discern cause from circumstance, see Hutson, *Circumstantial Shakespeare*, 3.

[5] Erasmus, *De Ratione Studii* [*Upon the Right Method of Instruction*], 162.

Polonius takes pride in the fact that he does not study or make notes ("played the desk or table-book"[6]) and also does not remain silent in order first to look within his heart ("given my heart a working mute and dumb"). He has not, in these ways, played the scholar—nor the close reader. No, he boasts, he is a man of action who, refusing merely to look on "with idle sight," has already gone "round to work."[7]

What Shakespeare reveals, though, is that just when Polonius thinks he is cutting through the world's illusions to the truth he is actually most lost in his own illusions. In more than one speech, Polonius extols brevity just at the moment when he is being most verbose:

> POLONIUS: My liege and madam, to expostulate
> What majesty should be, what duty is,
> Why day is day, night night, and time is time,
> Were nothing but to waste night, day and time;
> Therefore, brevity is the soul of wit
> And tediousness the limbs and outward flourishes.
> I will be brief: your noble son is mad.
> Mad call I it, for to define true madness,
> What is't but to be nothing else but mad?
> But let that go.
> QUEEN: More matter with less art.
> POLONIUS: Madam, I swear I use no art at all. (2.2.86–96)

On one level, Shakespeare seems to be critiquing in these scenes problems of overly elaborate courtly speech, as he does in other plays, such as in *King Lear*, where Goneril and Regan's elaborate and devious speeches are weighed against the plain, stripped-down, honest talk of their sister Cordelia and of the king's advisor, Kent.[8] Yet what is notable here, unlike in *King Lear*, is that the man most lost in words (Polonius) is the one who

[6] On the material aspects of tablebooks in *Hamlet*, see Stallybrass et al., "Hamlet's Tables."

[7] The attention Polonius does pay to language in other scenes comes in the form of rapid judgments that suggest he is holding a word or a phrase up to some pre-given standard. For example, Polonius responds to Hamlet's use of the phrase "beautified Ophelia" in his letter: "that's an ill phrase, a vile phrase" (2.2.109), without further explanation.

[8] Even Goneril's initial claim that her love for her father lies beyond words (1.1.55) reads as artifice, as a deployment of the rhetorical device often called the inexpressibility topos.

thinks he is offering plain words of straightforward counsel. Asserting that he is more interested in facts than in words, in truth than in art, Polonius claims to be cutting right to the heart of the matter: "I will be brief: your noble son is mad." However, he has already knit such a web of words that he appears to us—and to Gertrude—completely tangled in his own prolixity. She interrupts, "More matter with less art." The problem is that he thinks, in rejecting definition and the self-conscious use of words ("to expostulate / What majesty should be, what duty is, / Why day is day, night night, and time is time, / Were nothing but to waste night, day and time"), that is just what he is doing. To pay attention to words would, he thinks, be to waste his time—and therefore, the play suggests, he is lost in words.

Polonius's hastiness is part of what prevents him from thinking clearly, from reading accurately. In contrast to his relentless busyness, thought requires a "pause." In the famous soliloquy where Hamlet wrestles with the problem of suicide ("To be or not to be"), he articulates his question as that which "must give us pause" (3.1.67). Relatedly, when Claudius finally examines his own ill conscience, he uses this same language of the pause: "I stand in pause," he says (3.3.42).[9] Hamlet may exist in the public imagination as an indecisive prince (based in part on Laurence Olivier's 1948 film adaptation, which misleadingly frames the play by pulling out of context lines about a fatal flaw and adding a portentous, pretentious, and non-Shakespearean line, "This is the tragedy of a man who could not make up his mind"[10]). However, Shakespeare's play actually again and again questions the emphasis on speed, associating it with the play's overtly evil or bungling characters. Claudius and Polonius rarely suffer the debilitation of second thoughts. Rather, they are represented

[9] In a related mode, Macbeth tries to justify his killing the king's guards by accusing his passionate love for outrunning "the pauser, reason" (Shakespeare, *Macbeth*, 2.3.112). The pause for thought can also be faked and become a mere outward sign divorced from any inward reality—the kind of mere "seeming" that Hamlet warns can mislead people. Sending Hamlet away to England, Claudius says that the decision "must seem / Deliberate pause" (4.3.8–9).

[10] There is, among the romantics, precedent for this account of Hamlet as a dithering deep thinker. For example, August Wilhelm von Schlegel writes that Hamlet's "calculating consideration, which exhausts all the relations and possible consequences of a deed, must cripple the power of acting"; and Samuel Taylor Coleridge, admitting to having "a smack of Hamlet myself," remarks that "Hamlet's character is the prevalence of the abstracting and generalizing habit over the practical." See Bate, *Romantics on Shakespeare*, 308, 161, 160.

as almost constantly in a rush of activity—dispatching people, greeting people, dismissing people, hurrying from one place to another in a state of relentless busyness. They spew; they lurch; they command; they plot; they move distractedly, hastily—almost never pausing for attentive perception of themselves or of anyone else. Sometimes, Polonius is so busy doing things that he forgets just what things he is doing: "What was I about to say? By the mass, I was about to say something! Where did I leave?" (2.1.49–50). The king similarly acts with "quick determination" and "with speed" (3.1.167–68); his first speech in the Second Quarto does not even pause for a period until its thirty-ninth (and final) line.

Hamlet despises this haste. Of his uncle's marriage to his mother that followed so quickly upon his father's funeral, Hamlet's comment is telling: "O most wicked speed!" (1.2.156). Indeed, when Hamlet makes his worst mistakes, he is shown acting in a rush. For example, when he stabs Polonius through the arras, mistaking him for Claudius, Gertrude remarks on his disastrous haste: "O, what a rash and bloody deed is this!" (3.4.25). Hamlet then echoes her word four lines later when he discovers that he has killed Polonius: "Thou wretched, rash, intruding fool, farewell" (3.4.29), reminding the audience that Polonius also has acted too hastily.[11]

Polonius's actions are characterized by speed, and the precondition for this speed is often his tendency to misread: he imposes the already known or even the clichéd onto whatever object of study lies before him, applying past, proverbial knowledge to present situations. One way in which this repetition becomes evident is through Polonius's excessive use of commonplaces. These are aphoristic sayings, often associated with political counsel,[12] that supposedly express timeless truths that could be reapplied to new situations.[13] When, for example, Polonius advises

[11] The play associates the word "rash" with violence: Hamlet, grappling with Laertes in the grave, tells him that "though I am not splenative rash, / Yet have I in me something dangerous" (5.1.250–51). And the word recurs when, aboard the ship, Hamlet reverses the commission so that it orders not his death but the death of Rosencrantz and Guildenstern. Here the connotation is more positive, but the association with violence remains: Hamlet says he behaved "rashly" but, since he thereby saved his own life, "praised be rashness for it" (5.2.6–7).

[12] See Kiséry, *Hamlet's Moment*, 64–65, 71.

[13] On Renaissance commonplaces, see esp. Moss, *Printed Commonplace-Books*.

Laertes how to behave in France, he lists one commonplace after the next, concluding with the famous lines:

> This above all, to thine own self be true
> And it must follow as the night the day
> Thou canst not then be false to any man. (1.3.77–79)

For him, structures of meaning will repeat as though they were akin to the cycles of nature: "it must follow as the night the day." Marked in the First Quarto with gnomic pointers (that is with double inverted commas in the margin that were used to indicate to readers quotable lines),[14] these dictates are presented as laws, without human agents; ironically, even the mandate "to thine own self be true" can be folded into this logic of the inevitable, of the repeated, of the natural, of the authorless. According to Polonius's mode of thought, *what-was* is also *what-will-be*. Similarly, when trying to persuade Hamlet to forgo his mourning, Claudius tells the moping prince that the death of fathers is the order of the world:

> For what we know must be, and is as common
> As any the most vulgar thing to sense—
> Why should we in our peevish opposition
> Take it to heart? (1.2.98–101)

In these lines, the word "common" slides between at least two senses: the death of fathers is "common" in being a universal truth (all fathers die) and in being shared knowledge (we all know that all fathers die). This latter meaning is the basis of proverbial or *common*place wisdom. Claudius's lines suggest the complex effects of this kind of wisdom, which is not just explanatory about the past but also determinative of the future. That is, a consensus about how things have always been can become a template for what can exist in the future, for "what we know must be." The word "must" is important in this regard, hovering between seeming merely to acknowledge how things are independently of any agent (this is the natural order), and how they will be because of an agent (this is the order because I order it so). It is significant that Claudius articulates the self-evidence of this kind of knowledge by comparing it to empirical knowledge ("the most vulgar thing to sense") and also by expressing a

[14] Lesser and Stallybrass, "First Literary *Hamlet*," 376–78.

sense of personal detachment (his refusal to take the death "to heart")—a crucial set of associations to which I will return.

If there is something aggressive in all this repetition—this imposition of an old meaning on a new situation—that is also because it is part of a power struggle. The older generation is imposing its order onto the newer generation, and doing so by folding the meanings of particular events into generalities that are always and everywhere the same. Men like Claudius and Polonius mask the fact that a major power play has occurred (Claudius has usurped Hamlet's rights of succession) by naturalizing their violent retention of power as the workings of how things simply are. Through the lens of commonplace wisdom, we are not supposed to think about the particular circumstances of King Hamlet's death but about the truism that all fathers die. When the prince, in his first soliloquy, rants against this existing order, he does so by resisting its mere naturalness—or, more precisely, by complicating this idea of naturalness. He compares the world to "an unweeded garden / That grows to seed" (1.2.135–36). The garden metaphor picks up on Claudius's imagery of nature but transforms it by making nature the realm of a kind of art—a garden—that is, a world with agents, a world where "things rank and gross in nature / Possess it merely" (1.2.136–37). This is not a natural world where one thing follows another without human choice, but a natural world that has been corrupted through human choice—and, therefore, by implication, a world that could be otherwise.

Polonius and the other members of the old order constantly foreclose the possibility of what the world could become by hastily saying that it must be what it has already been. Polonius more than once creates lists of words in which the next word repeats the one that came before it: "That he's mad, 'tis true, 'tis true, 'tis pity, / And pity 'tis 'tis true: a foolish figure!" (2.2.97–98). While this list at first seems to construct the rhetorical figure known as the ladder or climax, where linked items on a list build on one another, this ladder leads nowhere (one nineteenth-century editor glosses the line, "It is no figure at all. It is hardly even a play with the words"[15]). Everything that follows seems already determined by what came before. The logic is predetermined, fast, and circular. "Take this from this if this be otherwise," Polonius says later in this same scene (2.2.153), again employing deictics with vague antecedents (as in

[15] MacDonald, *Tragedie of Hamlet*, 79; cited in *Hamlet*, 244.

2.1.99), which, in this case, seem to lead the listener in a circle. Shakespeare constructs similarly circular and pronoun-packed lines when he shows Macbeth plotting the murder of Duncan: "If it were done, when 'tis done, then 'twere well / It were done quickly" (1.7.1–2). It is as if there is no space for or possibility of a pause for thought or for choice. Hamlet's proclivity for non sequiturs (especially in his conversations with Polonius, such as when Hamlet refers to Jephthah at 2.2.339) could be understood as an attempt to disrupt the apparent seamlessness of the older courtier's repetitions.

For Polonius, art exists in service of this repetition of the always already known:

> HAMLET: You played once i'th'university, you say?
> POLONIUS: That did I, my lord, and was accounted a good actor.
> HAMLET: What did you enact?
> POLONIUS: I did enact Julius Caesar. I was killed i'th'Capitol. Brutus killed me. (3.2.95–100)

The idiocy of this interchange results from the fact that what Polonius flat-footedly presents as news about a performance (that Brutus killed Caesar) is that which is already pre-given in the old story. It is in keeping with Polonius's entire mode of reading the world that art is for him a repetition of the already known, rather than, say, an exploration of what is new, of what is (potentially) *in process* of coming into knowledge.

In contrast, Hamlet's version of literary and artistic composition opens toward emerging events—and therefore is not mere repetition. He aims for something different in the way that he inserts into art some reflection of what is actually unfolding in the world that exists around that artwork. Most famously, he requests that the players insert "some dozen lines, or sixteen lines" into *The Murder of Gonzago* (2.2.477), lines that crack the given play open from within.[16] That the number is unfixed (why twelve to sixteen lines?) may suggest a quality of suppleness in response to what the new situation requires. And a similar tendency is expressed in some less famous moments. Consider, for example, the moment when Hamlet responds to what he has learned from the ghost (i.e., that Claudius has

[16] Hamlet's method of working may loosely parallel in this respect the way Shakespeare himself worked with inherited texts, including with the so-called *Ur-Hamlet*. See Smith, "Ghost Writing."

murdered his father), "My tables! Meet it is I set it down / That one may smile and smile and be a villain" (1.5.107–8). Hamlet demonstrates here a kind of writing that attempts to take in what he is experiencing in the world—even as what he sets down, that people mask their villainy behind smiling faces, risks slipping into being its own cliché (as Horatio suggests, in response to a different remark of Hamlet's about villainy less than twenty lines later, "There needs no ghost, my lord, come from the grave / To tell us this" [1.5.123–24]). Later, Hamlet makes a related point in observing the way that tastes swing toward those in power:

> It is not very strange, for my uncle is King of Denmark, and those that would make mouths at him while my father lived give twenty, forty, fifty, a hundred ducats apiece for his picture in little. 'Sblood, there is something in this more than natural if philosophy could find it out. (2.2.300–305)

Hamlet tries to imagine, in however flawed a way, a kind of knowledge that would take in the way the world actually seems to be working—its strange way, in this case, of changing its values based on who holds power. What if the court's sycophancy, which presumes to lie outside the eternal truths of philosophy, could become the very matter of philosophy? For this to happen, he suggests, we would have to take into account the unknown and unnamed, the "something in this" that is "more than natural." Here truth is not necessarily mere repetition, not necessarily what unfolds according to timeless and inscrutable laws. Rather, truth could include what remains yet unknown, demanding that we become attentive to new experience. In this case, what he discovers is that the abdication of authorship—seeing everything as necessarily always already the way it is and therefore as agentless—may be motivated by an abdication to authority.

The well-known problem of close reading today is that it has too often entailed drawing a kind of circle around the text, separating it from its sociopolitical context. But if we take Polonius as an anti-close reader, we see that the opposite can be the case. The man who claims to have no time for close reading, seeming to know already the way things are, is the same man who conceals his own inscription into the power structure—committed, as he is, to repetition of that structure under the new king. Polonius is always in a rush—and in so being is unresponsive to the unique particularity and therefore to the not-yet-known actuality of what lies before him. Truly to attend to an object is also to attend to the place that the object holds in the larger sociopolitical world—and to the powers that shape and constrain this place.

2 Delusions of Distance: Aspiring to the Perspective of the "Seeing Unseen"

Polonius's role as an advisor to the king means that he often asserts his insider status. He wants to be privy to secrets and to other private intelligence—and to be "in the ear" (3.1.183) of any royal conference. At the same time, the methods he uses to seek out these secrets often demand his assertion that he does so from an objective distance. Polonius, I will suggest in this section, is an anti-close reader not only in being fast but also in adopting a distance from his object of inquiry.

Perceiving himself as dogged in his search for the truth, Polonius employs a method of investigation that several times involves separating himself from what he is studying. He twice hides behind the arras: first with the king in order to observe Hamlet's interaction with Ophelia and then a second time alone to observe Hamlet's interaction with Gertrude. In hiding behind the arras, Polonius adopts the perspective of what he calls the "seeing unseen" (3.1.32). Polonius associates this technique of self-concealment not with Machiavellian, Iago-like duplicity—but with impartiality. "'Tis meet," he says, "that some more audience than a mother / (Since nature makes them partial) should o'er-hear / The speech of vantage" (3.3.31–33). According to this line of thinking, Gertrude may be biased because, as Hamlet's mother, she is closely connected with him. Polonius's concern with her bias is an example of what Barbara J. Shapiro has called, in reference to the increasing objectivity in the field of law, the emerging "culture of fact."[17] Jurors, it was argued, should not be related to or allied with either party in a trial.[18] It was thought that a jury would behave more fairly if it did not know those involved in the case; the assumption was that closeness lessens—rather than increases—fair assessment and understanding. The emphasis must be on "Equity and Impartiality."[19] The problem for Polonius is that

[17] Shapiro, *Culture of Fact*.

[18] Shapiro, 26.

[19] *Exact Account of the Trial* (1689), 25, quoted in Shapiro, *Culture of Fact*, 27. Shapiro explains how this understanding of the jury as "fact evaluators" represented a

Gertrude is "partial," or even a *part* of Hamlet by the laws of nature. Two different meanings of the word *partial*—entailing, one, a part of a whole and, two, bias—appear here conflated, as though to be related is to be biased.

The ideal of a distance between investigators and the objects of their investigation can also be associated with the aims of an emergent empiricism. Francis Bacon, who was legal counsel under Elizabeth and James I (rising to serve as attorney general 1613–1617), will advocate for just such a distance in the field of science when he calls for observing "things themselves" by avoiding "mingling" the subject with the object.[20] His goal was to keep the viewing subject safely apart from the viewed object. In tracing the development of objectivity, Lorraine Daston and Peter Galison have aptly described the ideal of a perspective that will be free of the obfuscations of the researcher's involvement as "the viewpoint of angels,"[21] and Thomas Nagel has named this perspective, ironically, "the view from nowhere."[22]

By claiming not to be involved, Polonius aims for just such an objective distance. When he hides behind the arras, he wants to see his object of study as though he were not there. However, what Shakespeare reveals is that Polonius's denial of his own point of view is fundamentally flawed. The problem is that Polonius's distance turns out to entail or even to produce an unacknowledged projection of his own subjectivity. His claim of being on the outside is inseparable from his claim of being on the inside. Distancing turns out, paradoxically, to be inseparable from intruding.

This dynamic is perhaps most evident when Polonius sends Reynaldo to gather information about Laertes's conduct in France. Polonius instructs his man to "make inquire" into whether his son is misbehaving (2.1.3). Part of Polonius's difficulty in this scene is surely related to the way that, as András Kiséry has recently argued, he misapplies political knowledge to a personal situation—failing to maintain an emergent

departure from the jury's prior role: "Jurors were not initially fact evaluators but rather 'knowers' of the facts, selected locally because they were expected to bring some prior knowledge of the facts and/or litigants to the trial" (11). See also Hutson, *Invention of Suspicion*.

[20] Bacon, *Works*, 4:19, 54.

[21] Daston and Galison, "Image of Objectivity," 82.

[22] Nagel, *View from Nowhere*.

understanding of politics as its own discrete realm that requires professional knowledge and expertise.[23] But Shakespeare may also be engaging problems of an emergent empiricism. Polonius assumes that by not yet revealing himself to Laertes, Reynaldo will be better able to get at the truth of the situation. However, in order to encourage the exposure of this truth, Polonius instructs Reynaldo to drop hints that he has inside knowledge of Laertes's misdeeds: "there put on him / What forgeries you please. Marry, none so rank / As may dishonor him—take heed of that— / But, sir, such wanton, wild and usual slips / As are companions noted and most known / To youth and liberty" (2.1.19–24). The qualities that Polonius assumes belong to the object (to "youth and liberty") may, though, actually belong to himself, as he later suggests in an aside reference about his own youth, when he "suffered much extremity for love" (2.2.187); similarly, at another point, he says, "I do know / When the blood burns" (1.3.114–15). Polonius, when he thinks he is perceiving his object, is more often than not projecting, folding Laertes's possible misbehavior or Hamlet's madness into the always-the-same clichés of youth—a version, in this case, of boys will be boys—rendering these young men into repetitions of Polonius's own youthful self. In the scene with Reynaldo, Polonius asserts that his hints about Laertes's misbehavior should not dishonor his son ("none so rank / As may dishonor him"), but in spreading rumors that Laertes is drinking, gambling, and seeing prostitutes, that is precisely what Polonius is doing.

For all his dogged investigations, Polonius does not seem to know how to pause, how to listen, how, as Theodor Adorno would say, to let the object take the lead[24]; rather, Polonius imposes his preconceptions onto it. The aggressiveness of his investigative mode is suggested by the violence of his metaphors for this truth-seeking, which often rely on the language of the hunt: e.g., "If circumstances lead me I will find / Where truth is hid, though it were hid indeed / Within the center" (2.2.154–56).[25] He sees himself as trying to root out the truth, as though the effort of trying to understand put him in an adversarial relationship with the

[23] Kiséry, *Hamlet's Moment*, 87, 137.

[24] Adorno, *Aesthetic Theory*, 73: "the observer enters into a contract with the work, agreeing to submit to it on condition that it speak." Also, see Adorno, *Negative Dialectics*, 43.

[25] See also 2.2.46–49. For a discussion of this image of the hunt, see Lewis, *Vision of Darkness*, 43–111.

object rather than in a posture of receptivity to it. In interacting with his daughter, he demands of her: “Give me up the truth” (1.3.97). Polonius’s patriarchal demand is not just that she *give* the truth but that she *give up* the truth, that is, that she surrender or relinquish the truth to him.

Bacon will write in similarly adversarial terms about how “the nature of things betrays itself more readily under the vexations of art [that is, experiment] than in its natural freedom.”[26] According to this model, the effort of learning is antagonistic. When Hamlet makes his plan to stage the “Mouse-Trap,” he designs an experiment that is similarly adversarial—in order to “catch” the king’s conscience (2.2.540).

What Shakespeare shows, though, is that this mode of adversarial, seemingly detached proto-empiricist testing is not always as objective as it seems; rather, it can create its own illusions. After the scene in which Claudius and Polonius, from behind the arras, observe Hamlet discoursing to himself first about suicide (“To be or not to be”) and then railing against Ophelia (“Get thee to a nunnery!”), Ophelia laments: “O woe is me / T’have seen what I have seen, see what I see” (3.1.159–60). She experiences as a wound (“woe is me”) both what she has witnessed (in the present perfect, “what I have seen”) and what she continues to see as reality unfolds (in the present, “what I see”). In contrast, the king and Polonius present themselves as more evaluative and detached—and simpler in relation to time. The king assesses the situation: “Love! His affections do not that way tend” (3.1.161). Deciding that there is another reason for the prince’s madness, Claudius decides that Hamlet must be sent to England. But Polonius, significantly, can only perceive what he already knows:

> […] But yet do I believe
> The origin and commencement of his grief
> Sprung from neglected love. How now, Ophelia?
> You need not tell us what Lord Hamlet said—
> We heard it all. (3.1.175–79)

Polonius has put Hamlet in a kind of petri dish for observation, but what the old courtier sees only confirms what he already believed—that

[26] Bacon, *Works*, 4:29. Alan Fisher associates Polonius in passing with Bacon for yet another reason: they both use “indirections” in order to “find directions out” (2.1.63). See Fisher, “Shakespeare’s Last Humanist,” 45.

Hamlet's supposed madness is driven by frustrated love, which, he thinks, lies at the source of the prince's actions, at their "origin and commencement." Shakespeare makes us notice that Polonius does not let Ophelia speak: He may ask "How now, Ophelia?" but he then cuts her off, "You need not tell us what Lord Hamlet said—/ We heard it all." And the scene in fact ends nine lines later, with Ophelia never having had a chance to respond or to give her impressions of events. Polonius's claim of belief ("I believe") precedes his articulated observation ("We heard it all"). Judgments are not following from evidence, as Polonius thinks, but, rather, the reverse: he is producing evidence that follows from his own prejudgments.[27]

Polonius unknowingly projects his own experience onto new situations. It is Polonius who was overcome by love when he was young ("truly, in my youth I suffered much extremity for love, very near this" [2.2.186–87]) and who has universalized this experience. Sometimes, this unknowing self-preoccupation of Polonius's rises to the surface: When the king asks him about how Ophelia received Hamlet's profession of love, Polonius answers, "What do you think of me?" (2.2.126). His sexism here manifests as a failure to observe his daughter in her own separate reality. He may pride himself on his ability to root out the truth, but he is actually unable to get out of himself, unable to perceive the other as other. The term that Polonius uses for the hints he wants Reynaldo to give about Laertes's possible misbehavior in France is "distant knowledge" (2.1.13), that is, a removed comprehension. However, Polonius's distant knowledge turns out to entail the opposite of distance, and instead to involve something more like projection, smear, contamination.

For all his emphasis on distance, what characterizes Polonius is that he is constantly, to use Hamlet's word, "intruding" (3.4.29), repeatedly inserting himself into situations from which he thinks he has separated himself for the sake of objective knowledge. Polonius promises the king that, during Hamlet's discussion with Gertrude in her closet, "I'll be placed, so please you, in the ear / Of all their conference" (3.1.183–84). Polonius's apparent distance is actually an attempt at penetration; the detached outsider also wants to be the privileged insider. Recall the line that Ophelia says to him, after he warns her that she must fear Hamlet's intentions:

[27] Focusing on *Othello*, Joel Altman emphasizes this dynamic and, specifically, the figure of *hysteron proteron*. See Altman, *Improbability of Othello*, 184–99.

I do not know, my lord, what I should think. (1.3.103)

Shakespeare here analyzes in microcosm how Polonius has intruded into his daughter's thinking. Her line begins as a declarative negative statement ("I do not know") and then switches into the subjunctive ("what I should think"), possibly expressing how her thinking has started to become divorced from itself. (Indeed, Claudius will later describe her, once she has fully gone mad, as "divided from herself and her fair judgment" [4.5.85].) What marks the rupture in this line is, quite literally, "my lord" (Polonius), a phrase which, inserted into the center of her line, marks the divide from the declarative to the hypothetical—suggesting her increasing self-alienation. Later, reporting Hamlet's interaction with her in her closet, she responds to Polonius's question about whether Hamlet was mad for her love, "My lord, I do not know, / But truly I do fear it" (2.1.82–83), again negating her own experience of her thought, this time starting with "my lord." The point is that Polonius's investigations are inadvertently shaping events. What he thinks he observes from a distance is really that in which he is enmeshed. Simon Jarvis, evoking the way that the grasp at objectivity can entail an unconscious slide into subjectivity, writes that "The more rapidly and brutally thought cuts itself free from illusion, the more it is entangled."[28]

Returning to the question of close reading, Shakespeare's play offers a way to try to glimpse the self-deception that can be involved in too reductive an understanding of what it might mean to claim to use detached, empiricist methods to break through the illusions of subjectivity or partiality. The proto-Baconian empiricism that *Hamlet* scrutinizes is not totally unrelated to some modern understandings of literary objectivity, such as Franco Moretti's goal of "distant reading," which is also the title of his 2013 book. As founder of the Stanford Literary Lab, Moretti aims to circumvent problems of literary interpretation by using computers to examine data about books in order to produce a new kind of knowledge about them and about social and economic history. Data analysis surpasses, in his model, close reading. In articulating his empiricist method, Moretti echoes Bacon's language; pointing out that experiments are often described as "questions put to nature," Moretti says that "what

[28] Jarvis, "Adorno, Marx, Materialism," 80. His focus is on materialism and mystification.

I'm imagining here are questions—put to culture."[29] He may be referring to Bacon's well-known idea that we should put nature to the question through experimentation as one might interrogate a witness.[30]

Ultimately, it makes no difference whether Polonius thinks he is on the inside (in the ear of the conference for the sake of private knowledge) or on the outside (hidden behind the arras for the sake of detachment) because in both cases he is making the same mistake: he is aggressively seeking to master that which really needs to be listened to and attended to and patiently received.

3 Why Close Reading

"One might almost say," Adorno writes, "that truth itself depends on the tempo, the patience and perseverance of lingering with the particular."[31] Close reading, which uses a spatial term ("close") to evoke a reading based on proximity or even on intimacy (closeness), depends in this essay as much on tempo as on nearness: it is an art of slowness, of lingering, of *pausing*. It is a friend, to use Friedrich Nietzsche's description of philology, "of *lento*."[32]

In an age of intense productivity or at least of intense busyness, "of hurry, of indecent and perspiring haste," what we need, Nietzsche said in the nineteenth century, is an art that "does not so easily get anything done," a mode of reading that teaches us "to read *well*, that is to say, to read slowly, deeply, looking cautiously before and aft, with reservations, with doors left open, with delicate eyes and fingers."[33] This kind of painstaking, delicate, open-minded reading is slow because it treats the literary object as not yet known, as particular, as unsubordinated to pregiven generalizations—and therefore as unsubordinated to the way things

[29] Moretti, *Distant Reading*, 165. Moretti situates his method as against close reading at 48–49.

[30] "I mean…to examine nature herself and the arts upon interrogatories," Bacon writes in *Parasceve*. See Bacon, *Works*, 4:263. For an extended discussion of the conflict in the late sixteenth century between poetry and empiricism, with reference to Moretti, see Eisendrath, *Poetry in a World*, 1–23; esp. 18–19.

[31] Adorno, *Minima Moralia*, 77.

[32] Nietzsche, *Daybreak*, 5. Reuben A. Brower describes close reading as slow reading. See Brower, "Reading in Slow Motion."

[33] Nietzsche, *Daybreak*, 5.

have been. Close reading gently asks its text: *Who are you? How do you like to talk? What kinds of questions do you respond to? Teach me please how to read you.* In adopting this mode of inquiry, close reading becomes a practice by which readers open themselves to a new object, make themselves vulnerable to that which they do not yet understand. William Empson expresses a related need to treat a text as unknown: “In fact, you must rely on each particular poem to show you the way in which it is trying to be good.”[34] The text requires our receptivity in order that it can show us how to read it. The word that Adorno, writing about classical music, uses for this kind of attentive, effortful intellectual receptivity is “love.” He describes the necessary kind of intellectual listening as entailing simultaneously activity and passivity, the utmost rigor of attention and a kind of supple receptivity: listening is, he writes, “what demands work and effort on the part of the hearing, what demands strength of attention and memory, what demands, in fact, love.”[35]

Close reading in this way—with attentive receptivity to an object that is treated as not yet known—has implications for how we read both literature and also the world. Reflecting on the horrors of the twentieth century, Hannah Arendt argues that in order to perceive the outrageousness of events, we must break with “commonplaces.” She associates this word with pre-given patterns of understanding that immure us from feeling “the impact of reality and the shock of experience,” but we might also recall Polonius’s reliance on commonplaces in *Hamlet*. Instead of relying on such commonplaces, she says, we must find ways to perceive the actual historical moment so that we neither deny nor give in to its brutality. “Comprehension, in short, means the unpremeditated, attentive facing up to, and resisting of, reality—whatever it may be.”[36]

If Polonius’s mode of investigation turns out really to be a form of anti-investigation, a refusal to face up to reality by taking in the specificity of the events unfolding before him in a non-dominating way, this mode is also not unmotivated. His actions are self-serving. Although he claims to be seeking the truth, he actually ignores the particularity of whatever is newly emergent—he ignores, most importantly, the meanings by which

[34] Empson, *Seven Types of Ambiguity*, 7. Thanks to Anirudh Sridhar for directing my attention to this quotation.

[35] Quoted in Nicholsen, *Exact Imagination, Late Work*, 19.

[36] Arendt, *Origins of Totalitarianism*, viii.

the next generation of young people understand themselves—in order, ultimately, to preserve his place in the already-given power structure of the Danish court, that is, in the status quo.[37]

References

Adorno, Theodor W. *Aesthetic Theory*. Edited by Gretel Adorno and Rolf Tiedemann. Translated by Robert Hullot-Kentor. Minneapolis: University of Minnesota Press, 1997.

———. *Minima Moralia: Reflections from Damaged Life*. Translated by E. F. N. Jephcott. London: Verso, 2005.

———. *Negative Dialectics*. Translated by E. B. Ashton. New York: Continuum, 1973.

Altman, Joel. *The Improbability of Othello: Rhetorical Anthropology and Shakespearean Selfhood*. Chicago: University of Chicago Press, 2010.

Arendt, Hannah. *The Origins of Totalitarianism*. Orlando: Harcourt, 1966.

Bacon, Francis. *The Works of Francis Bacon*. Edited by James Spedding. 7 vols. London: Longman, 1870.

Bate, Jonathan, ed. *The Romantics on Shakespeare*. London: Penguin Books, 1992.

Brower, Reuben A. "Reading in Slow Motion." *In Defense of Reading: A Reader's Approach to Literary Criticism*, edited by Reuben A. Brower and Richard Poirier, 3–21. New York: Dutton, 1962.

Daston, Lorraine, and Peter Galison. "The Image of Objectivity." *Representations* 40 (Autumn 1992): 81–128.

Eisendrath, Rachel. *Poetry in a World of Things: Aesthetics and Empiricism in Renaissance Ekphrasis*. Chicago: University of Chicago Press, 2018.

Empson, William. *Seven Types of Ambiguity*. New York: New Directions, 1947.

Erasmus, Desiderius. *De Ratione Studii* [*Upon the Right Method of Instruction*]. In *Desiderius Erasmus: Concerning the Aim and Method of Education*, edited by William Harrison Woodward, 162–78. Cambridge: University Press, 1904.

Fisher, Alan. "Shakespeare's Last Humanist." *Renaissance and Reformation* 14, no. 1 (Winter 1990): 37–47.

Hutson, Lorna. *The Invention of Suspicion: Law and Mimesis in Shakespeare and Renaissance Drama*. Oxford: Oxford University Press, 2007.

———. *Circumstantial Shakespeare*. Oxford: Oxford University Press, 2015.

[37] For their insightful close reading of drafts of this essay, I am grateful to Derek Attridge, Julie Crawford, Heather Dubrow, Mir Ali Hosseini, Betsy Eisendrath, Anirudh Sridhar, and Timea Széll.

Jarvis, Simon. "Adorno, Marx, Materialism." In *Cambridge Companion to Adorno*, edited by Tom Huhn, 79–100. Cambridge: Cambridge University Press, 2004.

Kiséry, András. *Hamlet's Moment: Drama and Political Knowledge in Early Modern England*. Oxford: Oxford University Press, 2016.

Lesser, Zachary, and Peter Stallybrass. "The First Literary *Hamlet* and the Commonplacing of Professional Plays." *Shakespeare Quarterly* 59, no. 4 (2008): 371–420.

Lewis, Rhodri. *Hamlet and the Vision of Darkness*. Princeton: Princeton University Press, 2017.

MacDonald, George, ed. *The Tragedie of Hamlet, Prince of Denmarke: A Study with the Text of the Folio of 1623*. London: Longmans, Green, and Co., 1885.

Montaigne, Michel de. *Essais*. 3 vols. Paris: Garnier-Flammarion, 1969.

Moretti, Franco. *Distant Reading*. London: Verso, 2013.

Moss, Ann. *Printed Commonplace-Books and the Structuring of Renaissance Thought*. Oxford: Clarendon Press, 1996.

Nagel, Thomas. *The View from Nowhere*. Oxford: Oxford University Press, 1986.

Nicholsen, Shierry Weber. *Exact Imagination, Late Work: On Adorno's Aesthetics*. Cambridge, MA: MIT Press, 1999.

Nietzsche, Friedrich. *Daybreak: Thoughts on the Prejudices of Morality*. Edited by Maudemarie Clark and Brian Leiter. Translated by R. J. Hollingdale. Cambridge: Cambridge University Press, 1997.

Pritchard, William, Sir. *An Exact Account of the Trial between Sr. William Pritchard, Kt. and Alderman of the City of London, Plaintiff, and Thomas Papillon, Esq, Defendant*. London: Printed and sold by Richard Janeway, 1689.

Rose, Jacqueline, ed. *The Politics of Counsel in England and Scotland, 1286–1707*. Oxford: Published for the British Academy by Oxford University Press, 2016.

Shakespeare, William. *Hamlet*. Arden Shakespeare, 3rd ser. Edited by Ann Thompson and Neil Taylor. London: Thomson Learning, 2006.

———. *Macbeth*. Arden Shakespeare, 3rd ser. Edited by Sandra Clark and Pamela Mason. London: Bloomsbury, 2015.

Shapiro, Barbara J. *A Culture of Fact: England, 1550–1720*. Ithaca: Cornell University Press, 2000.

Smith, Emma. "Ghost Writing: *Hamlet* and the *Ur-Hamlet*." In *The Renaissance Text: Theory, Editing, Textuality*, edited by Andrew Murphy, 177–90. Manchester: Manchester University Press, 2000.

Stallybrass, Peter, Roger Chartier, J. Franklin Mowery, and Heather Wolfe. "Hamlet's Tables and the Technologies of Writing in Renaissance England," *Shakespeare Quarterly* 55, no. 4 (2004): 379–419.

CHAPTER 9

What Kind of Person Should the Critic Be?

Simon Grimble

In January 2013, the website *Critical Legal Thinking* published an interview with the American political theorist, Wendy Brown. In that interview, Brown was asked a question about how she conceived of her own role, along with that of other intellectuals, in the context of the Occupy movement and other political upheavals of the then present. In her answer, Brown described her annoyance with "the fetishism of 'the' public intellectual," but swiftly moved into another direction:

> The most important thing that we can do is be good teachers [...] Whatever we are teaching, whether it's Plato or Marx, economic theory or social theory, Nietzsche or Adorno, we need to be teaching [the students] how to read carefully, think hard, ask deep questions, make good arguments. And the reason this is so important is that the most substantive casualties of neoliberalism today are deep, independent thought, the making of citizens, and liberal arts education as opposed to vocational and technical training. We faculty still have our classrooms as places to do what we think is valuable in those classrooms, which for me is not about preaching a political line, but teaching students that thinking is fundamental to being

S. Grimble (✉)
Department of English Studies, Durham University, Durham, UK
e-mail: simon.grimble@durham.ac.uk

A. Sridhar et al. (eds.), *The Work of Reading*,
https://doi.org/10.1007/978-3-030-71139-9_9

> human and is increasingly devalued except as a technical practice. This is an old claim, from the Frankfurt School, but it's on steroids now. So I believe our most important work as academics is teaching students to think deeply and well. Our books come and go.[1]

The reason I quote this statement is not so much because of the broad brush of the argument, with which I am in general agreement: certainly, in the UK higher educational system, and specifically in the English variant in that, it can appear that "thinking is [...] increasingly devalued except as a technical practice." The arrival of annual university tuition fees of £9,000 and above following the passage of the 2011 Education Act means that we are seeing more and more students being pushed toward "vocational and technical training," as they, for all of the obvious reasons, try to secure greater chances of employability, an employability that they will need partly to pay off the debts that they have incurred as university students. This pattern has been most striking in secondary education, where the number of students taking English language or literature at A-level, the public examinations taken in the final year of school in England, Wales and Northern Ireland, has dropped by twenty-five percent since 2013, with, possibly, an increasing favoring of STEM subjects in its place.[2] At the same time, a certain rhetoric around employability has developed in UK universities, as universities try to justify the usefulness of the education that they provide, even if they are offering courses which are certainly academic, and which may have elements of the liberal and the humanist. One example of this would be that of the notion of "transferable skills," which is one way in which humanities subjects argue that the types of thinking and writing that they practice can form a training for employability in other areas outside of academia. In that sense, universities—as we see on module descriptions and other forms of academic bureaucratic life—try to translate the specific content of what happens in a classroom or lecture hall into other categories which have a manifest use-value. Clearly, the status of "thinking" in Brown's account does not fit easily into this process of translation. At the same time, one of the reasons that I quote Brown's statement is because of one phrase that makes me pause: you will note that the second of "the most substantive casualties of neoliberalism today" is, in her account, "the making of citizens." The

[1] Celikates and Jensen, "Reclaiming Democracy."

[2] Rustin, "Why Study English?"

reason that it makes me pause is not because the idea that universities in particular, and education in general, should be involved in "the making of citizens" is an unusual one in the history of thinking about the purposes of education: from the ancient Greeks to Rousseau to von Humboldt to John Dewey, we would have to say that this was a central idea, even if there have always been debates about how it should all work.[3] So, this is not the problem. The problem lies elsewhere: it raises the question of the social role of both the academic and the institution of which she or he is part. I can feel a small part of myself saying: "it's not part of my job description to make citizens. Who am I to make them? And what if they don't want to be so made?" In practice, if you bring up these possibilities with contemporary students, there is quite a strong possibility that you will meet at least some resistance, as they are often focused on the use-value and the transferable skills conferred by their university education, for all of the very unsurprising reasons described above. Resistance to these prevailing modes on the behalf of any particular academic can have very direct negative consequences in the context of the contemporary UK university: student complaints, poor results in module evaluation questionnaires, a general interruption of the smooth processes that university administrations would like to see characterizing what is now known in the United Kingdom as "the student experience"; a world where, as a friend and colleague at another Russell Group UK university has noted, rates of student satisfaction as registered in the National Student Survey have tended to rival the voting records for East European Communist Parties in the 1960s and 1970s, with rates of satisfaction of well over eighty percent.[4]

At the same time, I would say, as a citizen who is also an academic, that we cannot retreat from ideas about how education is related to citizenry, even if frankly corporatized universities sometimes appear to solely wish to preside over the smooth running of an instrumentalized process. And if we are interested in how education is related to citizenry, then we are also interested in the question of "what kind of person should the critic be." Are we interested in provoking what is known as "active citizenship"? I have to plead guilty here and say that I am interested in this, at least

[3] For example, see Trachtenberg, *Making Citizens*; Dewey, *Democracy and Education*; Heater, *Education for Citizenship*.

[4] See, for example, "Our Students among UK's Most Satisfied," on the Durham University website.

partly because the student who conceives of herself or himself as an active citizen tends often (although not always) to be a better reader, interpreter, and scholar. At the same time, I do not want to be extremely precise about exactly the nature of the dispositions that I am, for want of a better word, encouraging: people are different and will take things in different ways. But one should present them with possibilities. One possibility is described in Matthew Arnold's "On Translating Homer: Last Words," where he describes how he sees the role of the critic of poetry, and thinks about what kind of person they should be:

> The 'thing itself' with which one is here dealing, -the critical perception of poetic truth,- is of all things the most volatile, elusive, and evanescent; by even pressing too impetuously after it, one runs the risk of losing it. The critic of poetry should have the finest tact, the nicest moderation, the most free, flexible, and elastic spirit imaginable; he should be indeed the "ondoyant et divers," the undulating and diverse being of Montaigne.[5]

Is this something that one could put on a module description to say that this is what you would get from undertaking a particular course of study, that the students would emerge with "the undulating and diverse being of Montaigne"? Is that a transferable skill? Clearly not: it is a quality in itself, although you could take it into various locations. At the same time, I can sense a resistance in myself to Arnold's characterizations: it's not my place to be like that, or in another contemporary rhetoric in UK universities, it's above my pay grade. And this is because the notion of human emancipation that his conceptions involve can, in a divided society, look instead like something that is solely specific to a wealthy class who can afford cultivation. At a more general level, doubts about Arnold's statement may also exist because, in a market democracy like the United Kingdom, claims about intrinsic value are liable to be contested by more relativist notions, or by an understanding that the market should be the only source of deliberation because it at least can put a number on things.

At the same time, it should be clear that, in this contemporary landscape, these issues don't just disappear because they raise uncomfortable questions. Dispositions—of various kinds—are created in particular national, institutional, and disciplinary settings and have consequences of both immediate and delayed natures. One of the merits of Rita Felski's

[5] Arnold, "On Translating Homer," 89.

The Limits of Critique is that it very much focuses on the kinds of disposition that have developed in literary studies under the influence of what is known as "theory," particularly in the United States. Felski does not examine dispositions as such, but focuses instead on a pervasive "mood," which for her is characterized in the following way:

> Scholars like to think that their claims stand or fall on the merits of their reasoning and the irresistible weight of their evidence, yet they also adopt a low-key affective tone that can bolster or dramatically diminish their allure. Critical detachment, in this light, is not an absence of mood but one manifestation of it—a certain orientation towards one's subject, a way of making one's argument matter. It is tied to the cultivation of an intellectual persona that is highly prized in literary studies and beyond: suspicious, knowing, self-conscious, hardheaded, tirelessly vigilant.[6]

So, in one sense, and really irrespective of whether she recognizes it or not, Felski is speaking as a moralist here, just as Matthew Arnold was a moralist, and what she is against is this intellectual persona and the attributes with which it is associated: "suspicious, knowing, self-conscious, hardheaded, tirelessly vigilant." As Terry Eagleton noted in a helpfully reductive passage in his review of Felski's book, there are ways in which such a mentality can be related to long-standing issues in cultural history:

> Most critical writing of this kind stems these days from the United States, and in some ways it fits well enough with old-fashioned American Puritanism. The high moral or political tone, the air of spiritual superiority, the wariness of the aesthetic, the suspicion of outward appearances as deceitful, the search for an inner truth that's hard to come by, the anxious scanning for symptoms of impurity, which is also to be found in the cult of political correctness: none of this of course is peculiarly American, but it is probably no accident that it has flourished so prodigally there. Frank Kermode once wrote that reading a certain poem by Wallace Stevens made the hair on the back of his neck stand on end, a statement it would be as hard to imagine issuing from the lips of a young American professor in pursuit of tenure as it would be unthinkable in the writing of Georg Lukács. It is the kind of thing anybody might say, and academics are not paid for being just anybody.[7]

[6] Felski, *Limits of Critique*, 6.

[7] Eagleton, "Not Just Anybody."

It is possible that for some readers Eagleton's characterization seems both throwaway and bordering on the offensive (a border that, in his literary journalism, Eagleton likes to explore), but it does still direct us to the question of what kind of person should the critic be, as well as to the relation between that person and a set of cultural and historical circumstances. But in another sense, both Felski and Eagleton somewhat struggle to give voice to the alternative set of moral attributes that they do wish to attribute to the critic. In one way, this is understandable: Felski's book may be about the limits of critique, but it gives a critique of critique and therefore may have something of the same negativity as critique itself. There is a lot to be said for that negativity: as William Hazlitt said in his 1826 essay "On the Pleasure of Hating": "without something to hate, we should lose the very spring of thought and action [...] The white streak in our own fortunes is brightened (or just rendered visible) by making all around it as dark as possible."[8] Hating, for Hazlitt, is what makes thinking possible. At the same time, the attractions of particular dispositions must have a relation to their particular cultural moment. In that sense, Felski's dissatisfaction with that particular set of attributes must also relate to the question of what possibilities such attitudes open up or don't open up. One can see that those attributes *may* have sustained a particular literary critical identity, in conditions of political retreat where the world is conceived as at an "impasse," in Lauren Berlant's terms in *Cruel Optimism*; a world where you're hoping for the best but expecting the worst. We may be, in that sense, like the literary professors in R.E.M.'s 1998 song, "Sad Professor," who "try to rope in followers / To float their malcontent." As the song goes on, and as the speaker refers to himself, "As for this reader/I'm already spent."[9] Imagining a more constructive, a more hopeful, a more relational figure as the critic is a lot to ask for, given the world of inequality, stratification and eroded working conditions that many literary scholars (as well as other academics) now experience. But Felski's own dissatisfactions may be one sign of what is actually, if contrarily, possible.

[8] Hazlitt, "Pleasure of Hating," 308.

[9] Readers may be interested in the piece "Sad Professor" by the academic and critic John Sutherland, where he speculates that the "lit professor" in the song may be based on him, having met the lyricist, Michael Stipe, at around the time of the song's composition: "I would like to think it's me."

It may also be possible that what readers of Felski have responded to are not necessarily the details of her arguments, but her sense that literary scholarship and criticism should—and in important senses already does—matter. That sense of mattering has allowed her to depart from recent scholarly norms and to write in a fresher and livelier way, in ways which are less "vigilant" but more open. That freshness and liveliness has allowed her to give voice to the democratic spirit of the best kinds of criticism, and to depart from narrower, more inward-looking, more thoroughly professionalized forms. Some of that sharpness is also present in Joseph North's *Literary Criticism: A Concise Political History*. It is possible to disagree with North's selective history of literary criticism, which foregrounds I. A. Richards as a displaced founding father whose emphasis on aesthetic education is now something we should be making a return to, while admiring the vigor and clarity of much of the writing. The vigor and clarity are therefore of course related to the degree of confidence that North clearly has in the public role and responsibilities of the literary critic, and it is this confidence that allows him the freedom to be incisive, and to make judgments. The world of critique that Felski has attempted to summarize has tended to have less of this confidence: one attribute that we could—perhaps—add to her list of characteristics is that of being "buttoned-up." Felski and North are not exactly travelers on the open roads of democratic criticism, but there is some sense of liberation which is part of both of their projects. One of the consequences of critique as a mode in the way that Felski describes it is that it tends to be impersonal. To write in an impersonal way risks less exposure on the part of the critic; less of their self is displayed. This makes a kind of sense as a greater degree of self-exposure could lead to being open to more wounding types of criticism, from peer-reviewers or from other academic readers. So a preference for a type of impersonal critique is also an understandable preference for self-protection. Terry Eagleton is of course partially correct when he says in his essay on Felski that "it has always been an embarrassment to literary scholars that reading, along with talking about what you read, is something that a lot of non-scholarly people do as well," unlike the situation for "brain surgeons" or "analytic philosophers."[10] The perennially uneasy position of the academic literary critic, poised between literary matters of large public interest and

[10] Eagleton, "Not Just Anybody."

a specialized and often hierarchical academic sphere, is to move between these relatively more and less specialized poles. But if we are to move toward more affirmative modes in the practice of literary criticism that will necessarily involve some greater degree of personal rather than solely impersonal modes of writing. In a recent published lecture, the critic Simon During has asked the question: "Can you think personally and impersonally simultaneously? Yes, you can, and that's what I will be trying to do here." This approach enables him to use details of his own intellectual biography in order to develop an account of how the position of literary criticism has changed. As he summarizes his position:

> […] as we all know, the academic study of literature in 2018 is quite unlike that of the sixties. That is not just a matter of different ideas and methods, it's a matter of a different mood. Putting it simply: a shift from confidence and hope to flatness, even melancholy.[11]

Of course, the challenge for the melancholic literary critic is that of attempting to depart from their own melancholy. Combining personal and impersonal modes in one's writing is one way to gain a perspective on one's experience and in that sense to begin a process of reconstruction. It may well be difficult to maintain this process. As Lauren Berlant writes in relation to the feelings of impasse described above: "even with an image of a better good life available to sustain your optimism, it is awkward and it is threatening to detach from what is already not working."[12]

This is certainly true, and in that sense it may explain what Felski describes as the "allure" of critique but by turning it on its head: one could argue that critique is not so much an alluring mode as one that is particularly well-defended against the possibility of having to "detach from what is already not working." In that sense, the contemporary literary critic may end up in a particularly stuck position: drawn to a kind of oppositional politics, but then maintained in its own oppositionalism, as more relational ways of working and thinking become alien to it. Habits are of course important in this: if you are in the habit of critique, just as if you are in the habit of working in a different way, you are likely to continue to work in that way, even if the price of critique's vigilance might in the end be silence. In that sense we might all become rather like the

[11] During, "Literary Academia."

[12] Berlant, *Cruel Optimism*, 263.

Prince in *Hamlet*, and our position similar to that occupied by Hamlet in Act 4, Scene 4 as he considers Fortinbras setting out on his military adventure in Poland and in that sense showing a fortitude or a carelessness that he lacks: "How all occasions do inform against me / And spur my dull revenge!" Of course, the argument here is not that from "this time forth,/ My thoughts be bloody, or be nothing worth!" as Hamlet argues by the end of this soliloquy, particularly as his bloody thoughts will end, unsurprisingly, with his own death and his own silence.[13] Fortinbras's implicit recommendation of self-promoting military adventure, with great carelessness about the soldiers on both sides who will die in his enterprise, is not an appealing prospect either. The challenge instead is to try to sketch out our own constructive alternatives to the "impasse" that Berlant describes.

In that spirit, it will be worth considering and reminding ourselves about what is admirable and important in our existing practices. The focus of this volume is on close reading and, clearly, the sensitivity of this practice is a central concern. The best close reading is sensitive to the writing it attends to: it is highly conscious of the other, and aware of the manifold pressures, contradictions, and surprises that can be at stake in any given literary text. This sensitivity is precious and is in need of cultivation, both as a literary critical practice and as an emblem of the kinds of attention we need in our complex and fraught society. This is not an argument for saying that the right practice of literary criticism is the only way to develop these kinds of attention (far from it) but it is one way, and we should not be shy of saying so. To take an example from another discipline; as Wendy Brown has argued "democracy [...] requires a robust cultivation of society as the place where we experience a linked fate across our differences and separateness."[14] Close reading, and, in particular, the close group discussions required by this practice in schools, universities, and other educational institutions, is part of the "robust cultivation of society" that democracy requires. In Joseph North's terms, we could argue that this in some ways does represent a return to the example that I. A. Richards provided, where a central point of "practical criticism" was that it allowed citizens to develop critical intelligence that in turn allowed them to be better able to question "stock ideas" as they circulated in

[13] Shakespeare, *Hamlet*, IV, 4, 33–34, 65–66.

[14] Brown, *Neoliberalism*, 27.

society: Richards had been particularly concerned with how easy it had been for the British government to manipulate public opinion for nationalistic ends during the First World War. As Richards and C. K. Ogden wrote in *The Meaning of Meaning* (1923), "in war-time words become a normal part of the mechanism of deceit."[15] At the same time, Richards' methods were clearly not fail-safe in their mission to produce "intelligent, imaginative and discriminating" citizens,[16] partly because what is set up as pedagogical program was also so clearly a testing program, the means by which we, an already educated elite, find out who is able to appreciate the arts that "are our storehouse of recorded values."[17] In that sense, there was always a democratic and egalitarian problem built into Richards' approach: as Chris Baldick argues, "the consistency with which Richards attributes all 'failures in communication' in poetry-reading to various inadequacies and disturbances of the reader, rather than to the artist or to differences of history, language, and culture between the two, amounts to a systematic denigration of the reader."[18] Richards' pessimism about the possibilities of mass culture then produces its own intellectual and social problems, in the sense that his pedagogical methods tend to turn into an attempt to discover who is sufficiently worthy and thus able to gain access to the "storehouse of recorded values" rather than a route to open-ended literary education.

In this long history, then, we have to be careful that the re-prioritization of close reading does not lead back to some of the closed circle tendencies of this kind of approach. As Perry Anderson argued in his critique of F. R. Leavis, there can easily be a type of circularity built into these methods:

> When challenged for the rationale of his critical statements, Leavis always replied that they did not properly speaking have an affirmative but an *interrogative* form. The latent form of all literary criticism was: "This is so, is it not?" Thus Leavis wrote that his method in *Revaluations* was to get his readers "to agree (with, no doubt, critical qualifications) that the

[15] Quoted in Baldick, *English Criticism*, 134.

[16] Quoted in Baldick, 148.

[17] Quoted in Baldick, 148.

[18] Baldick, 153.

> map, the essential order of English poetry seen as a whole did, when they interrogated their experience, look like that to them also."[19]

In a spirit of the "robust cultivation of society across our differences and separateness" we have to be careful that the practice of literary critical education does not become "this is so, is it not?" Such tendencies have various effects: they tend, obviously, to protect and even to extend the role of the critic-educator, who is the guardian of the "storehouse of recorded values." Their authority is in some ways even better defended by the fact that he or she does not necessarily need to justify their choices of texts and what they find within them: "this is so, is it not?" appeals to feelings of implicit recognition that will be found to be the case amongst those who feel it "is so." Such methods always tend to promote an in-group among those who do all agree together, but it also is likely to create an out-group or groups who are alienated from both the methods and the common assumptions of the critic-educator. The tendency is therefore to get toward a single agreed meaning rather than to speak to citizens "across our differences and separateness."

In these senses, calls to return to close reading must be thoughtful about the problems that have always existed within this educational practice. It must also be admitted that some of these problems are very broadly spread and may be hard or impossible to escape entirely: in certain lights, they may be virtues rather than problems at all. One particular example of this is the feelings of recognition that are generated by close acquaintance with literary texts that do indeed "speak to you." In that sense all literary scholars, whether they are supporters of close reading or any other kind of literary theory or practice, tend to have some similarity to the reader described by Wallace Stevens in his "The House Was Quiet and the World Was Calm":

> The house was quiet and the world was calm.
> The reader became the book; and summer night
>
> Was like the conscious being of the book.
> The house was quiet and the world was calm.
>
> The words were spoken as if there was no book,
> Except that the reader leaned above the page,

[19] Anderson, "Components of the National Culture."

Wanted to lean, wanted much most to be
The scholar to whom his book is true, to whom

The summer night is like a perfection of thought.
The house was quiet because it had to be.[20]

Many literary critics (myself included) would want to be "the scholar to whom his book is true." Ironically, of course, this moment is imagined as one where we have moved from the world of the text—of messages that are written down to be read at a later date—to the world of the voice: "The words were spoken as if there was no book." We have moved from an impersonal address—to any reader—to a personal address, that is addressed to this particular reader. There is therefore a quality of intimacy that we are imagining. The tragic aspect, however, is that this feeling does only exist in imagination, at least in this poem: Stevens reminds us that the "reader leaned above the page," so he is still a reader, not a listener, trying to find the perfect angle to read the book which will guarantee, perhaps, their trueness to their book. Many different readers of many different books will find something to recognize in Stevens' account: the desire on the behalf of the reader to find the book that speaks to you. The other side of this, although, is the fact that this reader may then find it hard to explain to others what exactly is the nature of the book to which he wishes to be true. Stevens does not explain what is in "the book" and we know nothing of what it is about or what it is like: if these aspects were explained, then the book may have a more specific and a less general kind of appeal. But what the poem also demonstrates is that there may well be a powerful tendency among literary critics to defend their own moments of recognition that they have received from literary texts—and for important and not trivial reasons. The problem can come when these moments of recognition are then turned into a literary critical method—because we then find out that there are many who do not share these moments of recognition.

All of this is still voiced, of course, as a version of critique and in that sense I am departing no further than Felski and North from diagnosis toward the suggestion of positive alternatives. One of the problems suggested by the recent history of literary criticism in both Britain and the

[20] Stevens, "House Was Quiet," ll. 1–10.

United States is that it may find it hard to speak in an active, affirmative voice. As Felski says, "education is not just about acquiring knowledge and skills but about being initiated into a certain sensibility."[21] What if that certain sensibility is a negative one, a sensibility that is more about the defense of embattled values than it is about the establishment of good—or good-enough—alternatives? If this is the case, then it could certainly be argued that this sensibility has actually been passed down from Richards and Leavis to later generations of critics and theorists, even if they were ostensibly opposed to their ideas and methods, and thought that their embattled values were different from such precursors. In a more precise sense, this negativity is also related to the dominance of the historical-contextualist mode described by Joseph North—if we are all historians, of various kinds, then historians do not naturally go from what has happened—which they can describe with great skill—to what could or should happen. The answer to Lenin's question of "What is to be done?" does not come naturally—and we should acknowledge that it is an important question whatever one thinks of Lenin. But habits and dispositions can be refashioned as well as reproduced: we do not need to be, in terms of the title of Mark Greif's excellent collection of essays, "against everything."[22] Indeed, we need to be expanding the space for cooperation and sympathetic organization, in the worlds of literary criticism, as with the broader social and political context. One of the reasons we do not attempt this is because the *Kritiker* does not wish to be one of the sentimental dupes of ruling powers—but without linkages to broader society, our embattledness becomes a failed version of defense. One of the consequences of the set of changes to higher educational policy in the United Kingdom in the last ten years is that many academics in the humanities feel constantly under attack—for good reason. But those attacks have also made many of us conscious of our lack of ability to defend ourselves adequately: many of us have struggled to find the words to express why literary criticism, among other university subjects, should be funded out of general taxation, rather than through high tuition fees, as has been the case since 2012. Speaking in the affirmative voice would also include being better able to voice that determination—and in so doing not to

[21] Felski, *Limits of Critique*, 22.

[22] Greif, *Against Everything*, x.

be positioned as the view of the "producer interest" that has dominated public discussion of educational matters in the recent past.[23]

Of course, that affirmative voice requires confidence on the behalf of the literary critic: in Wendy Brown's terms, we need to be "robust." It can be difficult, although certainly not impossible, to combine that necessary robustness with the subtlety and sensitivity of the best literary criticism. Almost by definition, literary critics are extremely aware of variousness, of the wide variety of formal, historical, political, stylistic, and theoretical issues that may affect the particularity of any given text. This open-mindedness is a great advantage, in terms of both its ability to produce a rounded picture and its ability to transmit some of that capacity to other critics as well as to students and to wider publics. There is a clear civic virtue to such approaches. At the same time, that sensibility means that the literary critic may also fight shy of definitiveness, for fear of shutting down lines of inquiry or future debates. As Matthew Arnold wrote in "On Translating Homer: Last Words" (and this quotation directly precedes the section discussed at the beginning of this essay):

> To handle these matters properly there is needed a poise so perfect that the least overweight in any direction tends to destroy the balance. Temper destroys it, a crotchet destroys it, even erudition may destroy it. To press to the sense of the thing itself with which one is dealing, not to go off on some collateral issue about the thing, is the hardest matter in the world.[24]

The objection to Arnold's position would say: well, this is just gentlemanly cultivation that is being defended here, with Arnold trying to make himself look like the balanced center of the disordered world, the only person who can really reconcile sense and sensibility. And this objection would have a very strong point. But it seems to me that Arnold does have a valuable point about the kinds of attention that the best kinds of literary criticism can mark, which do "press to the sense of the thing itself with which one is dealing," and which don't "go off on some collateral issue about the thing." If we are to answer the question of "what kind of person should the critic be," then this kind of attention would be one of the things that we want. In that sense, we can make a polemical case for

[23] For example, see Bailey, "Anthony Seldon's Producer Interest."

[24] Arnold, "On Translating Homer," 89.

attentive open-mindedness as a central attribute of this critical persona.[25] Contemporary academic literary criticism may have its own "crotchets" and certainly its own "erudition," and both can be very valuable, and yet both could undermine this attribute. One key element here is the fact that examples of pressing to "the sense of the thing itself" may well happen in very various locations, and with very various critical or ideological affiliations. In Marco Roth's review of Joseph North's *Literary Criticism*, Roth questions North's own commitment to "open-mindedness," but from a position which is sympathetic to North's own critique of historical-contextualism. He comments on the relative shortage of actual "close reading" of literary criticism that features in North's book, with the exception of an analysis of a D. A. Miller reading of Jane Austen. For Roth, this is a lack:

> It's a good interpretation, but surely a century of criticism could yield something more inspiring, and indeed it has. Here is a partial list of practical critics, within and outside the university, who do not rate a mention or even a footnote: Randall Jarrell, R. P. Blackmur, Kenneth Burke, Harold Bloom, Geoffrey Hartman, Leslie Fiedler, Northrop Frye, Mary McCarthy, A. D. Nuttall, Frank Kermode, A. Alvarez, Susan Sontag, Iris Murdoch, George Steiner, David Bromwich, James Wood, Albert Murray, Stanley Crouch, Wayne Koestenbaum, Marina Warner, Terry Castle. Most of these names are not primarily associated with a "politics," although some have written on political subjects. Nor did they all benefit equally from the "institutional critical paradigm" of the mid-20th-century university as much as is commonly supposed. It's possible that North's commitments to the contemporary left renders all of them anathema, but it is legitimate to wonder whether any history of criticism whose terms ask us to ignore these voices is really making a case for greater open-mindedness.[26]

[25] At this point it would be possible to launch into a long *discursus* on the relationship between "critical personas" and the actual people who underly them. I won't be doing that: as suggested at the beginning of this essay, I do not wish to be prescriptive about the "actual people." However, if "the style is the man," then there is likely to be some relationship between the two entities, although this relationship is likely to be complex. In the age of MeToo and Black Lives Matter, unsurprisingly a series of debates have sprung up about the tone and conduct of academic life, as expressed in different disciplines and contexts: see, for example, Nagypál, "Economics Needs Reconciliation"; a very thoughtful reflection on the field of economics. These issues are as important in literary criticism as they are in any other discipline or indeed in any other part of society.

[26] Roth, "Tokens of Ruined Method."

The actual critics named here could be added to or exchanged with others, but Roth's central point surely remains: the essays of these writers are embodiments of attempts to press to "the sense of the thing itself." That does not mean that their attempts are therefore set in stone as unimpeachable examples of the way that we should do things: their variousness instead requires a later variousness of other critics, other students, other citizens. As John Ashbery writes in his "For John Clare," "there ought to be room for more things, for a spreading out, like."[27] The history of literary criticism has had many "things," but we need more things, more perspectives, wider publics, "democratic vistas" as Whitman said.

This variousness and open-mindedness in some ways sits at odds with other aspects of literary critical history, which exhibit instead the desire to categorize and, in some sense, to control the elusive and evasive literary text. It is noticeable that in Joseph North's book, while there is relatively little close reading of critics along the lines suggested by Roth above, there is actually no close reading by North of any particular literary text in the book. But this is a book that is recommending that a revised version of literary criticism should be a central element in a new kind of cultural politics. It is therefore striking that North chooses not to give an example of the virtues of his method in his book. Perhaps his concern was that a text's variousness could possibly overwhelm his own neat patterning: it's not possible to say. For Stefan Collini, in his review of North's book, the problem for North is that he is caught between two competing urges:

> This book, it seems to me, expresses two familiar, even admirable, impulses: the desire to write good literary criticism, and the desire to advance progressive political causes. North seems to feel he cannot do the first unless he can generate some general methodology which will ensure he is at the same time doing the second. But perhaps our intellectual and political commitments don't always marry up as neatly as this. Perhaps there is some value in being able to comment acutely on literature, and perhaps this ability can crop up in surprising or ideologically unsympathetic places. Perhaps the practice of criticism sometimes turns out to be richer and subtler than any of the abstract templates we claim should govern that practice. Perhaps, to adapt what he says of Miller, the critical voice that

[27] Ashbery, "For John Clare," 103.

> tells us this—North's voice—also seems to be trying to speak politically, but is making such a fuss of it that it keeps failing.[28]

This seems to me to be correct: North's determination to be expressing these two "familiar impulses" at the same time does indeed create problems with his argument. It is as if he is looking for the one approved example of how his method would work. He tries to find this example in the work of I. A. Richards, and yet a closer examination of Richards' writing—perhaps using some historical-contextualist tools—would likely lead to a collapse in confidence in Richards' abilities to unite these attributes. Instead, Collini is right to say that "the practice of criticism sometimes turns out to be richer and subtler than any of the abstract templates we claim that should govern that practice." North's desire to be doing his key tasks at once ends up making his project more difficult. Instead, we should be thinking about how a practice of criticism can work (and already has worked) to produce the ability to "comment acutely on literature." The preservation and the furtherance of this capacity is the political, perhaps more precisely, the social task. That is, we can further North's second "impulse" if we in fact concentrate on his first impulse. This social task then does involve the collective creation of certain dispositions and sensibilities: the preference for—here, in Collini's terms—the rich and the subtle over "abstract templates," while, at the same time, we cannot always do without the abstract: if we want the "robust cultivation of society," and we think that literary criticism can help in that process, then we need to think what "robust cultivation" is, as that too is an abstraction. In terms of "what kind of person should the critic be?" perhaps all we are left with is a series of adjectives: rich, subtle, robust, open-minded, free, flexible, elastic. These in turn can be compared with Felski's own list of adjectives that describe the mode of critique: "suspicious, knowing, self-conscious, hardheaded, tirelessly vigilant." We may prefer one set of these adjectives to another, but to say that there can be values at times in all of these adjectives is not to end up in a position of empty relativism. But, at this time, we may need to favor the first set over the second, in order to open up the lines of communication with broader society.

Dispositions are, indeed, everywhere. Frank discussion of how literary criticism, and the broader educational, social, and political cultures to

[28] Collini, "Lot to be Said."

which it is connected, participates in the creation and re-creation of dispositions allows us to think more fully about the values we are embodying (or deciding not to embody): this opens up intellectual space which in turn opens up social and educational space. This in turn allows a wider flourishing of critics, students, and citizens, who will create their various versions of the rich, the subtle, and the robust. In the medium-term, of course, these questions are acutely related to a broad set of practical questions about how literature and criticism are taught and passed on in educational establishments: as Marco Roth argues, "the split between 'education' as a professional field that trains teachers for public schools and 'literature,' which trains [academic] specialists, must be bridged."[29] The need for common civic cultures, while providing space for dissent, must be prioritized—and literary texts, in their endless variety do provide a space for thinking about these issues. For some readers, this may all be too much: too much of a revival of "humanism," too much of a revival of "the social mission of English criticism" or of "English as a vocation."[30] But if we are to turn away from suspicious reading, then we will need to put forward positive alternatives, and to think about what kind of person the critic should be.

References

Anderson, Perry. "Components of the National Culture." *New Left Review*, July/August 1968. https://newleftreview.org/issues/I50/articles/perry-anderson-components-of-the-national-culture.

Arnold, Matthew. "On Translating Homer: Last Words." In *Selected Prose*, edited by P.J. Keating, 85–98. London: Penguin, 1970.

Ashbery, John. "For John Clare." In *Selected Poems*, 103–4. London: Penguin, 1985.

Bailey, Tom. "Anthony Seldon's Producer Interest and Bad History of Higher Education." *Wonkhe* (blog), November 8, 2015. https://wonkhe.com/blogs/seldons-producer-interest-and-bad-history.

Baldick, Chris. *The Social Mission of English Criticism, 1848–1932.* Oxford: Oxford University Press, 1983.

Berlant, Lauren. *Cruel Optimism.* Durham, NC: Duke University Press, 2011.

[29] Roth, "Tokens of Ruined Method."

[30] Here I am recalling the titles of Chris Baldick's *The Social Mission of English Criticism, 1848–1932* and of Christopher Hilliard's excellent book on the Leavises and their broader impact, *English as a Vocation: The "Scrutiny" Movement*.

Brown, Wendy. *In the Ruins of Neoliberalism: The Rise of Antidemocratic Politics in the West*. New York: Columbia University Press, 2019.

Celikates, Robin, and Yolande Jensen. "Reclaiming Democracy: An Interview with Wendy Brown on Occupy, Sovereignty, and Secularism." *Critical Legal Thinking*, January 30, 2013. https://criticallegalthinking.com/2013/01/30/reclaiming-democracy-an-interview-with-wendy-brown-on-occupy-sovereignty-and-secularism/.

Dewey, John. *Democracy and Education: An Introduction to the Philosophy of Education*. New York (State): Macmillan Co, 1916.

During, Simon. "Literary Academia: Simon During Reflects, Part I." *Politics/Letters Live*, May 31, 2018. http://politicsslashletters.org/features/literary-academia-simon-reflects-part/.

Eagleton, Terry. "Not Just Anybody." *London Review of Books*, January 5, 2017. https://www.lrb.co.uk/the-paper/v39/n01/terry-eagleton/not-just-anybody.

Felski, Rita. *The Limits of Critique*. London: University of Chicago Press, 2015.

Greif, Mark. *Against Everything: On Dishonest Times*. London: Verso, 2017.

Hazlitt, William. "On the Pleasure of Hating." In *The Plain Speaker: Opinions on Books, Men, and Things*, vol. 1, 307–28. London: Henry Colbourn, 1826.

Heater, Derek. *A History of Education for Citizenship*. London: Routledge, 2004.

Hilliard, Christopher, *English as a Vocation: The "Scrutiny" Movement*. Oxford: Oxford University Press, 2012.

Nagypál, Éva. "Economics Needs Reconciliation If It Is to Be a Force for Positive Change." *Compassionate Economics*, July 7, 2020. https://compassionateeconomics.wordpress.com/2020/07/07/economics-needs-reconciliation-if-it-is-to-be-a-force-for-positive-change/.

"Our Students among UK's Most Satisfied." Durham University website, July 3, 2019. https://www.dur.ac.uk/experience/news/?itemno=39264.

Roth, Marco. "Tokens of Ruined Method: Does Literary Studies Have a Future?" *n +1*, Fall 2017. https://nplusonemag.com/issue-29/reviews/tokens-of-ruined-method.

Rustin, Susanna. "Why Study English? We're Poorer in Every Sense Without It." *The Guardian*, February 10, 2019. https://www.theguardian.com/commentisfree/2019/feb/10/study-english-a-level-university-government-taught.

Shakespeare, William. *Hamlet*. In *Complete Oxford Shakespeare*, edited by Stanley Wells and Gary Taylor, vol. 3. London: Guild Publishing, 1988.

Stevens, Wallace. "The House Was Quiet and the World Was Calm." In *Collected Poems*, 354–55. London: Faber, 1984.

Sutherland, John. "Sad Professor." *London Review of Books*, February 18, 1999. https://www.lrb.co.uk/the-paper/v21/n04/john-sutherland/diary.

Trachtenberg, Zev M. *Making Citizens: Rousseau's Political Theory of Culture*. London: Routledge, Taylor & Francis Group, 1993.

Close Reading

CHAPTER 10

"Slow Time," "a Brooklet, Scarce Espied": Close Reading, Cleanth Brooks, John Keats

Susan J. Wolfson

1 Mortification

My quotations are from two odes by John Keats, the first on a curiosity of historical endurance (*Ode on a Grecian Urn*) and the second from myth-history (*Ode to Psyche*). Quite far afield from *Frankenstein*: but they shared shelf-space in London's bookstores. Shelley's novel appeared early 1818; a year and a half on, Keats was writing those odes, to be published in, though not heralded by the title of, *Lamia, Isabella, The Eve of St. Agnes, and Other Poems* (1820). *Ode to Psyche*, like *Frankenstein*, stages a mind as a laboratory of creation, out to woo delight, but aware that shadowy thoughts, dark-cluster'd stir within—and without. Both works signal debts, deferred or paid, to *Paradise Lost*.

A sad episode of self-imaging in *Frankenstein* looks like a barbarous twist on the epiphanic moment of *Ode to Psyche*, a self-discovery, mapped onto a scene of self-recognition (the first human one) in *Paradise Lost*:

S. J. Wolfson (✉)
Princeton University, Princeton, NJ, USA
e-mail: wolfson@princeton.edu

A. Sridhar et al. (eds.), *The Work of Reading*,
https://doi.org/10.1007/978-3-030-71139-9_10

Eve's first view of herself, before she knows she is to be Adam's subordinate. Reading *Paradise Lost*, Keats scored the left margin next to these lines.[1]

> As I bent down to look, just opposite
> A shape within the watery gleam appear'd,
> Bending to look on me; I started back:
> It started back: but pleased I soon return'd,
> Pleased it return'd as soon, with answering looks
> Of sympathy and love. (4.460–65)

On one extended sentence, Milton forms a beautiful reciprocity in shaped returns of verse: responsive repetitions, parallel syntaxes. Sorry task for Eve then to know herself as a deformity in the male dispensation. No wonder she "oft remember[s]" this prehistory (4. 449; underlined by Keats, I:97).

Shelley's mordant parody has a humanly capable Creature (literate, instinctively benevolent) recount the shock of his deformity to Creator Frankenstein.[2] He had been incubating fond hopes of adoption by a family that he'd been aiding, watching, and imagining his own, unbeknownst to them:

> I had admired the perfect forms of my cottagers—their grace, beauty, and delicate complexions: but how was I terrified when I viewed myself in a transparent pool! At first I started back, unable to believe that it was indeed I who was reflected in the mirror; and when I became fully convinced that I was in reality the monster that I am, I was filled with the bitterest sensations of despondence and mortification. Alas! I did not yet entirely know the fatal effects of this miserable deformity.

This is Eve's answering look, gothic filtered. The Creature's last word, *deformity,* contrasts the *perfect forms* of cottagers: the possessive pronoun

[1] Keats's edition is the 2-volume Edinburg publication, 1807. The marks are on vol. I, p. 98. References to this edition hereafter use the form I:98. For the online site see Bibliography. References to *Paradise Lost* itself are from this edition and given by book and lines, in the form of the inset below.

[2] Shelley, *Frankenstein*, vol. II, ch. IV; Wolfson and Levao edition, p. 190.

my is heartbreak itself, more so against *myself. Deformity* makes substantive and inalterable what Milton reserves for adjective-form in his two-only usages in *Paradise Lost*, Death "dreadful and deform" (2.706), and the preview of mortal suffering Michael thrusts on Adam: "so deform what heart of rock could long / Dry-eyed behold? Adam could not, but wept" (11.494–95). For the Creature, it's total negation, *despondence, and mortification*: literally, fatal news. While Eve's enchantment by a beautiful form seems sheer opposite, it wavers on two registers. For a normal/normative male optics, it is erotic, still innocent. In postlapsarian reading, it is potentially monstrous (*Paradise Lost*'s only other fair she-form is Sin), an instinctual narcissism, primed for Satanic exploitation—so says a mostly male critical accounting. When Shelley reprises the scene for the Creature's self-regard, it is to expose deformity as *miserable* because culturally abjected. Was Keats "a monster of prevision?" Cleanth Brooks asks in 1957, saying he "must apologize for past blunderings and misreadings" of him.[3]

Close reading has been derogated as anti-context, especially anti-history; yet here is Brooks facing a past critic-self with remorse, and Shelley provoking close reading of a self-reading scene, sharpened not only by literary history but also by her historical moment, when whole categories of human beings—from slaves, to laborers, to women (non-men)—were susceptible of regard as deformations. Late twentieth-century cultural critique found it convenient to cite "literary" formations as insulated from socio-historical situations or collaborating in its culpable ideologies. The charge was influential. By 2013, Derek Attridge could say that "the primary focus of critical attention is still for the most part on historical context, on political and ideological issues, on the material, the economic, the psychological," with a "concentration on content and context" tending to "reductive and instrumentalizing readings of literature," and form "often simply left out of the account." He attributed this to "the historical failures of formal analysis," by which he meant both a repression of historical context in close reading practices, and the historical influence of this method for about four decades.[4]

As much as I value and continue to learn from Attridge's work, I resist this story of failures. It elides a substantial, still developing, bibliography

[3] Brooks, "Artistry" 251.

[4] Attridge, *Moving Words*, 8–9.

on historically informed attention to literary formings, and the critical force of these formations as a context for addressing complicated historical matters.[5] But it's the story that has taken hold. One linchpin was Terry Eagleton's "Ideology and Literary Form" (1976), the "Literary" working to contain, even repress, the "historical contradictions" of "Ideology."[6] Eagleton was at least a sharp close reader. Another lynchpin was Fredric Jameson's *The Political Unconscious* (1981), which cited literary aesthetics for "inventing imaginary or formal 'solutions' to unresolvable social contradictions."[7] This is the ground on which Attridge traces the "unacceptable ethico-political assumptions" shaping such icons of formal analysis as Brooks's *The Well Wrought Urn: Studies in the Structure of Poetry* (1947).[8] The sternest indictment, exemplified by Joseph North, goes like this: Brooks was a creature of John Crowe Ransom, both of them Southern agrarians, anti-urban, anti-industrial; Ransom, moreover, wrote some dismaying cultural criticism.[9] Brooks therefore was ransomed. Attridge does not ride this train of thought, but he knows the station stops of the North line, and he admirably regrets what gets passed by, passed off. Not least, the disparagements of "close reading" in favor of the master-mappings of "far reading" or the shallow paraphrasing operations of "surface reading"—at the expense of local texturings, complexities, and formations.

I want to recall the intervention that close reading presented to the 1930s and 1940s; the way this intervention has been caricatured; and the peculiar evolution of "Keats" in Brooks's work. I'll then turn to Keats's historically inflected poetic formations in the manuscript of his first truly experimental ode, *Ode to Psyche*—a venture that looks, uncannily, like a historically self-conscious production of avant-garde modernity for 1819.

[5] I draw this language from Breslin, *From Modern to Contemporary*, xiv, and Galperin, *Historical Austen*, 1.

[6] Eagleton, "Ideology," 114.

[7] Jameson, *Political Unconscious*, 79.

[8] *The Well Wrought* Urn is cited parenthetically hereafter.

[9] North, "'Close Reading,'" 141–42, 147–55. By the 1970s, Brooks and Warren had "moved quite far away" from the southern agrarianism (the "gallant" front for much segregationism) that Ransom and Warren championed with contributions to *I'll Take My Stand* (Louisiana State University Press, 1930); Brooks and Warren took special care that their anthologies "should carry no hint of any editorial belief in a self-perpetuating old-style southern culture if the Confederacy had triumphed" (R. W. B. Lewis, "Afterword," 419).

2 Brooks and Keats: "Scarce Espied"

In 1938, *Understanding Poetry* was a bold pedagogical intervention. It meant not only to professionalize the study of poetry (in parallel with other academic disciplines) but also to popularize a care for literature's ways of saying, its techniques, its distinct value. This was a conscious, not surreptitious, experiment in suspending biographical and historical background (along with philology, this was the oppression for Brooks's generation of graduate students, and the boredom for undergraduates, though frilled for them with murmurs of aesthetic appreciation). Brooks and coeditor Robert Penn Warren contended that "even if the interest is in the poem as a historical or ethical document, there is a prior consideration: one must grasp the poem as a literary construct before it can offer any real illumination."[10] The Table of Contents was, accordingly, organized by genre or device, not by author or historical period; no work is dated, let alone situated in the material circumstances of its production or publication. There was an appealing mix of canonical and new, high art and popular poetry, "difficult" poems and more accessible ones.

How does Keats fit in this agenda? The editors' preliminary "Letter to the Teacher" summons a popular textbook—unnamed, it was the standard at Louisiana State University, where the pedagogy of *Understanding Poetry* was pre-tested—to satirize its teaching of *Ode to a Nightingale*: "The song of the nightingale brings sadness and exhilaration to the poet and makes him long to be lifted up and away from the limitations of life." In reaction, Brooks and Warren coax, "Is not the real point of importance the relation of the paradox of 'exhilaration' and 'sadness' [...]?" and they object to the prompt to find "evidences of a love of beauty"

[10] Brooks and Warren, *Understanding Poetry*, iv–v. This anthology is cited parenthetically hereafter.

as shallow and over-driven.[11] But this is not entirely fair.[12] And *Understanding Poetry* doesn't exactly do any better by Keats's ode. Not first in its Keats inclusions, it comes after several encounters with Keats that have prejudiced the ground.

First off is *La Belle Dame sans Merci* in a unit of "Narrative Poems" (xvii)—a strange slot, since "narrative" is something it puts in question. *The Eve of St. Agnes* comes under "Implied Narrative" (xviii)—this, a not "fully presented" genre but "description" on narrative scaffolding (161). The next study of Keats is ready-made for the "Imagery" unit (xxii): the two similes in the sestet of *On First Looking into Chapman's Homer* (the watcher of the skies seeing a new planet and, famously, Cortez staring at the Pacific) (417). *To Autumn* is there for "Metrics" (xix), with an "Exercise" on "metrical variation, onomatopoeia, quantity, and hovering accent as related to the intention [!] of the poem" (245–47), and the first three stanzas of *Isabella* are summoned for lyric comparison to the "comic effect" of Byron's brisk ottava rima (265–68).

Ode to a Nightingale comes late, under "Imagery" (xxii) for an extended examination (407), but only to study its failures: a flimsy flow from reverie to awakening, with no "dramatic play of thought" on "the antithesis between the transience of beauty in the actual world and the permanence of beauty in the imagination" (410–11). In its "structure," "image leads to image" by an "association of ideas" that at best evokes *stream of consciousness*; in 1938 this new form gets italicized, and pointed to the *Glossary* (412). So used are we to readings of this *Ode* for its drama

[11] The textbook is James Dow McCallum's *College Omnibus* (1933); the comments cited are on 670, 826. The *Omnibus* was quite popular, a 4th edition by 1936, a 6th by 1947 (the year of *The Well Wrought Urn*).

[12] Like Brooks and Warren, McCallum addresses college students and general readers, emphasizing the connection of poetry to their lives in the world, but unlike Brooks and Warren, situating poetic forms and themes in relation to social and political upheavals, from the French Revolution to World War I, from the advent of science and industry. Brooks's citing Coleridge on the imagination as a force of "unity" (*Well Wrought Urn* 230) was preceded by McCallum (1019). McCallum's prompt for *Nightingale* is only one of nine questions; others concern poetic forms, themes, and historical diction. The 1936 introduction to Keats concludes with a close reading of the first stanza of *The Eve of St. Agnes* to show the accumulating effects of the imagery, and the bearing on a poem in which "high passion" blends into "sensory appeals to make it not only graphic but gripping" (1021). The first edition of *Omnibus* (1933) had more Keats than *Understanding Poetry*, the 4th edition (1936) still more, a selection that held through the 6th edition.

of thought that it's surprising to see that this wasn't always so—moreover, with pedagogical emphasis. *Understanding* this poem is seeing an "essential weakness" in its failing to make "a virtue out of the abruptness of the shifts and contrasts." The sole exception is the sudden double-play of *forlorn* from stanza 7 to 8: the ebbing of the nightingale's song into *faery lands forlorn* (end of 7), and the poet's sudden realization of his forlorn state, *Forlorn! the very word is like a bell / To toll me back from thee to my sole self!* (so starts 8). But even this verbal drama can't redeem the fundamental "defect" of "surface description" (412–13). (So what? a later generation devoted to this pedagogy might say.)

Ode on a Grecian Urn is happier fated, given cleanup position in *Understanding Poetry* as a final exercise in analyzing the "theme" stated in its last two lines (627):

> "Beauty is truth, truth beauty,"—that is all,
> Ye know on earth, and all ye need to know. (49–50)

The comma at the end of line 49 implies a summation and totalizing authority for the words in quotation. (Ironically) it has no textual authority.[13] Still sporting this hallucinated comma, *Ode on a Grecian Urn* finds welcome in *The Well Wrought Urn*, Brooks's public pedagogy for the 1940s. Here, it has the effect of reinforcing the aphorism, readying it for Brook's cautions against the conveyance of such language out of "dramatic context" (151). The comma is no emendation; it's a pedagogical misprision, a packaging mark for export.[14] Passage refused: Keats himself insisted that "axioms in philosophy are not axioms until they are proved

[13]There is no comma in the first publications, *Lamia & c* (116) or *Annals of the Fine Arts* 4.15 (January 1820), 639, nor even in any manuscript (Stillinger, "Transcripts").

[14]The tale of the comma is curious. It hangs on in the 2nd, 1950 edition of *Understanding Poetry* (476) but is gone, with scholarly-footnote fanfare, by the 1960 3rd edition (432); yet it's still in *Well Wrought Urn's* appendix of texts (263), 1947 and thereafter. My guess is that Brooks's immediate analogue, *King Lear*'s "Ripeness is all."—with this period (141, 151)—had him conjuring a similar punctuated summation for Keats's *that is all* (missing the enjambment to *that is all / Ye know*... for which syntax a comma has no sense). In a personal correspondence, Amanda Louise Johnson reports that she's also been on the comma-trail for an essay she's developing on a very different subject (August 26, 2020).

upon our pulses"—the pulsing in this *Ode* being an interpretive pressure (a battery of questions) toward this par-odic (*overwrought*) axiom.[15]

The Glossary for *Understanding Poetry* has another entry that will matter to Brooks's ongoing reading of Keats: IRONY. Here it's boilerplate on various contrasts of expectation (636), but just a year after *Understanding Poetry*, Brooks returns to Keats's repetition of *forlorn* under this sign, brushing it up as a "very brilliant case of qualifying irony," a "concentrated instance" of the *Ode's* very "theme." Keats is now to be admired for resistance to "didacticism" and "flat generalization," embracing "the complexity of experience." He is among those poets who "think through their images"—a rich *through*, too: by means of, and in the composition of.[16] The second edition *Understanding Poetry* (1950) has the longest study of *Ode to a Nightingale* (338–45); it reprises much of the first edition's, but adds a section (at 342) that resets Keats's "rich description" (339–41) in a structure of "apparent contradictions" that prove "meaningful and justified" in a series of overlapping "paradoxes" (343). A shorter unit in the third edition jettisons the itemizing of failures to describe a "very rich poem" of purposeful "complications [...] depth and significance," in a dramatic meditation on the contrary tugs of "the world of mankind and the world of the nightingale" (426–27).

In this edition, *Ode on a Grecian Urn* (the comma is gone, 432) focuses an exercise not about the theme of the last two lines, but on "paradox" and "ironic counterpoise": while the aphorism seems a "philosophic generalization," students are tuned to a dramatic situating that leaves it a tease and enigma (433). The score is drawn from *The Well Wrought Urn* (1947): the *Ode*'s "profound irony" is a "recognition of incongruities" (192). By the fourth edition of *Understanding Poetry* (1976), the 1938 sad-sack *Ode to a Nightingale* has been fully reformed into an "intricate verbal" work about the "burden of consciousness" that fuels the romance of the ever-easeful nightingale's song (358). It now bids fair to join the 1938 slot of "psychological development," in which "the images lead from one attitude and state of mind to another" in "close-knit [...] dramatic organization" (22–23). By Brooks's "reappraisal" of

[15] May 3, 1818; Keats, *Letters*, 1:279. I thank Christopher Rovee for the sharp catch of *overwrought* design and its agonized subjects (*Ode*, line 42) as the embedded antonym of *well wrought*.

[16] Brooks, "Wit," 31; "Notes for a Revised History," 238, and similar phrasing in "Artistry," 251.

1957, the "Keats" of the Great Odes may well "be one of the heroes of modernist criticism" (246) for his tough-minded integration of thoughts and images, formerly mistaken as "intellectual inconsistencies" but now more carefully read as "the dialectic of the poetry" (248). What brought this teacher to this pass?

He continued to teach himself. For Brooks, close reading is a verb, not a noun. Later reports notwithstanding, the literary attention and reflection that he brought to bear could change the literary object for him, opening up rather than closing down and ossifying it. The story Jane Gallop tells, in self-heroizing chiasmus, is only half right:

> In the New Critical framework, the value of studying literature lay in literature's intrinsic value, which justified the method of close reading. I suggest here the very opposite: it is the value of close reading that justifies the study of literature.[17]

What Brooks's long career of close reading shows is not an intrinsic value prior to method, nor a valuable method prior to its object, but a dialectic: decades ahead of Gallop, he invested close reading for surprising turns and returns on any seemingly well-wrought urn.

It is no little irony, given Brooks's polemic about aphorisms exported out of dramatic context, that *The Well Wrought Urn* (a title drawn from a dramatic context, Donne's *Canonization*, on 240) has been reified as a critical ideology, unmindful of its determinations, and so set (up) for minding by later critiques. A frequently cited symptom is the chapter "Keats's Sylvan Historian: History without Footnotes," notwithstanding the wit of this being the only chapter-title to have a footnote (139). Typically not contextualized is the experimental suspension of historical situation and context in Brooks's pedagogy.[18] At an historical moment when the differential of literary "structure" was no part of literary study, Brooks wanted to introduce this, against the practical danger of reducing poetry to historical symptom, or an instrument of political, religious, or moral systems of evaluation. He was aware of a "formidable objection": his having taken "too little into account" of the reigning protocol ("the

[17] Gallop, "Fate," 16.

[18] I've written about this in *Formal Charges,* especially in the Introduction. See also my fuller bibliography. M. H. Abrams provides an informative account of literary study in the era before Brooks's interventions ("Transformation of English Studies," 106–9).

only kind of reading possible") of "historical backgrounds" and "literary history" (x). While New Historicism would bring history out of any background and put it into "circulation" (Stephen Greenblatt, who never stopped being a close reader) or make it the determinative "ground" (Jerome McGann), Brooks was never set against history, just its imposition over and against literary study. He invited readers "to see what residuum, if any, is left after we have referred the poem to its cultural matrix" and "its historical context" (x). He later described this method of "calculated omissions" as a temporary "forfeiture," and was irked to see it translated (I'd say by those who may not even have read *The Well Wrought Urn*) into a programmatic dismissal.[19]

"The whole matter bears very definitely on the much advertised demise of the Humanities," Brooks contended in 1947 (*Well Wrought Urn*, x–xi), especially if literary critics were just second-order cultural historians and sociologists (199, 213). Then, as now. A poem is surely accountable to "human experience" in the world, he insisted (179). By 2007, in a commissioned essay for *PMLA*, "What is New Formalism?" my friendly opponent Marjorie Levinson litigated the issue, problematically. She identified both a *New* (as if it were a resurgence rather than a persistence) and an *ism* (as if an insistent regime), the full naming carrying a reactionary gleam from its various usages in the 1940s, 1950s, and 1980s. She answered her question by branding the twenty-first-century iteration as a movement without a "manifesto," a rear-guard pleasure-principle that evaded the rigorous contextual accounting of the other "New *-ism*": New Historicism. *New Formalism* was a "backlash," even a relapse to juvenile sentimental aesthetics, "a variant of the classic freshman complaint that analyzing literature destroys the experience of it."[20] Even Brooks had no such pedagogy.

The discursive (and pedagogical) hero of *The Well Wrought Urn* is "The Language of Paradox," its first chapter-title. Paradox is hailed as a language for literary complexity and for its informing consciousness (*of* works both ways: objective and subjective genitive). As a language, paradox may be a unifying "structure" (Brooks's keyword), but its

[19] Brooks, "New Criticism," 81–83.

[20] Levinson, "New Formalism?," 559, 562. For my reply, see "Formings without Formalism." Rigorously historicist that she is, I think she knows the signifying (political, cultural, and literary) of "New Formalist" in previous decades: a 1940s slur on academia, and an Eisenhower-era, then Reagan-era reaction against cultural license and laxness.

elements of contrast relate it to irony.[21] The structuring, moreover, is often dynamic rather than static, pressured rather than stable. Not usually noted in self-pleased critiques of *The Well Wrought Urn* is Brooks's frequent sighting of "thrusts and pressures," deflections, perversities, warps (192–93). He welcomes poetry that "raises far more problems than it solves" (x), structures built "by contradiction and qualification," with a "tendency" to be "disruptive," metaphor systems tilted into "discrepancies, contradictions" (8–9). He traced "conflict" (230) and "incongruities" (192).

Having just intervened with a case for *literary* structure, Brooks was not ready to go full-tilt post-structural, or deconstructive. But if he didn't privilege this grammar, he saw the syntax, and armed a harmonized "structure" of dominant and subordinate clauses to fend off his contrary sensations. The final paragraphs of his polemic on "The Heresy of Paraphrase" (an earlier essay, reset as the final chapter of *The Well Wrought Urn*) insist with *must* (15 times, 194–96) on the unifying mandate. On such overdrive, the genre of Critical Polemic shades into Critical Dramatic Monologue, Brooks arguing with himself, as he deflects the force of felt fissures, fractures, perversities, and incoherence. His criticism was always more unsettled and dialectical than later tales would have it. William Empson is the honorary ghost inside of Brooks's structure, the godfather of verbal theater operating only contingently in a dramatic context. Empson's wordwork is ambiguity rather than paradox; the structures are not formal coalescences but relays of complex words, patterns of thought rather than of art.[22] On this track, Empson (as signature adjective) made a rare appearance in *The Well Wrought Urn* as Brooks comments on how Wordsworth's paradox-symbology can "break down into outright confusion" that exceeds even the "Empsonian sense" of "rich and meaningful" ambiguity (115). All de Man had to do, flaunting insight into New Critical Blindness, was spring open Brooks's already vibrating lock.

What does remain unreconstructed in Brooks (Keats, too) is a formation of professional male identity that reinforces itself against female

[21] *Understanding Poetry*, 637.

[22] "The complexity of certain words," comments Michael Wood, "the accumulation of their many meanings and uses, defies the very notion of anything as stable as a structure" (*On Empson*, 21).

binaries, either for condescension or appropriation. Especially in *Understanding Poetry*, the discipline of literary study grabs the foil of unprofessional female readers and reading practices, book clubs versus the seminars in Ransom's convivial living room. Keats, manning up for his profession as poet, was not innocent of such moves.[23] Without going over this ground again, I turn to Keats's historical sense, spelled with a gently eroticized female figure, of his formative adventure in poetic modernity. He had just fallen in love with a real woman.

"Of course, literature is related to life [...] but what makes it literature, and what are those relations?" This was Brooks's question in 1943.[24] It is Derek Attridge's now (2020), about "enhancing understanding of not just the nature but also the value of literature."[25] And it was John Keats's, about 200 years ago.

3 History with Footnotes: "Ode to Psyche"

The next line in *Ode to Psyche* after "A brooklet, scarce espied:" is its rhymed situation:

> 'Mid hushed, cool-rooted flowers fragrant-eyed

—a line that the editors of *Understanding Poetry* conjure, out of context, to exemplify iambic pentameter (243). Allowing a "quantitative" hovering over the compound adjective, they still insist on "iambic pattern." While I'd also stress *cool*, especially with the assonance-hyphenation to *rooted* (and I'd keep Keats's *hush'd*), such dissent reflects, even so briefly, Keats's experiments against expectation.

Ode to Psyche is the least favored (except for *Ode on Indolence*, which Keats withheld from publication) of his Great Odes of 1819—those poems about which Stuart Sperry has commented, there was no method

[23] We know the stories from feminist and gender criticism, including my own, on Keats's vexed and wavering anxieties and operations. See my *Borderlines*, 205–84. In a unit on *Ode on Melancholy* in *An Approach to Literature*, 1953, Brooks and his coeditors describe with a pang the problematic aesthetic of the speaker's regard of his lover's "rich anger": "he patronizes her ... does not treat her as an equal"; "her anger is ... not a serious matter ... merely important as [it] sets off her beauty to advantage" for "connoisseur" savoring (357).

[24] Brooks, "Mr. Kazin's America," 56.

[25] Chapter 1, 1–19.

more ideal for reading than "the radical innovation of New Criticism."[26] *Psyche,* earliest written, is usually seen as a false start, a training exercise: smart moves but no *Urn, Nightingale, Melancholy,* or *Autumn.* The very genre had no title-role in Keats's last lifetime volume, *Lamia, Isabella, The Eve of St. Agnes, and Other Poems*, published in 1820. Even with better later attention to the genre, *Psyche* has remained something of an outlier. Yet conspicuously about its own genesis, it is quite suited for the question of historically and theoretically informed form-criticism, because this is its very project, its internal story, and its dramatic accomplishment.

> *You must recollect that Psyche was not embodied as a goddess before the time of Apulieus the Platonist who lived afteir the Agustan age, and consequently the Goddess was never worshipped or sacrificed to with any of the ancient fervor—and perhaps never thought of in the old religion* [...] *I am more orthodox that to let a hethen Goddess be so neglected—*
>
> *Ode to Psyche—*

This is Keats's letter-text.[27] On the odd slant of *you must* (... *pardon me, if I am being redundant*; or: *let me remind you*), Keats plays faux pedant on a self-constituting logic from what history *neglected.* He knows the etymology: *ne-legere* (not respected, not noticed, not *read*). What was *never thought of in the old religion* is a signpost for a modern *thought* poetry. Conscious of its own strategies, modernism, comments de Man, at once "engenders history" and is "bound to discover" the literary precedence of such assertions.[28] De Man's double-played *bound to* means not only that every "modernism" is bound to a history of modernisms, but also that modernism is bound to history for its self-constituting definition.

[26] Sperry, *Keats the Poet*, 242; Sperry pays exceptional attention to *Psyche* (249–61).

[27] Ms 1.52. sEquation 267. Hereafter cited parenthetically in text, by sequence number. I use the letter-text for its for its framing by Keats's historically inflected headnote and postscript. Compare *Letters*, 2:106–8, with minor variants. All print editions—the best is Stillinger' (364–66)—are based on the 1820 text of the ode. I apply my own line numbers.

[28] De Man, "Literary History and Literary Modernity," 150, 161.

Post-antiquity, the new grammar is *psychology*, the soul's word-system, eponym-bequest of *Psyche*.[29] *Oxford English Dictionary* says *psychology* first denoted soul-science (1654), then cognitive science: "Psychology, or the Theory of the human Mind" is a unit in David Hartley's *Observations on Man* (1749).[30] Keats writes *Ode to Psyche* about a poet discovering this language—in effect, an "Ode to *Ode to Psyche*." Autogenesis is the script, its actors a wordplay that reverses *never thought of* into modern poetry's *branched thoughts, new grown* (seq. 269). On this twist, the opening vocative is archly decadent:

> *O Goddess hear these tuneless numbers, wrung*
> *By sweet enforcement, and remembrance dear,*
> *And pardon that thy secrets should be sung*
> *Even ~~to~~ into thine own soft-chonched ear!* (1–4; seq. 267)

This muse is the lodge of *tuneless numbers,* new-tuned to close listening and close reading. On the sound of the vocative *hear* into the poet's *here,* Keats sets *rung* in *wrung*: what the very words have done, in wry contradiction to the sole instance of *tuneless* in his poetry. The very first rhyme, aptly, is *hear / dear.* Set at the end of line 2, *dear* is ready for rhyme-repetition in "soft-chonche*d ear*" (4), ringing back to *hear*. Keats wasn't sure what the participle should be—a draft also has *chonched*, so this seems deliberate[31]—just that it should end in *d*. Telling is both figured and prefigured—and modern to the core: words "juxtaposed in new and sudden combinations" with the charge of poetry to "dislocate language into meaning." This is T. S. Eliot, cited by Brooks in 1947.[32] By

[29] Keats had Lemprière's *Classical Dictionary* (1788) for Apuleius, with this entry for PSYCHE: "The word signifies *the soul*." Neither *psyche* nor *psychology* is in Samuel Johnson's *Dictionary of the English Language* (1755) but OED lists contemporaneous treatises in which *psychology* names a science of mind or soul.

[30] Hartley, *Observations,* Part I, Section III (p. 354).

[31] Gittings, 50–51. No dictionary has *chonched*; Keats's 1820 publishers tidied to *conched* (shell-like). I rather like the lexical mystery that Keats preserved in his two manuscripts.

[32] Brooks, *Well Wrought Urn*, 8, 192, without citing the essays of 1921 (in *The Sacred Wood*) and 1924 ("The Metaphysical Poets")—history without footnotes, here, anyway.

1957, Brooks would have Keats's wordwork prefiguring the modernism that figured him out.[33]

But why (*Even*) sing at all? The invocation by redundancy turns out to be, in the turn of a line, the consequence of a narrative begun in self-questioning, now rehearsed with stagey flair and its own grammatical game:

> *Surely I dreamt to day; or did I see*
> *The winged Psyche, with awaked eyes?* (5–6; seq. 268)

Ode to a Nightingale poses this question at its close, and leaves it hanging: *Was it a vision or a waking dream? ... Do I wake or sleep?* In literary memory, by sweet enforcement and remembrance dear, is Spenser's "Was it a Dream, or did I see it plain?" (*Sonnet* LXVII). Keats torques this formally balanced syntax into dramatic motion: *Surely I dreamt to-day* pauses at a coy semicolon, then pivots from *or* into a question, *did I see* ...? It's not just that dreaming feels like seeing. Keats arrays line 6 so that both *I see* and *Psyche* dovetail into *with awaked eyes*. *Psyche* and *I* are so poetically made for one another that a question-mark is pointless. It's a romance of poetry with its own grammar. Psyche is the muse of this amusement.

Keats's long game for Psyche-poetics begins with wordings which, were they Dante's or Spenser's, would signal epic errancy: *I wander'd in a forest thoughtlessly* (7; seq. 268). For Keats, it's pun-prologue to reparative thought-work, sparked *on the sudden, fainting with surprise* (8). Post-surprise, the narrator in the present reproduces the epiphanic scene: *two fair Creatures couched* (9), evoking the "loveliest pair" of *Paradise Lost* espied by Satan, <u>Under a tuft of shade that on a green / Stood whispering soft</u> (4.325–26), then, with peril, Eve <u>Half spied</u> alone in Eden (9.426). The underlines are alert reader Keats's (*1807* I:94, II:87), for remembrance dear. And so the poet's line of vision on that *Brooklet scarce espied:*

[33] Brooks summons Eliot's appreciation of metaphysical poetics to read Keats as a poet for whom senses and intellect are continuous "to the very nerve ends" ("Artistry," 246–47).

(12). It is a tableau vivant in halted vibration: *see* sounds in the middle syllable of *scarce espied*, a microplot for close hearing.[34]

This poet is not writing Miltonic code, however, but *hethen* romance, on a scoptic delicacy of *scarce espied*, *whisp'ring fan / Of leaves* and *trembled blossoms*. The adjective *trembled* (11; seq. 268) is canny: aligned with *couched*, it seems a past-tense verb; aligned with *whisp'ring*, a present reverberation. It gets *OED*'s only citation for the adjective: *made to tremble*. This fine effect unfolds espial in sequential prepositions: *couched side by side / In … beneath … where there*. It is voyeurism as aesthetic thrill, not Freudian trauma. The *calm-breathing*, the full embrace, the temporal uncertainty of *lips touch'd not, but had not bid adiew* (15–17; seq. 268[35]) tremble into interpretive foreplay, with poetic capital: *As if disjoined by soft-handed slumber / And ready past kisses to outnumber* (18–19) summons an infinitive verb unique in Keats's poetry, prefiguring the poet's hand at his own *numbers* (1). For this double logic, the two-timing of this scene at *tender eye-dawn* (20)—dawn of day and of seeing—is just right, winking at the *I* of *awaked eyes*, with a lovely reciprocal: *tender-eyed dawn* resounding *tender eye-dawn*. Keats revised to tune these phonics (the draft had *dawning* eye; Gittings 51).

On this soundstage, the odist sets *The winged boy I knew* (22) to contest its object-subject-verb syntax with the equation advanced by the lexical sequence of *winged boy I:* the successor-boy is the poet-I. This is the prehistory of *Ode to Psyche*. The disingenuous questions to the consort, *But who was though O ꝥ happy happy dove? / His Psyche true?* (22–23) are only rhetorical, dramatic cues answered in two shakes of an iamb's tail, and already by the presence of *Ode* itself. *Thou O* nicely inverts *O Thou*, the usual Odic apostrophe. The 1820 text turns the second question to sheer exclamation: *His Psyche true!* Such exclamation might finish a traditional ode's strophe. But instead of turning to an antistrophe, *Ode to Psyche* suspends this discovery-story, in order to stage its own event: an "ode" within the *Ode*, hailing a poetry of mind.

The name *Psyche* drops out, except by allonym: *O latest born …!* (24; seq. 268). A remainder of *all Olympus faded Hierarchy* (25), it supplies a signifying language for a modern odist's parody of past rituals: *Temple*

[34]The work of Garrett Stewart is the fount of this attention, beginning with *Reading Voices: Literature and the Phonotext* (1990). I've written a related essay on the occasion of Angela Leighton's *Hearing Things: The Work of Sound in Literature (2019)*.

[35]Keats affects a retro-Middle-English spelling of adieu.

thou has none, Nor Altar ... Nor virgin choir ... No voice, no lute, no pipe, no incense ... No shrine, no grove, no oracle, no heat (28–35; seq. 268–69). The repair-job is conspicuously post-Miltonic. Having teased Satan-scoptics in Eden, Keats evokes Milton's ode *On the Morning of Christ's Nativity* (1629) for outright reversal. Milton gloats at the expulsion of the heathen gods and the ruining of the Temple at Delphi: *No nightly trance, or breathèd spell, / Inspires the pale-ey'd Priest from the prophetic cell* (*The Hymn* XIX). Keats captures and rebrands the words for modern *thought* poetry, wittily launching its very letters in "*though* Temple hadst *thou* none," even recalling *thou* from *who wast thou?* The poetry is the event, the mind's medium of words.

The belatedness of *too late for antique vows, / Too, too late for the fond believing Lyre* (36-37; seq. 269) is no abjection, but readiness for rescue. The modern poet rings *antic* in *antique* (the old ring), shades *fond* with thoughtful irony. For the claim, *I see and sing by my own eyes inspired* (43; seq. 269), Keats deftly tunes his phonotext. The prior pairing of *I* and *Psyche* yields to *I ... my ... eyes.* Who needs her? The lead-up grammar is a dramatic event in itself:

> *Yet even in these days so far retir'd*
> *From happy Pieties, thy lucent fans,*
> *Fluttering among the faint Olympians,*
> *I see, and sing by my own eyes inspired.* (40–43; seq. 269)

The adjectival phrase *far retir'd / From* seems set to govern all the way to the end of line 42: retired from *happy Pieties* and from *thy lucent fans* (those wings). There may even be a faint hint of wry modernity in a punning of *fans* as devotees (abbreviated *fanatics*, *fane*-worshippers). Wrong! The caesura comma at *Pieties* (41) turns out, in retraced reading, to be a differential: *thy lucent fans* is the direct object of *I see and sing*. Not even an allonym, Psyche is just this ghost-effect, *lucent ... Fluttering*. This is a poet who has read and metamorphosed the material of Lemprière: "Psyche is generally represented with the wings of a butterfly, to intimate the lightness of the soul, of which the butterfly is a symbol." From *symbol* to intimation to *representation* to self-authorizing poetic language, "Psyche" becomes modern.

Capitalizing on all the *I* puns, this poet declares he is *by my own eyes inspired* (43). The next line, *O let me be ...* (44), initiates a verbatim reparation of the litany of Olympian neglect. Amid this rehearsal of what works now, *these days* (40), Keats slyly torques one repetition: the lovely phonological chiasmus of *no incense sweet / From chain-swung Censer* (32–33; seq. 269) becomes lovelier yet with *s winged Censer* (47). Keats means *swinged,* but the slightly separated *s* releases *winged* for a modern, unchained verbal capture of *winged* Psyche and *winged* boy (6, 21; seq. 268). The letter-wit plays across echoes so deliberated as to feel like calculated puns. That restaged "*fainting* with surprise" (8) in the embodied origin story is succeeded by disembodied *fans* among the *faint* Olympians (41-42), then summoned into modern poetry's *fane* (50) of mind, and "all" that "*fan*cy e'er could *feign*" (62; seq. 270).

To ironize this flux of success, a handy foil is Spenser's love-struck Britomart, prone to "feigning Fancy."[36] The poet who declares, *Yes I will be thy Priest and build a fane / In some untrodden region of my Mind* (50–51; seq. 269) knows his fictions—Keats tested *frame* for *feign* (seq. 270)—knows this frame of Mind, knows the impossible reproduction of another Spenserian foil:

> Her Temple fair is built within my Mind,
>   In which her glorious Image placed is,
> On which my Thoughts do day and night attend,
>   Like sacred Priests that never think amiss.[37]

Too, too late for this antiquity, the retro-interior décor that Keats volunteers for his miss makes no visionary claim. What he builds before our eyes is a flagrantly psychedelic poetry: *branched thoughts* (52) structuring *the wreathed trellis of a working brain* (60; seq. 270)—that's the rhyme for *fane* and *feign.* We might sense he's already there with the strange allure of *hush'd, cool-rooted flowers, fragrant eyed* (13). Not just promised, *Ode to Psyche* itself presents a radical brain poetics in succession to wandering in a *forest thoughtlessly* (7). All the old gods *shall be lull'd to sleep* (57)—lull'd in the sounding that Keats's first thought, *charm'd* didn't give (seq. 270)—so that a brainscape of *wide quietness* (58) can open up, and hiss the sensation. *Phoebes sapphire-region'd star, / Or Vesper* (26–27; seq. 268) evaporates into a constellation of *stars without a name* (61). Keats actually wrote *mane.* He meant *name*, of course, but the anagram came to his ear on the arc of rhyme from *brain* (60) to *feign* (62).

[36] Spenser, *The Faerie Queene*, III.IV.5.

[37] Spenser, Sonnet XXII: 5–8.

Keats's grammar of *shadowy thought* (65; seq. 270)—the ode's last sounding of *thought*—is mindful of Wordsworth's pledge to "shadowy ground" in making "the Mind" the "haunt, and the main region of my Song."[38] Keats ups the ante to brainful physiology: those *branched thoughts, new grown with pleasant pain, / Instead of pines shall murmur in the wind* (52–53; seq. 269). In a phonic ambush, he sounds *groan* rung unsweetly from *grown* and, with semantic float, a *Mind / wind* sight-rhyme. Branched thoughts figure surreally into psychic poetics:

> *Far, far around shall those dark-cluster'd trees*
> *Fledge the wild-ridged mountains steep by steep* (54–55; seq. 269)

Here, too, falls the shadow of Wordsworth, from a poem that drew Keats's admiration of its *dark passages: Tintern Abbey* (*Letters* 1:279). Wordsworth interiorizes, his thoughts intensifying what he beholds, not only in visual measure but with wordings that impress Keats's thoughts:

> steep and lofty cliffs,
> Which on a wild secluded scene impress
> Thoughts of more deep seclusion. (5–7)

Keats sends his thoughts into, onto the steeps with Psyche transformed: as *dark-cluster'd* quietly rings a new formation, *dark-luster'd,* her feathers metamorphose into a dynamic verb, *Fledge*. It's no far-fetched pun. Keats soon tells Fanny Brawne of his half-thought "To let the verses of an half-fledged brain tumble into the reading-rooms and drawing room windows" (July 1819; *Letters* 2:130). Out of the drawing rooms and reading rooms, and onto the mind's mountain-steeps, Keats casts a poet on the wing. John Ruskin was inspired to bring his own mind to the scene: so taken was he by Keats's "figurative pines" that he couldn't help adding a visual supplement, "the pine in exquisite fineness," detailed by branches "in fringes" (he printed the final stanza entire, with emphasis on *fledge the wild-ridged mountains*).[39] Keats's exponential linguistic intricacy has this strange phenomenological force.

[38] Wordsworth, *Excursion* (1814), Prospectus, xi–xii. Keats echoes the last phrase in a letter, May 3, 1819 (*Letters*, 1:279). *Letters* cited hereafter parenthetically.

[39] Ruskin, *Modern Painters*, 88.

Keats's conclusion opens a romance of modern poet and modern muse, ironic only in being a provisional, an infinitive stretch into possibility:

> *A bright torch, and a casement ope at night*
> *To let the warm Love in* - (66–67; seq. 270)

The arc of the ode, comments Stuart Sperry, "is given a kind of circularity by its opening lines, which both prefigure and complete the irony of its conclusion." Reversing his smart spin, we might say, with Christopher Miller, that the conclusion is "a frame of mind ... rather than an *object* of thought."[40] I'd put it this way: for *Ode to Psyche*, the object of thought is this frame of mind. In the letter of April 30, 1819, it's not even Keats's last word. In a campy voice of "antique vows," he postscripts (seq. 270) with a quaintly feigned verb (not in *OED*):

> *Here endethe ye Ode to Psyche*

Endethe, but open. Such is an "avid ... intellectual-emotional experience of reading" in "delight." These words could be Keats's for the liveliness of reading, ever vibrant and alert. Scarce espied, they are Cleanth Brooks's.[41]

What of our historical moment, a COVID contingency in which many are readers again: re-readers, slow-readers, readers in conversation with other readers? Derek Attridge advocates for discovery, or rediscovery, of "the deeply pleasurable experience" of engaging "literature that offers challenges and surprises, that inspires admiration for its craft and subtlety, and that takes the reader into unaccustomed realms of thought and feeling."[42] Keats's *Ode to Psyche* is not only an experience of his surprise into modernity; it also, with surprises of canny ode-forming, engages readers with thoughts and feelings that might be theirs. A fable about New Criticism is that it "severs" poetry "irretrievably from both psychology and history."[43] *Ode to Psyche* not only is never so severed but is proactively versed in, informed by psychology (psyche) and history (the grounds for poetic modernity). Often cited for escaping history, Keats is

[40] Sperry, "Romantic Irony," 249. Miller, *Surprise*, 216.

[41] Brooks, "In Search of," 2.

[42] Chapter 1, 1–19.

[43] Mao's characterization (which his essay incisively contests); Mao, "New Critics," 227.

never really far, as Brooks saw, from history: his own, literature's, even (or especially) in his shapings of new adventures. In 2020, we can access manuscript archives and rare books that previously required time, financial support, travel, and now a safety in health. New technology has opened these resources to us, to nuance our historical accountings. Keats would have died for such a lode of riches. Even so, he lives in the genealogy of a theoretically and historically informed pleasure of close reading, and would have been the ideal collaborator for Reuben Brower's advocacy for "slow reading": "slowing down the process of reading to observe what is happening, in order to attend very closely to the words, their uses, and their meanings"[44]—in other words, reading.[45]

References

Abrams, M. H. "The Transformation of English Studies: 1930–1995." *Dedalus* 126, no. 1 (1997): 105–31.

Attridge, Derek. *Moving Words: Forms of English Poetry*. Oxford: Oxford University Press, 2013.

Breslin, James E. B. *From Modern to Contemporary: American Poetry, 1945–1965*. Chicago: University of Chicago Press, 1983.

Brooks, Cleanth. "Mr. Kazin's America" (commentary on *On Native Grounds: An Interpretation of Modern America*). *Sewanee Review* 51, no. 1 (1943): 52–61.

———. *The Well Wrought Urn: Studies in the Structure of Poetry*. New York: Reynal & Hitchcock, 1947.

———. "The Artistry of Keats: A Modern Tribute." In *The Major English Romantic Poets: A Symposium in Reappraisal*, 246–51. Edited by C. D. Thorpe, C. Baker, and B. Weaver. Carbondale: Southern Illinois UP, 1957.

———. "Notes for a Revised History of English Poetry." In *Modern Poetry and the Tradition*, 219–44. New York: Oxford University Press, 1965.

———. "Wit and High Seriousness." In *Modern Poetry and the Tradition*, 18–38. New York: Oxford University Press, 1965.

———. "In Search of New Criticism." In *Community, Religion, and Literature*, 1–15. Columbia: University of Missouri Press, 1995.

[44] "Reading in Slow Motion" (1959); *In Defense of Reading*, ed. Reuben A. Brower and Richard Poirier (New York: E. P. Dutton, 1962), 5–6.

[45] I'm very grateful to Chris Rovee and Garrett Stewart for alert conversation on my essay, and to Eta Nurulhady for timely research assistance.

———. "New Criticism." In *Community, Religion, and Literature*, 80–97. Columbia: University of Missouri Press, 1995.

Brooks, Cleanth, and Robert Penn Warren. *Understanding Poetry: An Anthology for College Students.* New York: Henry Holt, 1938. 2d edition, 1950; 3rd edition (Holt, Rhinehart and Winston, 1960); 4th edition, 1976.

Brooks, Cleanth, Robert Penn Warren, and John Thibaut Purser. *An Approach to Literature: A Collection of Prose and Verse with Analyses and Discussions.* Baton Rouge: Louisiana State University Press, 1936.

De Man, Paul. "Literary History and Literary Modernity." In *Blindness and Insight*, 2nd edition, 142–65. Minneapolis: University of Minnesota Press, 1983.

Eagleton, Terry. "Ideology and Literary Form." In *Criticism and Ideology. A Study in Marxist Literary Theory*, 102–61. London: NLB, 1976.

Empson, William. *Seven Types of Ambiguity.* London: Chatto & Windus, 1930.

———. *The Structure of Complex Words.* Chatto & Windus, 1951.

Gallop, Jane. "The Fate of Close Reading." *ADE Bulletin* 149 (2010): 15–18.

Galperin, William H. *The Historical Austen.* Philadelphia: University Pennsylvania Press, 2003.

Gittings, Robert. *The Odes of Keats & Their Earliest Known Manuscripts in Facsimile.* Ohio: Kent State University Press, 1970.

Greenblatt, Stephen. "Culture." In *Critical Terms for Literary Study*, 225–32. Edited by Frank Lentricchia and Thomas McLaughlin. Chicago: University of Chicago Press, 1995.

———. *Renaissance Self-Fashioning: From More to Shakespeare.* Chicago: University of Chicago Press, 1995.

Hartley, David. *Observations on man, his frame, his duty, and his expectations. In two parts.* London: various printers, 1749.

Jameson, Fredric. *The Political Unconscious.* Ithaca: Cornell University Press, 1981.

Keats, John. "Ode to Psyche." In *Lamia, Isabella, The Eve of St. Agnes, and Other Poems*, 117–21. London: Taylor and Hessey, 1820.

———. *The Letters of John Keats.* Edited by Hyder E. Rollins. 2 vols. Cambridge: Harvard University Press, 1958.

———. *The Poems of John Keats.* Edited by Jack Stillinger. Harvard University Press, 1978.

———. *Milton's Paradise Lost.* Edinburgh: 1807. Keats's marked edition. http://keatslibrary.org/paradise-lost/plviewer.php.

———. *Ode to Psyche.* Manuscript transcription in a letter to George and Georgiana Keats, April 30, 1819. Harvard Keats Collection: https://nrs.harvard.edu/urn-3:FHCL.Hough.10385405?n+267, 268, 269, 270. MS Keats 1.53, seq. 267–72.

Levinson, Marjorie B. "What is New Formalism?" *PMLA* 122, no. 2 (2007): 558–69.
Lewis, R. W. B. "Afterword." In *Cleanth Brooks and Robert Penn Warren: A Literary Correspondence*, 417–24, Edited by James A. Grimshaw, Jr. Columbia: University of Missouri Press, 1998.
Mao, Douglas. "The New Critics and the Text-Object." *ELH* 63 (1996): 227–54.
McCallum, James Dow. *The College Omnibus*. New York: Harcourt, Brace, 1933.
McGann, Jerome J. "Keats and the Historical Method in Literary Criticism." *MLN* 94, no. 5 (1979): 988–1032.
———. *The Romantic Ideology*. Chicago: University of Chicago Press, 1983.
Miller, Christopher. *Surprise*. Ithaca: Cornell University Press, 2015.
Milton, John. *Paradise Lost*. See under "Keats.".
North, Joseph. "What is 'New Critical' about 'Close Reading'?" *NLH* 44, no. 1 (2013): 141–57.
Rovee, Christopher. "Reading Keats Together," chapter manuscript.
Ruskin, John. *Modern Painters*, vol. 5. London: Smith, Elder, 1860.
[Shelley, Mary W.]. *Frankenstein; or, The Modern Prometheus* (1818); *The Annotated Frankenstein*. Edited by Susan J. Wolfson and Ronald Levao. Cambridge: Harvard University Press, 2012.
Spenser, Edmund. *The Works of Mr. Edmund Spenser.* 6 vols. Edited by John Hughes. London: Jacob Tonson. 1715. This is the edition that Keats read and marked.
Sperry, Stuart M. "Romantic Irony: The Great Odes of the Spring." In *Keats the Poet*, 242–91. Princeton: Princeton University Press, 1973.
Stillinger, Jack. "Keats's *Grecian Urn* and the Evidence of Transcripts." *PMLA* 73 (1958): 447–48.
Wolfson, Susan J. *Formal Charges: The Shaping of Poetry in British Romanticism*. Palo Alto: Stanford University Press, 1997.
———. "Keats and Gender Acts" and "Gendering Keats." Sequential chapters in *Borderlines: The Shiftings of Gender in British Romanticism*, 205–84. Palo Alto: Stanford University Press, 2006.
———. "Reading for Form without Formal*ism*." *Literary Matters* 3, no. 2 (2010): 2–3, 14–15. http://www.literarymatters.org/wp-content/uploads/2017/07/LiteraryMatters_3_2.pdf.
———. "Romantic Poetry: Formings Without Formalism." In *Oxford Handbooks Online in Literature*. Edited by Colin Burrow and Thomas Keysmer. Oxford: Oxford University Press, 2016. https://global.oup.com/academic/product/oxford-handbooks-online-literature.
———. Review of Angela Leighton, *Hearing Things: The Work of Sound in Literature. Essays in Criticism* 69, no. 1 (2019) 95–103.
Wood, Michael. *On Empson*. Princeton: Princeton University Press, 2017.

Wordsworth, William. *The Excursion*. London: Longman, 1814.
———. *Poems*. 2 vols. London: Longman, 1815.

CHAPTER 11

Poem as Field, Canon as Crystal: Geoffrey Hill's Historical Semantics

Anirudh Sridhar

Whatever the ends of literary criticism might amount to, it is founded, or so I—perhaps naïvely—will claim, on theory and canon: the reader will notice, theory without a capital "T," canon without the definite article. I take "theory," in this context, simply to indicate any synthesis of understanding about a body of works institutionally recognized as literary. Michael Oakeshott in *On Human Conduct* dissects the term as follows: "*Thea*: [...] the observation of a 'going-on'. *Theorein*: to distinguish [...] a going-on. *Theoria*: the activity of [...] seeking to understand. And *Theorema*: what emerges from this activity."[1] Theoretical reflection, says Oakeshott, can thus never be a substitute for an understanding already enjoyed but only an elaboration of the conditions of such understanding. Oakeshott's latently prescriptive formula slantly mirrors that of David Hume, for whom the "frequent survey or contemplation of a particular

[1] Oakeshott, *Human Conduct*, 3.

A. Sridhar (✉)
University of Oxford, Oxford, UK
e-mail: anirudh.sridhar@bnc.ox.ac.uk

A. Sridhar et al. (eds.), *The Work of Reading*,
https://doi.org/10.1007/978-3-030-71139-9_11

species of beauty" is the index of "experience in those objects"—experience necessary to "mark the distinguishing species of each quality": following which, it becomes clear to any critic why Milton belongs in the canon while Ogilby does not.[2]

Now the canon may have been, once, the preserve of vested sentiment, and lately, a weapon for politics styled radical, but it is plain that the dominant creed of literary criticism today advances the canon in ways barely resonant with "understanding" or "experience."[3] What is expected of most graduates and academics, by default, is a kind of "theory-lite": that the theory advanced and works adduced for evidence will come from a "heavy accumulation of data" as opposed to an "intensity of perception."[4] In this phase of "empirico-historicism,"[5] the canon has served to filter, more than anything else, and make of an unwieldy past a serviceable history—serviceable, at any rate, to the theory (or theory-lite) advanced. Literary works have, in this way, come to occupy the role that records of physical behavior have in science. A scientist, according to Thomas Kuhn, will select from amidst a rabble of data the set of facts that balances best between scope of representation and fitness to formula.[6] That literary artifacts have in our time become factual evidence mustn't, however, come as shock, as the late avatars of most surviving disciplines have been as ghostly sublimations of positivism.[7]

The "professionalism" that scientism confers on the fields into which it advances cannot be easily resisted—it has been the most potent intellectual force of the twentieth century and betrays no sign of exhaustion. Nevertheless, I will attempt in this essay to make a case for appointing poets, rather than "facts," the arbiters of theorization, and the canonization that that entails. I began with the assumption that the burden of theorization lies in sharing the conditions of an understanding already

[2] "Of the Standard of Taste" in *Dissertations*, 221, 210.

[3] A word or line quoted for the first time in double quotes ("") will in all subsequent mentions be marked in single quotes ('')—this is necessary for the close reading in section III, as words and phrases from the poem therein will be repeated many times.

[4] Hill, *Collected Critical Writings*, 350.

[5] It is characterized thus by Derek Attridge in the Introduction to this volume.

[6] See Kuhn, *Structure of Scientific Revolutions.*

[7] A similar argument is forwarded about the scientific pretensions of twentieth century historiography by Hayden White in "The Historical Text as Literary Artifact"—history, he says, is but narrative stitched from a selection of facts from a neutral registry of data.

enjoyed and must now, to make good my case, demonstrate that those conditions for the literary critic are set by the peculiar doings of poets in a shared lyric past—what gets said may be material to the workings of novels but that is not my present subject.

1 Canon

Altogether outside the turmoils of twentieth-century literature departments, the lyric canon has continued to shape itself within-and-into the lived world of poets and their readers, as if a protean manual or uncodified constitution. The term "canon," in literary studies today, holds but a faded significance, a vestige of "quality" almost redundant to the business of gathering and processing data. In this essay, I intend the term in a purely *functional* sense: arguing that for a body of works to hang together, meaning within must be a function of the forces mutually exerted by constituent members. Seen historically, we may say that between two poems in a canon, the doings-with-words that make of the first a poem will be a condition necessary to the distinctive doings-with-words achieved in the second.[8]

It is critical for the rational study of this process that canons be conceived as subject neither to individual origination nor impersonal afflatus. An axiomatic privileging of the creative ego has beset with specious biographical contention the academic attempts of the last fifty years to establish literary canons. W. Jackson Bate, for instance, looking for a "way of taking up the whole of English poetry during the last three centuries,"[9] came to the pithy conclusion that all great poets labor under the burden of the past:

> In confronting a brilliantly creative achievement immediately before him in his own language [...] Dryden's situation as a seventeenth-century poet was almost unique. He is the first great European [...] example of a major

[8] The tenets of Russian Formalism (OPOJAZ, especially) do not govern this view—for as regards the shifting boundaries between poetic form and the lived world, I frame no hypothesis: except to point out the impossibility that the theorems of Gödel proved, of finding within any formal system the proof of its consistency.

[9] Bate, *Burden of the Past*, 3.

> writer who is taking it for granted that the very existence of a past creates the necessity for difference.[10]

It is indeed remarkable, however, that Dryden's sense of being bound by ancient forces and patterns towards new words and figures can be made so closely to resemble the professional preoccupations of American academics. Bate's theory of poetic influence was later tweaked by Harold Bloom into a Freudian family romance, of all things, so that the poet, now, looked to the precursor with the anxiety of a son contemplating his father's legacy.[11] Although literary allusion is at best tangential to our present concern, it may be worth noting that Christopher Ricks's *Allusion to the Poets* also framed "the poet as heir."[12] In all these works, there are moments of real insight into the nature of poetry, as when Bloom says the "poem is now *held* open to the precursor, where once it *was* open, and the uncanny effect is that the new poem's achievement makes it seem to us, not as though the precursor were writing it, but as though the later poet himself had written the precursor's characteristic work"[13]—but they are altogether individual in their focus. While Bate et al. seem mindful of the semantic forces of the past propelling the outcroppings of canon, they analyze the phenomenon in fusty terms, of political economy and psychoanalysis, competition and discontent. Perhaps these are the liberal sentiments of a generation seeking to distance itself from the modernist vision of poetry as a collective scriptive endeavor: of poets as striving through their cumulative definitions to overcome, in some extraordinary way, the forbidding inertia of language.

When Pound says "the poet's job is to define and yet again define until the detail of surface is in accord with its root in justice,"[14] he might be speaking of words across an oeuvre but quite possibly, the body of poetry itself. Semantic entanglement across the history of a lyric corpus, however, is attested to most plainly in Eliot's "Tradition and the Individual Talent"—in the tantalizing idea that what happens in a

[10] Bate, 31.

[11] Bloom, *Anxiety of Influence*, 8.

[12] Ricks, *Allusion to the Poets*, Section I.

[13] Bloom, *Anxiety of Influence*, 16.

[14] "Letter to Basil Bunting" in Pound, *Letters*, 277.

new poem happens simultaneously to all the works that preceded it.[15] Although Eliot observes the fact in a characteristically gloomy mood, "every genuine [...] poet fulfills once and for all some possibility of the language, and so leaves one possibility less for his successors,"[16] one might as plausibly hold that the poet in the very act of completing one possibility is giving rise to another.[17] Henry Staten draws from Aristotle a more optimistic—and indeed, non-individualistic—vision of a lyric canon shaping itself through the organic evolution of poetic *techne*, instanced in the hand of individual poets, but unfolding, all the same, to a full intended *physis*.[18] Staten quotes elsewhere Stephen Halliwell's redaction of the *Poetics*: the history of poetry, says Halliwell, "has to be comprehended [as] channeled into acts of human discovery of what was there to be found,"[19] namely, a culturally evolving *techne* manifested in a functionally held-together canon. The growth of such a canon, like the formation of crystals with which it is compared in the chapter title, can be *rationally* traced—though not predicted—by the close reader of poetry. The arbitrations over competing biographies that govern canonization today provoke the elementary question—resembling disconcertingly the cruder doubts of data-enthusiasts, 'distant readers', so-called—of whether grave decisions of exclusion and inclusion, importance and relevance, are best left to the caprice of literary professionals. *Epistêmê* shifts rather more randomly than *technê*.

We do not, in this essay, take full measure of the means of poetic *techne*—"how the poem means"[20]—, which one might abbreviate, however inadequately, to syntax, rhythm and diction; I deal mostly with the latter. But it will hopefully become apparent in the following sections that an aspect central to the unfolding of poetic *techne* is, to borrow

[15] Eliot, *Sacred Wood*, 49–50.

[16] Eliot, *Classic*, 24.

[17] Unless, of course, one is partial to the *Timaeus*: and sees history itself as the moving image of some Eternity subsisting whole. But that is for another day.

[18] See section III of Staten's essay in this volume, 'Is the Author Still Dead,' for a fuller account of poetic *techne*.

[19] Halliwell, *Poetics*, 49; Also see Staten, "The Origin," 48–9.

[20] Alluding to John Ciardi's *How does a Poem Mean?* (1961).

a phrase from the Futurists, "the unfolding of the word as such"[21]—which, to again reconcile discovery with invention, we might also recast in workmanly terms: "the poet," declares Lévi-Strauss, "behaves with regard to language like an engineer trying to form heavier atoms from lighter ones."[22]

2 Field

> "Poetry/ Unearths from among the speechless dead. // Lazarus mystified" [23]
>
> —Geoffrey Hill

Besides privileging the career of poetry over that of poets, I mean in this essay to propose another amendment to the empirico-historicist conception of the artwork. And that is to view, as Derek Attridge does in the Introduction to this volume, the literary work as an event,[24] and poetry, as "a way of happening."[25] To view a poem as an event in the world is, I believe, to secure it ontologically from the exploitations of fact, the Baroque agglomerations of detail that encircle works of art today. The notion upon which empirico-historicism rests, that beneath the mayhem of sense and scatter of emotion lies an inert substratum available for forensic analysis, can be dispelled if the fundamental state of a poem is itself taken, with William Carlos Williams, as a "field of action."[26] That is not to dissolve the poem's corporeality into occult forces but to keep its constituent masses themselves in an evental state. Or as Wallace Stevens once put it, "a poem is the cry of its occasion, / Part of the res itself and not about it."[27]

[21] Steiner, "Formalism," 11.

[22] Lévi-Strauss, "Signs," 85.

[23] Hill, "History as Poetry," ll. 3–6 (*King Log*).

[24] See chapter 4 of *The Singularity of Literature* for an analysis of the literary work as event.

[25] W. H. Auden, "In Memory of W. B. Yeats," ll. 41 (*Another Time*).

[26] Williams, *Selected Essays*, 287.

[27] Stevens, *Poetry*, 404.

To treat a poem as a way of happening, its utterance as other than mimesis, creates interesting difficulties for interpretation. The disciplinary demands of "setting down" meaning lead often to an artificial stabilization of the poetic field. Even the foremost practitioners of close reading today at times regard poems as painting pictures. For instance, *The Craft of Poetry*, beginning with the radical aim of remaining at "the level of how [the poem] works [...] rather than [...] of meaning," weighing its various operations in accordance with function, goes on to imply that the "bedrock of interpretation" lies in the "little narrative" that the poem paints.[28] The mid-century tools of reading—"speaking situation," "visual narrative"—that have congealed into our contemporary practice, in the hands of exegetes less alert than Attridge and Staten, can have the effect of rendering poems sclerotic. Under our current reading protocols, the poem is taken as "primary material" documenting an original event, whose lineaments, once extracted from the poem, are then reset in "secondary material," which is in turn promoted to the primary in the pages of reception history, and so on, until the poem, eventually, is all but lost in the tangled networks of description. Our best efforts at keeping meaning alive—through repeated calls for critical modesty and hermeneutic pluralism—thus prove insufficient to check the reification that renders a poem to empirico-historicism.

Jonathan Culler says, "disrupting narrative, invocation, or address makes the poem an event in the lyric present rather than the representation of a past event."[29] But even here, I would argue that the simple fact of residing in the generic present is not enough to distinguish a thing—speech-act or otherwise—as an event. We discriminate events from whatever else is extant, or so the votaries of Whitehead will argue, chiefly through the experience in sense-awareness of activity. It is, I will claim, in the intensity of interaction between diction, syntax and rhythm, that the poem ultimately manifests itself as an event. While I agree with Attridge and Staten that the test for an interpretation lies in whether "the poem as a whole hangs [in it] together,"[30] I would add that a successful reading

[28] Attridge and Staten, *Craft of Poetry*, 8, 21, 22. Although "narrative" is only taken as foundational for the poem at hand—Dickinson's "I Started Early"—it becomes clear from the ensuing exegesis that the poem's main work is proprioceptive: to *feel* body in sea.

[29] Culler, *Theory of Lyric*, 8.

[30] Attridge and Staten, *Craft of Poetry*, 15.

will also show the whole hang*ing* together: for only in the present continuous does an artifact become once again an artwork. Walking through the aisles of Chartres, for instance, if observers no longer feel the flying buttresses pressing inward against the ribbed vaults, the vaults pressing downward on the columns below, and the colossal ribcage thus *being held up*, the erstwhile work of art, despite erudite plaques annotating its stony scripture, can only be described as a relic. To improvise again from Oakeshott and Hume, we may say that to "understand" a poem *is* to "experience" it: that the event of the poem relies for its renewed occurrence on its lines not only activating memory and intelligence but invoking *soma* into its doings. And close reading, I therefore believe, is better off chasing the "simple, sensuous, and passionate"[31] movements of a poem than finding a picture at the terminus of narrative.

Although I will develop Williams's "field of action" mainly with respect to diction, such models have in the past also proven useful for the exploration of syntax and rhythm. Donald Davie, in *Articulate Energy*, borrows from Fenollosa a theory of poetic syntax as the "*transference of power*:"[32] sentences, as redistributing force from subject, via verb, to object, much like "the transferences of force from agent to object, which constitute natural phenomena."[33] Charles Olson, on the other hand, converts "the large area of the whole poem, into the FIELD [...] where all the syllables and all the lines must be managed in their relations to each other."[34] Diction and syntax in Olson's field are to obey the semantic governance of sound; meaning, he declares, originates in the inflection of voice and modulation of breath in pronouncing the syllable. He employs the concept of the "field" to invest the "space" of a poem "with physical quantities as velocity [and] force."[35] An event in physical space, for Olson, sets off the poetic act thus: the buffeting of bodily nervure among the elements foments the event which, conducted through the "well-weighed syllables" of a poem, culminates in the reading body, where the shock of

[31] How Milton thought poetry should be studied.

[32] Davie, *Articulate Energy*, 36.

[33] Fenollosa, "Chinese Written Character," 44.

[34] "Projective Verse" (1950) in Olson, *Prose*, 243.

[35] "Equal, that is, to the Real Itself" (1958) in Olson, *Prose*, 123.

the poet's primeval experience resonates.[36] The poem, therefore, is not "the act of thought about the instant," but "the act of the instant"—not descriptive symbolism but physical undertaking.[37]

I consider Davie and Olson, in this essay, as fellow travelers only insofar as they attend not to the question of what the poem means but what the poem *does* when it means—when it tries, that is, to overcome the quotidian torpor of *parole*. "That commonplace image," writes Hill,

> founded upon the unfinished statues of Michelangelo, 'mighty figures straining to free themselves from the imprisoning marble,' has never struck me as being an ideal image for sculpture itself; it seems more to embody the nature and condition of those arts which are composed of words. The arts which use language are the most impure of arts [...] However much a poem is shaped and finished, it remains to some extent within the "imprisoning marble" of a quotidian shapelessness and imperfection. At the same time I would claim the utmost significance for matters of technique and I take no cynical view of those rare moments in which the inertia of language, which is also the coercive force of language, seems to have been overcome.[38]

I similarly proceed in this essay under the—possibly mistaken—notion that the forces most pivotal to what a poem does steeped in the density of its polluted medium are the discursive *energeia* of words—that syntax and rhythm are ultimately forces that release and direct the ample realization of semantic potential in "complex words."[39]

I must try and secure this dynamic animation of a poem now, and will attempt to do so, conversely, in the still images of Ben Jonson. Jonson was a poet of pacific occupation and often found in words astute ways of trimming the passions. Take the country-house, "Penshurst," through whose ancient idyll he gently escorts us, praising, all the while, its modesty and provision. "Now, Penshurst," he salutes, withdrawing, "they that will

[36] A sneak nod to Sidney's *Apology* and to Attridge's first book, whose work on meter is still of central importance to close reading.

[37] As I hope in this essay to show that the reading body has been left out unjustly from our established close reading practices, I stand indebted to Olson's writings on "Proprioception" (1962) (*Prose*, 181). Nevertheless, I proceed in this matter without a theory of the breath as origin of bodily hermeneutics.

[38] From "Poetry as Menace and Atonement" (Hill, *Collected Critical Writings*, 3–4).

[39] Recalling Empson's *The Structure of Complex Words*.

proportion thee / With other edifices, when they see / Those proud, ambitious heaps, and nothing else, / May say their lords have built, but thy lord dwells" (99–102). The poem, it seems to me, can only achieve that still serenity in "dwell" by an engineered resistance to "built." The countervailing forces of the final line, however, are already buttressed by an interaction in the previous lines between "proportion" and "heap." If proportionate, a thing cannot be, as "heap" seems to suggest, amorphous. However, the proud edifice with polished pillars and Baroque design, when mounted over Penshurst in generations to come, can by the very dint of its ordonnance come to seem inordinate. This channels the tension between "built" and "dwells." The Renaissance equation of nobility with proportion is all but undone in the word "dwell," whose harmony flourishes precisely in the absence of contrived symmetry. The muscular and commemorative pride in building so central to seventeenth-century culture is thus confronted with an exalted state of dwelling. A sylvan askesis, we might venture, comes to rest on the word "dwell" by a careful manipulation of forces in-and-through the lines prior.

Although such instances of "ample realization of semantic potential" might seem in the moment of achievement absolute, the historical evolution of poetic *techne* will usually show them to be conditional. Action in a future poem's field will, in other words, come to be constrained and induced by external forces from the shared lyric past. "An implication," says Empson, "is not a sense at all, but it often becomes one later in its [the word's] career."[40]

One might reasonably wonder, at this point, why such etymological concerns are not better suited to the lexicographer than literary critic. In fact, Empson recommends that "the interactions of the senses of a word should be included" in all serious dictionaries.[41] And Hill assents, arguing in a cranky review of the *Oxford English Dictionary's* second edition, that the lexicographical practice of listing senses has resulted in a great disservice to the genius of language.[42] In Milton's, "Hee unobserv'd/ Home to his Mothers house privat returnd," says Hill, "the play between 'unobserved' and 'privat' so modifies the pitch of the latter word that, while fulfilling the terms of the *OED*'s simple definition ('privately,

[40] Empson, *Structure of Complex Words*, 49.

[41] Empson, 391.

[42] "Common Weal, Common Woe" in Hill, *Collected Critical Writings*, 265–79.

secretly'), it holds something of its signification in reserve," namely, "the capacity of the imagination to be at once constrained and inviolable."[43] More crucial to the point, even, are instances when the different senses of a word mutually annihilate one another. Hill recalls Melville's Union soldiers, who will "die experienced ere three days are spent— / Perish, enlightened by the vollied glare." The men are "illuminated" and "extinguished" in the "blaze of musketry," while simultaneously "instructed" in the nature of brute reality—their "ignorance," thus, "erased in an illuminated instant, together with their lives."[44] In this way, the dictionary's distinctions, between the physical and metaphysical connotations of "enlightened," are rendered by Melville void. But despite Empson's and Hill's riveting discoveries of lexicographical inadequacies, I am unable to see how the explosive and implosive reactions of words in their poetic field can adequately be demonstrated in the stable medium of dictionary paraphrase. For instance, Empson, I think, would have seen "dwell" as a "complex word" for its potential to reveal senses beyond its denotative strictures. But my list of synonyms for "dwell" do not reveal very much without a re-reading of the poem with the salient lines of force accentuated.

Of course, in observing forces within the "poetic field," we have gotten no closer to characterizing the crystallization over time of poetic canons. Indeed, there are poems for which the tracing of external forces from the lyric past will seem perverse, merely, to their self-sufficient doings. This is often the case when the semantic legacies upon which the poem builds have been assumed almost entirely by public, even colloquial, understanding.[45] Be that as it may, reading a poem's semantic field through its canonical history will more often than not enrich understanding. And to that "understanding," on which I began claiming the theories of literature depend, we are able now to adjoin the following: the observation and identification of "complex words" as "living powers"[46] embodied in and negotiating identity through a lyric corpus will serve as the conditions for any such understanding of poetry as begets theory. While it is the poem that discloses a past poem as its perlocutive precursor, the distinguishing

[43] Hill, 274. From *Paradise Regain'd* (1671).

[44] Hill, 277. From "The March in Virginia" (1866).

[45] This seems the case in most Yeats poems.

[46] Coleridge, *Aids to Reflection*, xix.

of this disclosure will yield for the theorist both theorem and canon—a canon determined, ultimately, by poets through the poems they reveal as limiting and liberating the semantic field wherein they toil.[47]

3 Crystal

Frank Kermode ventured once that "every verse is occultly linked, in ways to be researched, with all the others; the text is a world system."[48] I hope, however, to demonstrate in this section, how we can treat the arrowed links between poems of a crystallizing "world-system," or canon, in a manner not occult. The crystallizing process can be studied from a number of examples. I will approach the matter instead from a single poem which has largely baffled critics to see if my proposed methodological assumptions cannot also be defended on grounds of hermeneutic capacity. Hill's early masterpiece, "To the (Supposed) Patron," closes his first collection, *For the Unfallen.*

Prodigal of loves and barbeques,
Expert in the strangest faunas, at home
He considers the lilies the rewards.
There is no substitute for a rich man.
At his first entering a new province
With new coin, music, the barest glancing
Of steel or gold suffices. There are many
Tremulous dreams secured under that head.
For his delight and his capacity
To absorb, freshly, the inside succulence
Of untoughened sacrifice, his bronze agents
Speculate among convertible stones
And drink desert sand. That no mirage
Irritate his mild gaze, the lewd noonday
Is housed in cool places, and fountains
Salt the sparse haze. His flesh is made clean.

[47] I use Austin's terminology, somewhat loosely, to talk of the "forces" that speech-acts have beyond sense-and-reference (*How to do things*, 100); and use perlocution to compass the intended (in the present poem) and unintended (in the past poems) forces of words, when the Hebrew 'davhar'—a word that is also an act, a bringing forward of something—will also do.

[48] Kermode, *Forms of Attention*, 75. I thank Ronan McDonald for directing me to this brilliant work in his essay in this volume.

For the unfallen—firstborn, or wise
Councillor—prepared vistas extend
As far as harvest; and idyllic death
Where fish at dawn ignite the powdery lake.[49]

The lines insinuate the rich man's presence in a grammar designed as if to *glance* him. The words mouthed in passive voice cast over-and-around the rich man in subjective and objective genetives, unfolding in a long chain of stubbornly subordinate clauses, interpolated with terse main clauses. "He," in fact, is active in only the first main clause (of line 3)—a circumstance to which we must return later.[50]

Perhaps the most striking example of "glancing grammar" is in lines 5–7, where the subject, in a happy marriage of form and content, is itself a "glancing." In the construction, "at his entering, the barest glancing," he seems barely present, like a shock that struck the autonomous nervous system, whereupon the body has twitched and current passed before the brain has registered an effect. The choice of "at," rather than "upon," together with the continuous "entering" hold him, as if, in the ephemerality of the event. Despite his fugitive appearance, the display of wealth and power is almost stilled and eternalized in the moment of his "entering, glancing," as if gerund is giving way to a phantom gerundive: i.e., that the flash of silver and gold "suffices" to materialize the rich man's "tremulous dreams"[51] seems a presumed state of affairs, a foregone conclusion, rather than an actual happening, which might demand such travails as go into the excitement of obedience.

The freak writhings of syntax from which the utterances of the poem are given off should readily indicate to us that a formal understanding will not be served, at all, by the modernist procedures of elaborating a "speaking persona" and "visual narrative." The bearing of a speaking-voice, if there is one, is disclosed in but one line of the entire poem. But taking line 4 as an opinion, or asseveration, even, will be, or so I hope to show, to stray from where the force of language is guiding understanding.

[49]This poem is used with the kind permission of the literary estate of Sir Geoffrey Hill; all rights reserved. As the essay is a full reading of the poem, the use can also be considered fair in copyright terms.

[50]The active voice reappears in the last sentence but not while the poem is describing him.

[51]Viz.: the pun on 'secured' ensures that the 'dreams' cloistered in his imagination are *simultaneously* taking shape under his purview.

For the Unfallen was published in 1959 and collects poems written in Engand from 1952 to 1958. It is an England diminished by war. Visceral signs of a vanished past are everywhere to be seen. The great beneficiary from the stirrings of honor and shelling of sacrifice in the decades past has proven America: who has won mastery, somehow, by sheer will of capital. In "The Troublesome Reign," an early poem in the collection, the poet is sick with "Reluctant heat" for a disdaining lady—not Beatrice quite—who fairly considers him ridiculous. When finally, "She was his," "Her limbs grasped him, satisfied, while his brain / Judged every move and cry from its separate dark // More dark, more separate, now, yet still not dead" (14–17). Their detached and lingering Eros, almost wholly Agape now, has stiffened to custom, discharged as if to keep a crumbling moral architecture up: "By such rites they saved love's face, and such laws / As prescribe mutual tolerance, charity / To neighbours, strangers, those by nature / Subdued among famines and difficult wars" (21–24). The millennial caritas of Christianity, whose lineaments are visible now only in stark convention is late in the collection all but overrun by what its rites had so long existed to subdue. In "Of Commerce and Society,"[52] "The tables of exchange [are yet again] overturned" (V. 4) as "The bells / In hollowed Europe spilt / To the gods of coin and salt" (I. 5–7). "To the (Supposed) Patron," composed under these anarchic upheavals, declares, finally, "There is no substitute for a rich man."[53] The illocutionary forces in-and-on these words show, however, the assertiveness of the line giving way, slowly, to *resignation*—and I hope to show that such goings-about-words will remain masked, almost fully, if the poem is read as the confessions of a speaking voice in a speaking situation.

Now there is no reason why external forces on the poetic field cannot arrive in the form of syntax; Hill's grammar, like his diction, means through tradition.[54] In a lecture as Professor of Poetry at Oxford University, Hill declared that "a deep dynastic wound" afflicts the grammar of

[52] Hill, *Unfallen*, 48–53.

[53] I have probably furnished more external material than is strictly necessary; but I have made much of sharing the "conditions of one's understanding," and so, having read the collection chronologically, have shared what was called up to me when reading the poem. "England in the 1950s," however, is likely sufficient context, and saying much more severely risks diminishing the pitch of the poem with gross historical particularities.

[54] As regards rhythm, see Llewelyn Morgan's *Musa Pedestra* for an account of how metric tradition influences meaning in Roman lyric poetry.

poetry. The opening stave of *Paradise Lost* (Canto 1, lines 1–26), says Hill, "is designed to embody and project simultaneously the hegemonies of derived rebellious power and the hierarchical grammar of salvation." In the opening canto,

> the main affirmative clause comprising three words only, is not heard until the first half of line 6, and after a comma, the subordinate clauses take up again until the second main clause at lines 12 and 13 ends also with a comma, flowing into three further lines of adjectival and adverbial phrases until we reach the first full period at the end of line 16.

Hill wonders why Milton compromises economy in such a defiant manner. "The shape of the syntax," he concludes, "is sinuous or serpentine, a form appropriate to a tragedy of deviant ethics"—and we can do much worse than that to characterize the adjectival and adverbial phrases coiling periphrastically around our "(Supposed) Patron."

The serpentine syntax glancing the rich man, revealing in flashes a presence as terrific as Lucifer's, works ultimately—or so I have argued—to direct and release the forces latent in diction. But to see how diction stands to syntax, we must first observe what the words themselves are getting up to in their crisscrossing semantic orbits. Seen—with Williams—as actions or forces, the senses (both *Sinn* and *Bedeutung*) of words interact to posit the rich man to the world, and—with Stevens—as masses, the cacophonies (or texture) of words induce the "sensuous intelligence" of the reader into the poem's semantic field.[55] As regards the former, we shall begin with how "prodigal" is modified by "absorbs." Lines 10–11 describe a body that remains "untoughened" after sacrifice, abiding, as if, for the rich man's "delight." A carcass will ordinarily flush its muscles with lactic acid—converted *post mortem* from glycogen—and keep, thereby, tender, pink, and flavorful; but if the animal was stressed before slaughter, the release of adrenaline will have used up the glycogen and stiffened the muscles thereafter. The violent ritual of sacrifice, one might usually suppose, is enough to quicken flesh into *rigor mortis*. But the rich man, we know, from his 'barest glancings,' enjoys a certain effortless way the world: and it seems, dismayingly, that beasts are as resigned as the natives

[55] Poetry should be "alive with sensuous intelligence" (Hill, *Collected Critical Writings*, 439).

to the pall purport of his bare presence.[56] Now that he should *absorb* their preserved "succulence," that their supine offering should be rivaled by his inert accepting—in the lack, we might infer, of the craving that motors teeth and mandible to rip and grind—modifies backwardly the "prodigal" of line 1. "Prodigal" seems at first to improbably suggest "a wasteful nature"—improbable, because the object of "prodigal," "barbecue," would not have called up to the poem's readers the extravagant soirees of American backyards: instead, the measured hewings of bone, the patient curing of marrow, the orderly arrangement of parts, with such knowledge of anatomy as might be expected from an "expert in the strangest faunas." We can thus square his surgical dealings with flesh—carnal though they may be—with a "prodigal" nature only if we draw from "absorb" a more general suggestion that any interaction with bodied world is for the rich man not a matter of import. It is not so much that the "prodigal first-born" wastes his graces away—like the "fair youth" of Shakespeare's sonnets—but that grace itself—of which meat is surely a sign—seems wasted on him: "for the unfallen" stand indifferent to "the gathering of bestial and common hardship" (9)[57] wherein effort and sustenance yet remain inextricably bound.

We have seen how syntax flashes a presence and sense defines its nature; but texture, I have said, implicates the reading body into proceedings. The articulate violence in the words, "absorb freshly the inside succulence of untoughened sacrifice" appeal directly to body. The enclosing labials in "ab"-so-"rb" fatten the mouth, preparing the bursting and swift closing of the stressed "fresh," and the lisping sibilants, "inside succulence sacrifice," issuing thereafter: as if to read is to be viscerally involved in rupturing, gushing, sucking. Proprioceptive awareness is thus heightened—as in the working senses of the blind—by the words rendering themselves opaque to picturing in any immediate or sensible way. That the lack of sensory participation implied by "absorb" is only available to apprehension *sensuously*—i.e., through the somatic impacts of sound—is a formal circumstance crucial to the workings of the poem. The beginning of the subordinate clause, where the occurrence was indemnified, as if, "for his delight," and the far-fetched implications of "absorb," brought

[56] There is a possibility of the rich man absorbing the gifts of Christ's self-sacrifice like Marlowe's Faustus drinking Christ's blood from the firmament; but I haven't here the space to countenance that possibility with my reading.

[57] "Picture of a Nativity" in Hill, *For the Unfallen*.

out in its interaction with "prodigal," seal the rich man off, as if in aegis, from the very experience whose articulation awakens in us a sensuous intelligence.[58]

This hermeneutic paradox was formally prepared in the title itself, in the enigmatic brackets enclosing (supposed). But this becomes clear only upon brawling some way through the sinewy lines. The newly rich man is unfallen, so without desire—for the Earth is already his paradise. And so, he needn't patronize the artist to win him favor with God, who, once, we will recall, had made it harder for a rich man to enter the kingdom of heaven than for a camel to pass into the eye of a needle.[59] The tone of "supposed" might at first blush show a poet, writing under plutocracy, yearning for an old god-fearing aristocrat. The brackets, however, complicate proceedings. In one sense, brackets make what is confined intimate—so implicit as to not require saying; and in another, they render the presence within not-full—suggested, though inexplicit. While the act of "supposing" is intimate, what is supposed, or posited—the patron, i.e.—is rendered by the brackets spectral. At the same time, the enclosure—coupled with the passive form—prevents the "yearning" enshrined in "supposed" from slipping into narrative (say, of a speaking voice lamenting a bygone system of benevolence and patronage). "Yearning" becomes thereby no more nor less than the condition of the Fallen—to which, of course, the unfallen are not subject. From the supposed patron and his wayward graces being yearned after, desire is itself abstracted, immured in brackets, and branded, it seems, like a stigma on the dying body of the poet. Having excited mind thus to its durance in body, the poem suffers the reader to *undergo* what the rich man (and I hope to activate both senses of the word here) *fore-goes*.

I began noting the fact that "he" is active only in the grammar of the third line: "He considers the lilies the rewards"—active, in the simple present of "considers" and the purposiveness with which he contemplates the flowers. For if consideration was enjoyment, merely, "regards" would surely have done, if only for the assonantal reprise in "rewards." But why he should consider so, I submit, remains entirely a mystery unless we

[58] I take the tropes of close reading I've tried to avoid—dramatic situation, speaking voice—as tied and giving rise to the "amygisme" which might approach the poem by picturing a pagan ritual or, worse yet, a 'lewd noonday housed in cool places.'

[59] Matthew 19:24.

depart from the poetic field to the historical forces of the poem's perlocutive precursors. "Consider the lilies of the field, how they grow; they toil not, neither do they spin: And yet I say unto you, That even Solomon in all his glory was not arrayed like one of these."[60] And over the exhortation looms the injunction, "cursed is the ground beneath thee; in toil shalt thou eat of it all days of thy life; [...] In the sweat of thy face shalt thou eat bread, till thou return unto the ground."[61] Given the rich man of our poem seems luridly free of toil, and physical constraints in general, the Biblical verses together appear to bring forth the following sense: he considers the condition of the lily, glory without effort, the reward.

Empson, in "Doctrinal Point," compares the state of the flower (he prefers the magnolia) with that of modern man, who enjoys some such faith as that the facts of life, when answered by science, will bring him finally to grace: to the state of the flowers that the poem says, "Are right in doing anything they can think of" (12). By the end of the poem, scientific man has discovered the formula for grace: and "The duality of choice becomes the singularity of existence; / The effort of virtue the unconsciousness of foreknowledge" (18–19)—a "singularity," we might note, that our poem's rich man evidently enjoys with the world around him. But such unconscious ease, Empson's lines seem to suggest, when programmed into human being, will erode that being, flatten it, rather than add up to grace. And therein lies the difference: although life for Hill's man seems automatic, his being not quite somatic, he is far from the diminished organism that Empson foresees in his poem. Our rich man thrills into the world, his glory, far from faded. "Doctrinal Point," also invoking Matthew, continues in its conclusion that the luster of the petal will always outshine "That over-all that Solomon should wear" (20)—"over-all," the worker's habit, suggesting even mighty Solomon had to spin and toil for his wisdom. Empson argues that "Man was given authority over all creatures, but this involves much toiling,"[62] unlike the flower, whose effortless allure and full life of impulses come with the condition that it enjoys no earthly powers. That is God's deal and it is broken by the rich man.

[60] Matthew 6:28.

[61] Genesis 3:17 and 3:19.

[62] From notes-section (Empson, *Poems*, 278).

But it is not the first time: rich men have in the past also been like "the summer's flower," "to the summer sweet," while for themselves, but lived and died. And so, following the mystery of the lilies and the rewards, we come to Shakespeare[63]: "They that have power to hurt and will do none, /[...] Who, moving others, are themselves as stone, / Cold, unmoved, and to temptation slow: / They rightly do inherit heaven's graces" (1, 3–5). Empson, in his famous exegesis of Sonnet 94,[64] describes the powerful and enigmatic figure of the poem as an "arriviste," whose "impudent worldliness [...] Shakespeare finds shocking and delightful."[65] The cold individual is "symbolically chaste" like the lily, inscrutable and unmoved, however in accordance with sensuous impulses he might live.[66] Just so, Hill's patron is a "prodigal of loves" yet indifferent to appeal.[67] The perlocutionary force, however, comes from the closing caution of the sonnet that this kind of life is not for long tolerated: "For sweetest things turn sourest by their deeds; / Lilies that fester smell far worse than weeds" (13–14). The lily's career in perfection is brief. Its fallen petals warn in their rot: "no one can rise above common life, as you have done so fully, without in the same degree sinking below it."[68] But even so, the rich man of our poem "considers the lilies the rewards."

The lyric past of lilies can, however, be countenanced with line 3, if we observe before "the rewards" an implicit comma. This would lever "rewards" into a special zone of interest. Indeed, "reward" has had a past almost as darkling as the lily's, to which I'm able to attend, now, only in summary. (1) "light reward and recompense were found/ Fleeting like feathers in the wind" (George Gascoigne, 1572)[69]; (2) "Natheless the villain sped himself so well/ [...] Yet not escapèd from the due reward/ Of his bad deeds" (Spenser, *Faerie Queene*, Book 3, Canto V). The two texts neatly divide "reward" into its positive and negative

[63] Sonnet 94 is also perlocutive precursor to "Doctrinal Point."

[64] "They that have Power" in Empson, *Some Versions of Pastoral*, 85–115.

[65] Empson, 87.

[66] Empson, 88.

[67] "Love" here is not Christian. The jaded Agape of the early poems is now wholly animal Eros.

[68] Empson, 97.

[69] See Braden, *Sixteenth-Century Poetry*, 99.

applications: positively, whatever is bestowed above just due—the "recompense"—is reward; negatively, "reward" is weighed equally against the committed sin; here, reward *is* recompense. But from this relative equanimity between the senses, the English of the Bible releases in "reward" a willful caprice.[70] One of the delights of heaven, we are told, is the high-view from which can be relished the torments of the damned: "Only with thine eyes shalt thou behold and see the reward of the wicked."[71] Now it should be clear that whether, in line 3, he considers the lilies *as* his rewards or the lilies *and* the rewards, the very mention of "reward"—in conjunction with the Biblical flower—has loosed on the poem its terrible miasma.[72]

But whether such a reward indeed awaits the rich man remains yet unclear. Luckily, there is a simple test: "For the unfallen, prepared vistas extend as far as harvest." I will take "far" here as a spatial metaphor for time, for the world does not impose on the unfallen physical limits; all vistas, we may assume, are prepared for them. "Harvest" demarks instead the time of year when what is sown is to be reaped. And two rewards await thereupon: (1) "idyllic death;" and (2) "the powdery lake." Unlike Shakespeare's oblivious patron, who past his prime, one way or another, will meet judgment, the rich man of our poem glides over shifting circumstances, untouched, it seems, by *tempus edax rerum*: and passes into death, casually, as if to another province.

"Idyllic death," we may yet protest, is but an ominous reprieve before the real—and the full force of the Psalms will now apply—reward begins. Indeed, the "powdery lake" seems readily to invoke the "burning Sulphur" of Milton's "lake of fire."[73] Unnervingly, though, the drama of Hell seems for the rich man but last entertainments, staged on his fish-pond, set up, as if, immaculately for his pleasure, like the noonday, the beasts, and the new provinces.[74] If the lily is his reward, it is his triumph over Divine will, and if the reward, his torment, the punishment

[70] Not yet in the Wycliffe, already in the *King James*.

[71] Psalm 91:8.

[72] The voyeurism was curtailed, somewhat, in the Hebrew original, wherein the elect behold "the *shillumah* (recompense) of the wicked;" here, the privilege is an ever-lasting lesson rather than entertainment.

[73] Lines 69 and 280, both from Book 1 of *Paradise Lost*.

[74] For the bobbing fish to ignite the lake, the powder must also signify gunpowder; but that equation is already latent in *Paradise Lost*.

is subsumed onto the world, now all made stage, for his delight.[75] Both are in effect.

The final victory of William Morris's "anarchical plutocracy"[76] over the millennial struggle for what Chesterton calls "mystical communism,"[77] seems, for Hill, to close the Christian chapter just so—a tragedy, then, not of deviant ethics but deviant theodicy. In a late poem in the collection, "Of Commerce and Society," the gods of coin "Destroy only to save"—because "America," for all its exploits, is "Well-stocked with foods,/ Enlarged and deep-oiled" (VI. 10–11).[78] The line, I think, is a mordant evocation of Schumpeter, in whose writings the leveling and remaking of worlds by magnates and tycoons had received their vindication as acts of "creative destruction."[79] The tone of "destroy only to save," which seems plain, is insufficient, however, to prepare the complex feeling of line 4: for "To the (Supposed) Patron," I will maintain, cannot be understood in terms of dissent. The poem, it seems, has taken distant measure of what has happened and tells what it has seen as if from ancient eyes: "There is no substitute for a rich man"—not protest, nor assertion, but resigned utterance.

Coda

> Do words make up the majesty
> Of man, and his justice
> Between the stones and the void? [80]
>
> —Geoffrey Hill

Such a tracing of canon, the skeptical reader will surely have noted, does not solve, fully, the problems of exclusion that have vexed the benevolence of Cultural Theorists; but it has in its expansion, or so I have attempted

[75] With due apologies for 'subsume *onto*'—I hope, however, it is clear why "divest" or "discharge" would not have done.

[76] Morris, *Signs of Change*, 191. Hill, in a video interview with *The Economist*, says he thought he had invented the term "plutocratic anarchy" until he read "anarchical plutocracy" in Morris.

[77] Chesterton, *History of England*, 92.

[78] The connotation, here, of Arab oil, will I hope make up, somewhat, for my not dealing with the rich man's 'bronze agents' that 'drink desert sand.'

[79] Schumpeter, *Capitalism*, 83.

[80] "Three Baroque Meditations" in *King Log*.

to argue, the virtue of revealing what actually transgresses the canon—as opposed to the charitable tallying of new biographical identities. Crystallized through the *Faerie Queene*, *The Book of Matthew*, Sonnet 94, Psalm 91, and "Doctrinal Point,"[81] the complex pasts of "lilies" and "rewards" seem in the poem to have been, in some measure, overcome, and thereby, set forth anew for coming times.[82] If, as the votaries of Wittgenstein held, "a sense of language is also a feeling for ways of living that have meant something,"[83] and as Ransom said, "the density [...] of poetic language reflects the world's density,"[84] then the poem, in the very act of transgression, can be seen as countenancing the bearings of history and displaying the posture of affairs. It is in some such way, I think, that the question of literature's *relevance* to political reality must be approached—for only when secure in this will we devote literary criticism guiltlessly to the task of close reading.[85]

References

Auden, W. H. *Another Time*. London: Faber & Faber, 1940.

Austin, J. L. *How to do things with Words*. Edited by J. O. Urmson and Marina Sbisa. Oxford: Oxford University Press, 1975.

Attridge, Derek. *The Singularity of Literature*. London: Routledge, 2004.

Bate, Jackson W. *The Burden of the Past and the English Poet*. London: Chatto & Windus, 1971.

[81] There are other, less obvious ones I have omitted, and perhaps more obvious ones I have missed. Because it is the present poem that reveals past poems as perlocutive precursors, the expansion of the canon in this method takes place not only in the present but also in the past, where neglected poems like "Doctrinal Point" might be rendered to critical attention by future poets.

[82] That such an endeavor in semantic tracing might direct the understanding of a poet reading another, and thereby influence, in some small way, the growth of the crystal, will be fortuitous, I think, to the immediate tasks of criticism.

[83] I am quoting Rush Rhees, student and literary executor of Wittgenstein (*Answers*, 150).

[84] Ransom, *New Criticism*, 79.

[85] "To the (Supposed) Patron" was introduced to me many years ago by the polymath Hans Mathews. His vision of the poem has remained powerful in imagination. But to the extent possible, I have tried to render this reading through my own discoveries of its workings. Two crucial points, however, deserve mention: (1) he read line 4 (albeit with a different emphasis to mine) as an 'assertion subtending concession'; and (2) he discovered Sonnet 94 and *Paradise Lost* as necessary precursors to the poem.

Bloom, Harold, *The Anxiety of Influence: A Theory of Poetry*. Oxford: Oxford University Press, 1997.

Braden, Gordon. *Sixteenth-Century Poetry: An Annotated Anthology*. Oxford: Blackwell Publishing, 2005.

Chesterton, G. K. *A Short History of England*. London: Chatto & Windus, 1917.

Ciardi, John. *How does a Poem Mean?* Edited by Miller Williams. Boston: Houghton Mifflin, 1975.

Coleridge, S. T. *Aids to Reflection and the Confessions of an Inquiring Spirit*. London: George Bell & Sons, 1884.

Davie, Donald. *Articulate Energy: An Inquiry into the Syntax of English Poetry*. London: Routledge, 1976.

Eliot, T. S. *The Sacred Wood: Essays on Poetry and Criticism*. London: Methuen & Co., 1920.

———. *What Is a Classic? An Address Delivered before the Virgil Society on the 16th of October, 1944*. London: Faber & Faber, 1945.

Empson, William. *The Complete Poems*. Edited by John Haffenden. London: Penguin, 2000.

———. *Some Versions of Pastoral*. London: Chatto & Windus, 1935.

———. *The Structure of Complex Words*. London: Chatto & Windus, 1951.

Fenollosa, Ernest. *The Chinese Written Character as a Medium for Poetry*. Edited by Lucas. Klein, Jonathan Stalling, Haun Saussy, and Ezra Pound. New York: Fordham University Press, 2008.

Halliwell, Stephen. *Aristotle's Poetics*. Chicago: University of Chicago Press, 1986.

Hill, Geoffrey. "A Deep Dynastic Wound." Professor of Poetry Lectures, Oxford University, April 30, 2013. https://www.english.ox.ac.uk/professor-sir-geoffrey-hill-lectures.

———. *Collected Critical Writings*. Edited by Kenneth Haynes. Oxford: Oxford University Press, 2008.

———. *For the Unfallen*. London: André Deutsch, 1959.

———. "Interview: Poems should be Beautiful." *The Economist*, December 2, 2011. https://www.economist.com/prospero/2011/12/02/poems-should-be-beautiful.

———. *King Log*. London: André Deutsch, 1968.

Hume, David. *Four Dissertations*. London: A. Millar, 1757.

Jonson, Ben. *Bartholomew Fair*. Edited by Eugene M. Waith. New Haven: Yale University Press, 1963.

———. *The Poems of Ben Jonson*. Edited by Robert Bell. London: Charles Griffin, 1870.

Kermode, Frank. *Forms of Attention*. Chicago: University of Chicago Press, 1985.

Kuhn, Thomas S. *The Structure of Scientific Revolutions*. Chicago: University of Chicago Press, 1962.

Lévi-Strauss, Claude. "Art as a System of Signs." In *Art Theory and Criticism: An Anthology of Formalist, Avant-garde, Contextualist and Post-modernist Thought*, edited by Sally Everett, 80–88. Jefferson: McFarland, 1991.

Milton, John, *Paradise Lost*. Edited by A. W. Verity. Cambridge: Cambridge University Press, 1910.

Morris, William. *Signs of Changes: Lectures on Socialism*. Vol. 23 of *The Collected Works of William Morris*. Cambridge: Cambridge University Press, 2012.

Oakeshott, Michael. *On Human Conduct*. Oxford: Clarendon Press, 1975.

Olson, Charles. *Collected Prose*. Edited by Donald Allen and Benjamin Friedlander. Berkeley: University of California Press, 1997.

Pound, Ezra. *Selected Letters of Ezra Pound, 1907–1941*. Edited by D. D. Paige. New York: New Directions, 1971.

Ransom, John C. *The New Criticism*. Norfolk: New Directions, 1941.

Rhees, Rush. *Without Answers*. London: Routledge, 1969.

Ricks, Christopher. *Allusion to the Poets*. Oxford: Oxford University Press, 2002.

Schumpeter, Joseph A. *Capitalism, Socialism, and Democracy*. New York: Routledge, 1994.

Shakespeare, William. *Sonnets*. Edited by Katherine Duncan-Jones. London: Thomas Nelson and Sons, 1997.

Spenser, Edmund. *The Third Booke of the Faerie Queene*. Edited by R. S. Bear. London: Grosart, 1882.

Staten, Henry. "The Origin of the Work of Art in Material Practice." *NLH* 43, no. 1 (Winter 2012): 46–61.

Steiner, Peter. "Russian Formalism." In *Cambridge History of Literary Criticism*, vol. 8, *From Formalism to Poststructuralism*, edited by Raman Selden, 11–29. Cambridge: Cambridge University Press, 1995.

Stevens, Wallace. *Collected Poetry and Prose*. Edited by Frank Kermode and Joan Richardson. New York: Library of America, 1997.

The Bible: Authorized King James Version. Oxford: Oxford University Press, 1998.

White, Hayden. *Tropics of Discourse: Essays in Cultural Criticism*. Baltimore: Johns Hopkins University Press, 1978.

Williams, William C. *Selected Essays*. New York: Random House, 1954.

CHAPTER 12

Criticism and the Non-I, or, Rachel Cusk's Sentences

Tom Eyers

When I think about what I do when I read literature closely, I think about the granular movements of sense and nonsense that may both propel and still a poem or a narrative, that might motor it toward historical import or, just as usefully, refuse, or remain indifferent to, its time or place. But I'm also compelled to consider the kinds of knowledge and non-knowledge that close reading elicits; to examine whether close reading can ever produce a true account of a text, and what truth would even mean in that case; to question whether "closeness" is the correct metaphor for what we do when we run ourselves full tilt at, or sit meditatively alongside, or perhaps consciously distance ourselves from a poem or narrative; and to ruminate on whether literary form might itself engender an immanent literary historicism radically different in kind from those that currently reign supreme over the literature departments.

T. Eyers (✉)
Duquesne University, Pittsburgh, PA, USA
e-mail: eyerst@duq.edu

A. Sridhar et al. (eds.), *The Work of Reading*,
https://doi.org/10.1007/978-3-030-71139-9_12

Nevertheless, the question of close reading also promotes a drawing back to contextual concerns: to the various political indictments, long-past and recent, of formalistic reading, for instance; to the long-overdue widening and worlding of the canon that such critiques have resulted in; to the fear that any defense of close reading must risk a regression to aestheticist ideology, even to gentlemanly belle-lettrist amateurism. Once upon a time, "theory" was considered an enemy of close attention to literary, figural complexity, and this despite the pronounced commitment to microscopic rhetorical reading that American deconstruction, at least, loudly proclaimed. Today, theorists—I am, I suppose, a member of that embattled species—are in the strange position of defending a practice, close reading, that we were previously assumed to have raffishly disdained. While I cannot promise that all or even a majority of these quandaries will receive adequate treatment in what follows, all of them whir incessantly in the background whenever I write philosophically about literary matters: this essay is no exception.

I intend here to make the case for a new way of thinking about the relationship between narrative, the narrative voice or subject, and the question of literature's historicity. I will approach these theoretical thickets by way, first, of a reconsideration of the concept of the subject as it was variously deconstructed, banished, or radically redrawn in the moment of 1960s French structuralist anti-humanism. Secondly, I will assess free indirect style for its ability to produce narrative voices beyond the confines of the subject/object dichotomy, voices that might at the same time be said to call back to that same distinction; voices, in any case, comparable in their liminality to the reconfigured subject or self-proposed by the French anti-humanists. Finally, I will turn to the path-breaking sentences of the contemporary British novelist Rachel Cusk, who, I will argue, has constructed an immanent, unique theory-in-action of the literary subject or what I will call her "non-I," one premised on a qualified evacuation of narrative interiority not unlike some of the anti-philosophical maneuvers of the French anti-humanists, and yet in some respects superior to them, and certainly more appropriate to our times.

Cusk, I will argue, permits us to re-historicize the subject of narrative in a fashion oftentimes foreclosed in the radical anti-historicism of French high structuralism, a historicization nonetheless substantially and usefully different from the archival-empiricist, frequently positivist historicisms now hegemonic in literary studies. The curious "non-I" that results from Cusk's experiments is not a narrative subject in the conventional first-person sense, but neither is it the equivalent to the wide-shot capaciousness of the third person, or the free-floating halfway house of free indirect style, to which I will turn in the middle section of this essay—or, indeed, to the absolute cancellation of character selfhood, or even consciousness per se, that one might associate with various early to mid-twentieth-century literary and artistic avant-gardes. The very impossibility of assigning Cusk's "Non-I" to any of these categories, is a sign that it may help open us to new ways of thinking about the possibilities of narrative as recording device or fever chart, not of history as an external, public, empirically verifiable procession of events, and not of subjective interiority as the private counterpart to, or denial of, the latter, but of some hitherto obscure admixture of, or alchemical solution beyond, the two.

I will slowly build up to a reading of these stunning (which is also to say *stunned*, anesthetized) experiments in subjective narrative voice by, in the first instance, turning to the moment of French high structuralism, as it pushed beyond the legacy of the Cartesian cogito, and so invoked outlines of a new experimental subject that may be said to have prefigured, at an historical distance and in a different national context, Cusk's contemporary advances. This initial section asks: what to retain from the most compelling, and yet most esoteric moment of "French theory," at least with respect to the question of the "I," and insofar as those exuberant theoretical experiments might help us think, once again, the "I" of narrative?

1 Between the Subject and Its Negation: Paris, 1966–1969

The apex of French high structuralism arrived with the attempt to synthesize the psychoanalytic structuralism of Jacques Lacan, and the structural Marxism of Louis Althusser. That venture found its most ambitious iteration in the still little-known journal *Cahiers pour l'Analyse*, published between 1966 and 1969 by students of the aforementioned *maître penseurs*, including a young Alain Badiou, and featuring contributions from Jean-Claude Milner, Jacques-Alain Miller, and Luce Irigaray, among others.[1] The journal is difficult to characterize in the terms of the exceptionally broad-brush narrative that intellectual history has tended to impose upon this storied moment in French philosophy. Often enough, French structuralism, itself a category, like all categories, that begins to break down when peered at long enough, is said to have mounted a full-frontal attack on the Cartesian subject, leaving in its wake only a subjective processes and structures, and a space for the subject only as epiphenomenon or ideological effect. There were, it is true, many polemics around the *humanist* subject in this period, but the fate of the subject per se was more productively murky.

Inevitably, the question of the subject was parsed differently depending on the intellectual and political investments of those doing the parsing. I won't tease out the varying approaches tested in this historical moment, except to say that, for my purposes, the most intriguing theoretical interventions tended to demur from any rejection of the concept outright, in favor of attempts to produce the concept anew, shorn as much as possible of humanist and metaphysical baggage. Many, if not most of these attempts were noble failures, but they remain a compelling resource for thinking about rather different recent and contemporary attempts to renew the literary subject, and more specifically the subject of narrative as the latter may balloon out beyond, or shrink between the lines of, our inherited narratological categories or, indeed, individual sentences, paragraphs, or texts.

The editions of the *Cahiers* stage multiple debates and controversies, but perhaps the defining disagreement occurs between Jacques-Alain Miller, soon to become Lacan's son-in-law and then the inheritor of his intellectual estate, and Alain Badiou. The debate concerns the status of the subject in both psychoanalysis and in the natural sciences, and it more broadly involves, if only implicitly, the charged legacy of Cartesianism as vaunted historical bearer of French intellectual pride. It would take us beyond the ken of this essay to fully map this fascinating, if now vertiginously distant, discussion—one that was clearly motivated at the time by

[1] I write at length about the journal across the totality of Eyers, *Post-Rationalism*. Crucial articles from the journal were translated and published in Hallward and Peden, *Concept and Form*. A superb open access website, featuring much of the journal in translation as well as useful synopses and concept definitions may be found at http://www.kingston.ac.uk/cahiers.

the heat of political and theoretical urgency. Instead, I will briefly summarize its stakes, before rather brutally excising a single quotation with which to begin to think through the distinct form-problems posed by Rachel Cusk's recent experiments in narrative point of view.

Jacques-Alain Miller's "Suture (Elements of a Logic of the Signifier)" appeared in February of 1966 in the first edition of the journal.[2] Miller's essay boldly extends some of Lacan's contemporary arguments into a broader manifesto for the Lacanian theory of the subject—the subject, that is, "of the signifier"—insisting on the relevance of the theory for domains beyond psychoanalysis, and most especially for the philosophy of science. If it is commonplace to ask whether psychoanalysis is a science, the *Cahiers* authors were minded instead to ask what "science," and philosophy too, would come to mean were psychoanalysis to be taken as paradigmatic of what "science" is.

Science is here understood according to its most formalizable guises, with mathematics its purest means of expression. Such an explicitly rationalist, anti-empiricist (and hyper-Cartesian!) theory of scientific knowledge arises from the tradition of French historical epistemology, epitomized by the writings of Georges Canguilhem, Alexandre Koyré, Jean Cavaillès, and others.[3] For Miller, the highly formalized procedures of the mathematized sciences, whose very self-understanding is formed by their pious refusal of the particular and subjective, are nonetheless surreptitiously reliant on the very thing, the subject, that they make a show of denying.

More particularly, he argues that the position of the zero in Fregean logic, as vanishing condition for the succession of natural numbers (1, 2, 3…), is formally equivalent to the position of the subject as it fades before but nonetheless supports, the irruption of the signifier. For Lacan, recall, the subject or self is not the vast and yet mappable rational and emotional interiority of humanist lore. Rather, it is a breach, an interruption, formally equivalent to the unconscious in psychoanalysis, one that irrupts upon the deceptive ideological continuities of the Imaginary and the Symbolic—a "constitutive exception" that is, nonetheless,

[2] Hallward and Peden, *Concept and Form*, 91–103.

[3] I cover the grounding of French anti-humanism in historical epistemology in Eyers, *Post-Rationalism*. See also Canguilhem, *Vital Rationalist*; Koyré, *Infinite Universe*; Bachelard, *Atomistic Intuitions*; Cavaillès, *Theory of Science*.

most often immediately swallowed up by that to which it is an exception. Miller in turn insists that, whatever the ideological self-image of the mathematical, physical sciences, their very existence relies on the constitutive exclusion of the subject that they nonetheless presuppose, just as the train of numbers (1, 2, 3...) is only logically sustainable if one posits a non- or negative number, a vanishing point of grounding—zero, this is to say—that then tacitly underwrites the sequence that follows.

The objections to our *Cahiers* authors are predictable enough: Miller and others are wrapping such an analogical para-logic, that of the constitutive exception, over the starker computations of Frege and company, and so they are arguing, not from formal equivalence or even more family resemblance, but from loose analogy. Alain Badiou, in his riposte to Miller, goes further. For the young Badiou, whose essay "Mark and Lack: Of the Zero" was published in the final number of the *Cahiers* in 1969,[4] it is not simply the means by which Miller makes his argument that is deficient, but rather the content of the argument as such. For Badiou, it is a fundamental misconstrual of the autonomous character of scientific knowledge to presume that it must find support in anything outside of itself.

As he writes, "[*Both*] Frege's ideological representation of his own enterprise *and* the capture of this representation in the lexicon of the Signifier, of lack and the place-of-lack, mask the pure productive essence, the process of positing through which logic, as a machine, lacks nothing it does not produce elsewhere."[5] There can be, then, no "subject" of mathematized science for the young Badiou, whether that subject is imagined within the terms of the older humanisms, with reflective interiority center stage, or psychoanalytic as recast by Lacan, the subject-as-lack, always just out of frame. From this defining moment in French high structuralism, we are presented with two mutually antagonistic attempts to redraw the relations between scientific knowledge, its various "outsides" (ideology, signification in the everyday and unconscious sense), and the subject. While in what follows, I will locate in literary form recastings of the subject that rather outstrip the sometimes arid formalism of Badiou et al., I wish to retain this emphasis on abstraction, on the hidden possibilities opened up by theoretical maneuvers that at first blush seem austerely

[4] Hallward and Peden, *Concept and Form*, 159–87.

[5] Hallward and Peden, 160.

removed from the subjects or voices that we encounter when we read literature closely.

If Badiou offers us one extreme, Miller's post-Lacanian subject offers us, not exactly a "third way," but rather a subject emergent only upon the moment of its fading; a "non-I" that occupies a liminal space, a liminality illuminative of, but not entirely sufficient to, the stunned inside-out quality of Cusk's narrative voice.

Here is Miller:

> [W]hat in Lacanian algebra is called the relation of the subject to the field of the Other (as the locus of truth) can be identified with the relation which the zero entertains with the identity of the unique as the support of truth. This relation [...] cannot be integrated into any definition of objectivity [...] What constitutes this relation as the matrix of the chain must be isolated in the implication which makes the determinant of the exclusion of the subject outside the field of the Other its representation in that field in the form of the unique, the one of distinctive unity, which is called 'unary' by Lacan.[6]

Where to start? Some key terms are in need of definition. The "field of the Other" is equivalent to what Lacan named the Symbolic, namely language, convention, law, all that is to be understood structurally—which is to say, as defined by relations rather than positive terms. Why "Other"? Because, for Miller after Lacan, we are always alienated from ourselves by virtue of our reliance on external, "other," signifiers and images to be what we are. Why does Miller insist that this "field cannot be integrated into any definition of objectivity"? For two principal reasons: first, because the field of the Other, or Symbolic, is never totalizable—there is no obvious means by which one could demarcate where it begins and where it ends. And, second, because the field is rendered inconsistent from within, so to speak, by what Miller refers to above as the "unique," the "one of distinctive unity," a signifier whose exceptionality in the field (it sits apart from the relations that give the field its illusion of self-sameness) makes of it the stand-in for the subject in the latter's necessary absence.

The reader will have noticed the similarity of this logic with that of the "constitutive exception" described above. What is novel here is

[6] Hallward and Peden, 100.

that the formative exception that allows the "field of the Other" to cohere is the subject itself, the very entity who, by stark contrast, was centered in philosophy, at least from Descartes onwards, as itself center*ing* self-consistent condition for knowledge of the very "field" to which Miller refers. It is novel, too, because that constitutively excluded subject nonetheless makes an appearance in the Symbolic from which it has been banished, by way of its errant representative, that unique isolated signifier sat at a position internally askance from its surroundings.

We are left with the overlap between two lacks or exceptions: the subject itself, that which "fades," to use Lacan's favored term, in the face of the Other, and the lack in the Other itself, represented by a "floating" signifier whose contentlessness makes it potentially emblematic of both nothing—the nothing, that is, of the subject evacuated of its interiority and eclipsed by the signifier that is its permanent representative—and anything at all. The very means by which some, Badiou for instance, moved to banish the subject entirely, namely the importation from mathematics of a purely relational *combinatoire*, here motivates the positing of a new, uncanny subject, one there where it is not, with "it" here meaning something substantial, easily definable, unproblematically locatable in space and time. To paraphrase a later Lacanian epigram, this new, uncanny not-not there subject *is* where it is not. I want to leave these brief philosophical reflections by remarking this idea of a subject that is neither that of Cartesian stability, nor that of epiphenomenon or mere ideological excrescence. Quite what that apparently new subject *is*, I would argue, is better captured in literary writing than it is in a strictly theoretical register.

2 Close Literature

Within narratology specifically, and in the practice of prose narrative more generally, one might identify any number of narrative shapes that may be said to approximate that in-between, *not*-not subject explored above in the context of French high structuralism. Instead of attempting comprehensiveness, I will discuss only one such candidate in this section, free indirect style, before showing how Cusk's sentences mark an advance on it, perversely by reversing one of its principle freedoms. The history of free indirect discourse is usually told as the opening up of narrative freedom, and yet one of the lessons of both the experimental theory of the subject of psychoanalysis discussed above, and the radically distanced narrative subject of Cusk's sentences, is that the putative shutting down of narrative possibility and choice, and the modeling of a practice of close reading that is severe rather than expansive, gives us access to narrative-subjective worlds otherwise hidden from view. In all that follows, I will think these different narrative options as much in terms of the kind of close reading they might enjoin in a reader, as in their inherent formal possibilities or features.

Why should free indirect discourse come to mind when considering models of subjectivity that move beyond conventions of interiority and exteriority, of a simplistically imagined inside and outside of subjective experience? Most obviously, because it is a narrative convention that explicitly interlaces aspects of the third person with aspects of the first-person narration. The technical definitions that are usually given rarely capture the sometimes effortlessly weightless, sometimes awkward effect of this invasion of the first-person reflection into the objective pretensions of the third person. Consider this, from the entry on the device in the *Oxford Research Encyclopedia of Literature*:

> In free indirect discourse (FID), the narrative discourse of a text incorporates the language and subjectivity of a character, including emotional coloring, deictics, judgments, and style, without an introductory attributing frame like "she thought that" and without shifts in the pronouns or the tense sequence to accord with the character's perspective. By combining the immediacy of direct quotation and the flexibility of indirect discourse, FID allows for the seamless integration of a character's thought or speech, with all of its distinctive markers, into the narratorial discourse.[7]

This summary usefully highlights the "immediacy" and "flexibility" of the style. "Immediacy" is here associated with direct quotation, or the unmediated intervention of first-person speech, while "flexibility" is associated with the ranginess of third person, with its always somewhat tendentious air of the objective. To say, however, that the style "combines" these things, while technically true, doesn't quite capture how, at least when one is primed to read for it, the use of the style in narrative may suggest first-person voice invading, even collapsing the distance of third-person narration or, perhaps more intriguingly, the opposite, how it may

[7] Gunn, "Free Indirect Discourse."

induce a sense of subjective voice itself becoming object, taking a stance outside of itself. Consider the following (to demonstrate how unexpected even the most expected or familiar instances of free indirect style, I have chosen an eminently canonical, perhaps even hackneyed example):

> Her soul, worn out by pride, was finally finding repose in Christian humility; and, luxuriating in her own frailty, Emma watched the annihilation of her own will, which would leave the path wide open to the irresistible forces of grace. There existed, therefore, greater joys beyond mere happiness, a different love transcending all others, a love without interruption or end, which would grow greater throughout eternity![8]

The key descriptors in the technical definition of free indirect style given above are "immediacy," "flexible," and "seamless." Read from a certain angle, these would seem appropriately explanatory of the quote from *Madame Bovary*. To be seamless is to be without seam, to be without a border that marks the end of one thing from the beginning of another. In this sense, the move from the third person of the first sentence, to the second, bearer of free indirect style, is indeed seamless. There is a flexibility here, a light travel between modes. On such a reading, the free indirect style would seem to free up narrative voice, pluralizing it to a certain degree, while nonetheless confronting rather than covering over the inherent ambivalences of voice, the fact that from one angle of approach a subject looks like an object, and vice versa. The Flaubert that speaks for Emma's life does so, not from an Archimedean point of objective security, but neither entirely immanently, through the marked-off language of her own thoughts or speech; his voice is half-submerged, awkwardly intercalated, in the scene that his voice seeks to describe, and thus occupies a liminal position that it would be hard to diagram or stabilize in advance. And so what might at first blush have seemed like an unproblematic opening up of possibilities takes on a subtly darker hue, for there is nothing especially certain or secure in this new freedom. What might have seemed to grant less artificial access to a character's thoughts in fact multiplies our uncertainties as to where each voice—the narrator, and the narrated—is to be situated.

[8] Flaubert, *Madame Bovary*,189.

We are dealing here with something of a dialectic of freedom and unfreedom, of the apparent relaxation of limits, and their stark reimposition. It is apposite, then, that the quote from Flaubert above precisely concerns Emma's yielding to weakness, perhaps even the blurring of the outline of her individuality, it is smudging into the divine ambient surrounds of grace. And yet, this becoming-liquid of Emma is presented, not through one long sentence, say, but rather through two sentences, conventionally separated by a period. Indeed, the two narrative techniques are walled off from one another, even as the combination of third and first person is used to evoke the gradual indistinction of Emma from something divine that is in excess of her. There would seem to be a useful mismatch of form and content here, or rather a dance between different formal and thematic resonances that never quite resolves: two narrative devices that are presented in distinct separation, side by side, the combination nonetheless meant to induce a sliding of one voice into and through another; a character's epiphany carried out by means of a certain dissolving of distinctiveness, the episode shoring up all the more our sense of that character's inner life.

I mentioned above the possibility that free indirect style, rather than passively combining the "immediacy" of first-person speech with the "flexibility" of third-person narration, might instead confer on character subjectivity something of a rigidifying objectivity, a neutrality or passivity, a stalled outwardness, that would seem to belie any hope that the technique might give us further entrance to interiority. This may be one effect of the removal of markers indicating that it is indeed a distinctive character's speech that we are reading, and it is surely only one moment in that aforementioned dance of formal and thematic possibilities, of tentative freedoms (the freeing up narrative voice to move between registers, Emma's subjectivity melting into grace) and productive constrictions (our sense of a character fastened by a newly available clarity and distinctness all her own). And yet it is worth emphasizing that all of this is made possible by the *occlusion* of those deictic markers that usually specify, clarify, make firmly available to us, the difference between one voice—that of the narrator—and another, that of a character.

We have returned, it would seem, to the dilemmas raised by Jacques-Alain Miller, after Lacan. There, as here, a new vision of the subject, or subjects, comes into view, only upon the "eclipse" of its or their agency, its or their fading in the face of language (or the Other) per se, with its limitless tricks. There, as here, there is not one voice in question, but at least two: that of the subject of the unconscious and that of the obscuring and yet enabling Other, in the psychoanalytic instance; here, the ostensibly objective third-person narrator, and the quietly and yet determinedly intercalated speech of Emma, neither quite subject nor object; and yet a third position seems also legible, a position that seems too impassive to quite count as a voice or subjective position at all. Flaubert marks this emergence of a third scene, so to speak, with the irony that was his forte—with an exclamation point, this is to say, the typographic mark least suited, and so with a rather blunt irony *most* suited, to the diaphanous result of his scrambling of form and theme, subject and object, direct and indirect. This is the generalized narrative indistinctiveness I mentioned above, and this is nothing but the point of view of the reader herself: impassive, because for all the complex narrative machinery of free indirect style, the reader is deposited on a rather neutral plane, unencumbered of the need to jump effortfully from narrator to character, from interior to exterior. The close reader of free indirect style is a rather benumbed spectator, languidly leaving and arriving at quietly announced shifts in perspective—a passive receptacle.

3 Rachel Cusk's Sentences

Where the theoretical experiments of Miller, Lacan, et al. provides a skeletal framework for thinking new figures of subjectivity, the immersion of those figures in narrative makes a compelling case for the experimental capacities of literature itself. One of the standard criticisms made of the high structuralism that Miller and his cohort represented is that it couldn't think historicity; that, in its rush to reject Hegelian teleologies, it neglected to articulate structure and historical time. This is a hasty judgment indeed, and it doesn't hold up upon closer inspection; but we would nonetheless do well at this juncture to address the problem of historical time head-on.

Might literature be capable of producing historical logics all of its own? How might these be bound up with the kind of close reading that particular literary forms elicit? It is here that Rachel Cusk's extraordinary novel *Outline* will allow us both to consolidate the insights thus far garnered from theoretical psychoanalysis and free indirect style, while moving some way beyond them. To begin, let me recapitulate the curious mode of readership that, I claimed in the previous section, is one potential outcome of free indirect style's production of an impassive third voice: namely, the placing of the reader within a languorous movement between voices, without the need ever quite to acknowledge the differences between them. There is a neutrality to free indirect style, one related, I would argue, to the preponderance of abstraction that defined the high structuralists' attempts to break beyond Cartesian limits.

There are something notable here about the productive effects of apparently neutralized, withdrawn or especially abstract structures or uses of language. These seem especially to accompany the most fertile attempts, in philosophy and literature both, to produce new figurations of the subject at least removed from, if not entirely free of, the legacy of foundationalist accounts of selfhood. How to relate these experiments to their historical situation? Must these experiments remain ahistorical, and if not, what mode of historicization do they permit? How might that mode relate to the question of close reading?

To get a grip on these questions, I will turn to a fairly lengthy quotation from near the beginning of Rachel Cusk's 2014 novel *Outline*. Because it is impossible to get a proper sense of Cusk's innovations in a short, circumscribed excerpt, I will use ellipses in what follows in order to get as much of Cusk's technique as possible in view:

> It was nearly thirty years since his first marriage ended, and the further he got from that life, the more real it became to him. Or not real exactly, he said—what had happened since had been real enough. The word he was looking for was authentic: his first marriage had been authentic in a way that nothing ever had again. The older he got, the more it represented to him a kind of home, a place to which he yearned to return... All the same, it seemed to him now that that life had been lived almost unconsciously, that he had been lost in it, absorbed in it, as you can be absorbed in a book... Never again since had he been able to absorb himself; never again had he been able to believe in that way... Whatever it was, he and his wife had built things that had flourished, had together expanded the sum of what they were and what they had; life had responded willingly to them, had treated them abundantly, and this—he now saw—was what had given him the confidence to break it all, break it with what now seemed to him to be an extraordinary casualness, because he thought there would be more.
>
> More what? I asked.
>
> "More—life," he said, opening his hands in a gesture of receipt. "And more affection," he added, after a pause. "I wanted more affection."[9]

[9] Cusk, *Outline*, 15–16.

There is a meta-literary commentary here that ghosts the text: a symptomatically unassuming meta-reflection, this is to say, one tightly wedded to the text upon which it comments. This commentary notes the ebbing and flowing of proximity and distance, but it ultimately comes down repeatedly on the *side* of distance, so to speak; of an ontological numbness that might well convert, at a slight shift in one's angle of approach, to something as profound as an historical diagnosis—in prose, nonetheless, that ostentatiously shrinks from the loud import of such a thing. Notice, for instance, the repeated references to distance, to absorption, to unconsciousness: the very first line of the above quotation refers to a marriage that appears more real the more the character in question is removed from it.

The utilitarian clip of the prose, at one with its clinical precision, enforces this sense of removal all the more, in a manner significantly distinct, I would argue, from the familiar post-Hemingway style of reduction that defines many a contemporary Anglophone middlebrow novel. The quote is consistent with the novel as a whole, in that the narrator seems subsumed, lost, within the stories of others, in this case that of a man she has sat next to on an airplane. Cusk has referred in interviews to her narrator as a blank, as someone whose life circumstances have left her hollow, receptive only to what comes at her from outside herself.[10] But for our purposes, I think it possible to glean the outline (fortuitously the title of the novel) of a new way of thinking the subject, entirely immanent to Cusk's experiments in narrative form. If, for Miller after Lacan, the subject fades in the face of the Other that is its only support, Cusk's narrative non-I would similarly seem immersed entirely in its outside.

Consider, for instance, how Cusk, in the above quote, marks off the speech of the man speaking to the narrator but leaves the narrator's speech without quotation marks. How might we compare this strategy to free indirect style, analyzed above? In uses of the latter, the thoughts or speech of another character intrude upon that of the narrator, such that the two subjectivities are momentarily mixed. I have commented above on the manner in which this apparent relaxation of character difference may also result in a paradoxical resolidification of the lines between characters. In Cusk's prose, I would suggest, the removal of quotation marks from the speech of the narrator effects something like a reversal of this

[10] Thurman, "Cusk Gut-Renovates the Novel."

storied narrative trick. For, instead of allowing the voice of a second character to situate itself serenely within the space of the narrative voice, it is Cusk's non-I that moves beyond its bounds, by only ever being made present, so to speak, by the thoughts and actions of others. And yet, even as it does so, one never gets the sense of this self having entirely dissolved *into* its surrounds. To the contrary, it is always clear that the stories told to the narrator are told by characters distinct from that narrator; indeed, Cusk is at pains to emphasize the yawning gap between the endless self-reflection, the limitless interior self-inspection, of the people the nameless narrator meets, and that narrator's having absolutely no comparable inner life of her own.

Indeed, it is this extraordinary evacuation of interiority from a narrative "I" that nonetheless retains its sense of distinctiveness, its difference from the other characters that populate the novel, that is Cusk's real coup, and that prompts my calling this new prose subject the "non-I": just as Lacan coined the term "non-all" to designate a set that is neither closed nor entirely without boundaries, so Cusks' non-I is neither a full-blown repudiation of the subject (think of the young Badiou's position, discussed above), nor a subject with inner depths. Rather, Cusk's narrative subject appears to be both entirely immersed outside of itself, insofar as it appears mostly as a passive receptacle for the stories of others (signaled again by the lack of quotation marks around its speech), and entirely abstracted from the world, entirely other to, absolutely irreducible to, the characters she meets.

The fading of the subject that Lacan repeatedly referenced is here augmented by the idea of an "I" that is somehow, simultaneously, entirely moved outside its own bounds, and entirely withdrawn: anonymously lacking, and yet everywhere all at once. It is noteworthy that Cusk achieves this paradoxical sense of distinctiveness for her "I" in a manner directly opposed to the usual mechanics of first-person narration, whereby a character is rendered distinct through the presentation of an inner life; here, it is the very absence of such a life that makes the novel's non-I so perspicuous. Notable, too, and as I have already had cause to mention, is the further difference here from that older species of narrative liminality analyzed above, free indirect style; if the latter has been deemed appropriate to its historical moment of emergence, negotiating between the newly privatized "individual" and the latter's putatively objective, social responsibilities as citizen (this being Franco Moretti's argument; see note 12 below), then perhaps Cusk's ambient subject, her an-aesthetic, might tell us something about the very times in which we now live, times that often seem to have made "history," in its bold, nineteenth century, capitalizable sense of recordable progress, all but impossible.

Cusk, then, in having us think differently how we might read for history and subjectivity both, would have us read for absence, for the outline of a subject whose not quite being there is the surest testament to its importance, and for a logic of historical time that is similarly pronounced in its lack. I am tempted, then, to mark this as the ethic of *close reading* that Cusk's narrative practice implicitly proposes. Such an ethic would have us read for what is missing from contemporary writing and indeed from contemporary life, to note the failings or the trailing away of durable public selves, but also to mark a pervasive lack of a sense of historicity itself, the partial incapacity of contemporary events, at least in the rich North, to lend themselves to long-term inscription.

If, in the high theory of Jacques-Alain Miller and Lacan, the subject's lack is in part what makes it a quasi-transcendental entity to some degree absent from the particularities of historical time, it is, I think, in the present-absence of Cusk's non-I that a certain position on history, on the knowability of the present, takes hold. Throughout *Outline*, this is to say, one gets the impression of history almost having given up on itself, just as its characters immured in the glazed indifferences and peturbabilites of high capitalism have rather given up on it. While Cusk's non-I travels to Greece, teaches students creative writing, and so on, the inverted nature of the subject that does these things—its inability to record itself, to know itself, to make durable its presence in the world—allegorizes a broader numbness, a broader inability to make of experience something memorable, memorizable, inscribable, something definitively oriented toward a sharable future.

We are past due to another quote from the book; following on not far from where the previous quote left off, the following describes the scene in the airplane from the narrator's perspective:

> The plane seemed stilled, almost motionless; there was so little interface between inside and outside, so little friction, that it was hard to believe we were moving forward. The electric light, with the absolute darkness outside, made people look very fleshly and real, their detail so unmediated, so impersonal, so infinite. Each time the man with the baby passed I saw the network of creases in his shorts, his freckled arms covered in coarse reddish fur, the pale, mounded skin of his mid-riff where his T-shirt had

> ridden up, and the tender wrinkled feet of the baby on his shoulder, the little hunched back, the soft head with its primitive whorl of hair.[11]

If our previous quote described a muted drama of proximity and distance, with distance the overriding logic of the passage, then here it is the push and pull of abstraction and immediacy, of the particular and the general, that comes into focus. The particular, even the "fleshly," is amply represented by the close-up details of bodily hair, of the creases in skin, and so on. But these attain their distinctiveness, their sharpness of focus, only because of the broader abstraction, even impassivity, of the scene. Even as the passage begins with some clear, particular details—people reading, sleeping, talking—they are encased within a more general miasma of stillness, of an apparent lack of movement: "there was so little interface between inside and outside, so little friction, that it was hard to believe we were moving forward."

For Franco Moretti, recall, free indirect style in the nineteenth century served as precisely an interface, a formal literary hinge between inside and outside, between privatized individual freedom and social incorporation—one oiled, one might speculate, by the friction that it both tried to resolve and that, in so doing, it helped to preserve.[12] What is such a hinge or interface, I would ask, but the assumed possibility of the ongoingness of historical time itself, which is to say a sustained belief in the unrolling permanence of history, the faith that one might always inscribe where one is, and where one might come to be. Just as there is no friction in Cusk's airplane, no discernible interface between inside and outside, so there is no historical mediation that might make the experiences of the novel anything other than particulars to be noted and moved on from.

In Cusk's novel, this to say, no lever between the general and particular exists. Its absence is registered in the icily precise scenes of description, such as that of the airplane above. There, general and particular parallel one another without resolution, such that incommensurable properties (stillness, movement, fleshly detail, generalized impassivity) must simply coexist. And it is registered, too, in the curious mechanics of the narrative voice itself, which is piercingly exact in its absorption and accounting of its surroundings, while nonetheless always never less than an absence, a

[11] Cusk, *Outline*, 16–17.

[12] Moretti, *Bourgeois*, 96.

subjective cipher for, among other things, history's logics of collectivity having appeared to have dropped entirely out of the frame.

Cusk's narrator's intensity of sensory reception is, to conclude, a kind of reading, and, as I have argued, that receptivity is a constituent part of a novel para-theory of the literary subject, what I am calling the "non-I." *Outline* would have us to scan the present for its missing pieces, always with the suspicion that the most meaningful missing piece might be ourselves, inhabitants of protracted, history-scrambling crises for whom non-knowledge, especially of our own selves, may be just as consequential, for better or worse, as positive knowledge per se. All of this places us at a useful distance from both the form-negating contextualist historicisms that are currently hegemonic in literary studies, and from any nostalgic aestheticism that would be too enamored of its texts' bejeweled interiors to say much about our baleful present.

References

Bachelard, Gaston. *Atomistic Intuitions: An Essay on Classification*. Translated by Roch C. Smith. Albany, NY: SUNY Press, 2018.

Canguilhem, Georges. *A Vital Rationalist: Selected Writings from Georges Canguilhem*. Edited by François Delaporte. Translated by Arthur Goldhammer. New York: Zone Books, 1994.

Cavaillès, Jean. *On Logic and the Theory of Science*. Translated by Knox Peden. London: Urbanomic, forthcoming.

Cusk, Rachel. *Outline*. New York: Farrar, Straus and Giroux, 2014.

Eyers, Tom. *Post-Rationalism: Psychoanalysis, Epistemology, and Marxism in Post-War France*. London: Bloomsbury, 2013.

Flaubert, Gustave. *Madame Bovary: Provincial Manners*. Translated by Margaret Mauldon. Oxford: University Press, 2004.

Gunn, Daniel P. "Free Indirect Discourse." *Oxford Research Encyclopedia of Literature*. June 25, 2019. https://oxfordre.com/literature/view/10.1093/acrefore/9780190201098.001.0001/acrefore-9780190201098-e-1020.

Hallward, Peter, and Knox Peden, eds. *Concept and Form*. Vol. 1, *Selections from the "Cahiers pour l'Analyse."* London: Verso, 2012.

Koyré, Alexandre. *From the Closed World to the Infinite Universe*. Baltimore: Johns Hopkins Press, 1957.

Moretti, Franco. *The Bourgeois: Between History and Literature*. London: Verso, 2013.

Thurman, Judith. "Rachel Cusk Gut-Renovates the Novel." *New Yorker*. August 7 and 14, 2017. https://www.newyorker.com/magazine/2017/08/07/rachel-cusk-gut-renovates-the-novel.

CHAPTER 13

Ecocide and Objectivity: Literary Thinking in *How the Dead Dream*

Anna Kornbluh

A calamitous near future, already present for many, is wrenching art, literature, and the ways we talk about them. The more profound the emergency and urgency, the tighter the vise vitiating representation. Defictionalization, documentarism, expressivism, and a torqued "realism" appear as the available avenues for responsible representation. The planet is on fire, the accelerant monopolized and the burns socialized; art can be an extinguisher if only it slides into Instant Messages. Such conscriptions of art and literature as lovely adornment of ineffectual facts or as humanization of large-scale far-off problems are ubiquitous and beguiling, with creatives and critics alike beating the drum for more personalizing human-interest angles, more literalist disaster stories, more realistic climate depiction. Exigency declarations are de rigueur opening salvos for every humanities think piece, every critical theory monograph, and they are now becoming prescriptions for aesthetic production.

A. Kornbluh (✉)
University of Illinois, Chicago, IL, USA
e-mail: kornbluh@uic.edu

A. Sridhar et al. (eds.), *The Work of Reading*,
https://doi.org/10.1007/978-3-030-71139-9_13

Within this matrix of immediacy, directly presenting crisis and catastrophe is essential work. But what if literature is not employee of the month? Its qualifications slacken through indirection and tropes, defamiliarization and displacement, imaginativeness and mediation. It is a formal mode for syntheses, but not a communicative mode for propositions. If an edited collection on the ongoing matter of close reading could expectably incant these singularities and evanescences, this essay aims at something rather different: articulating literature's specific *objectivity*, the conceptual energies activated by its mediacy. Especially on the most pressing crisis—that of the ecocide—this mediacy, this distance from instrumentalism and resistance to extractive logics, this quality of being composed rather than expressed, this intervening in the ordinary, constitutes an exceptionally crucial competency.

Blossoming literary ecocriticism regularly underrates this talent for objectivity, enunciating instead more and more poignant calls for literalism. Critics like Amitav Ghosh lament that climate fiction has more often taken the particular shape of science fiction than of brutal mimesis, charging fiction writers with depicting the present or very near future in known settings.[1] Film scholars, newspaper critics, and even Hollywood producers now call for "more realistic" [2] representation, entreating the industry to directly feature "a successful transformation of society"[3] or effective acts for individuals, so as to surpass dystopia paralysis. "Realism" of the sort that volubly elaborates facts while "touch(ing) people's hearts"[4] appears now in our critical gaze as the very best that art can do.[5] But literature affords more than the prettification of science or subjectification of the facts—it is the composition of new, unusual abstractions; the thickening and calibrating of thinking; the vectoring of our senses beyond the merely sensible. Such objectivity is arguably an even greater resource for the present than the various subjectivisms and literalisms activated by the demands for immediacy.

"Objectivity" in this sense means the quality of independence from individual perception or personal feeling; the quality of relating to the

[1] See Ghosh, *Great Derangement*.

[2] Ryzik, "Movies about Climate Change."

[3] Buckley, "Scared of Climate Change."

[4] Ryzik, "Movies about Climate Change."

[5] This mimetic, referential, indicative conception does not exhaust realism.

object rather than the subject. Although literary critics—to say nothing of feminist epistemologists or historians of science—instinctually question such a divide and its implied differentiation between the arts and sciences, the regular mode of this questioning involves exposing the constructedness and unavailability of objectivity, its latent subjectivity.[6] It should, however, be possible to flip the question—to pursue the latent objectivity in the putatively subjective knowledge domains. Such at least was the wager of Theodor Adorno, who prized the internal necessity of an artwork's form as an aesthetic modality of objectivity. For Adorno intrinsic unity in good works actuates the object's own objectivity, a specifically intellective agency: "art is rationality which criticizes rationality without withdrawing from it."[7] Taking inspiration from Adorno, what I want to pinpoint with "objectivity" in these pages is a capacity for conceptuality, a faculty for synthesis, which runs perpendicular to, but also parallels, the quantitative or the empirical, the phenomenal and the embodied. Literature is capable of thinking, not only of eliciting feeling or immediately expressing the personal or contextual. Literary language exercises mediacy, soliciting methods attuned to mediation rather than fixated on immediate uptake in affect or data. We critics have widely accepted these two poles, championing quantification or empathogenesis as our best justifications in the time of post-disciplinarity and decommissioned education, of private knowledge and self-expression. But the objectivity of the literary itself opens a different avenue. Literature's mediacy and its intrinsic abstractions model the kinds of imaginative projection integral for responding to the dismantled university, social inequality, and climate catastrophe. We need literary objectivity if there is to be any hope of imagining better spaces and composing better states, of synthesizing different values and instituting infrastructure more conducive to human flourishing.

While these prospects of literary utopianism, literary world building, and literary conceptuality have always been modern, they look differently by the dusking light of the Anthropocene. Now the facts amass and the conceptual complexities swell: How do humans fathom their own

[6] In their book *Objectivity*, note both that "Objectivity has a history" and that "the history of scientific objectivity is surprisingly short. It first emerged in the mid-nineteenth century" (27). See also Donna Haraway's exploration of the pitfalls of constructedness in Haraway, "Situated Knowledges."

[7] Adorno, *Aesthetic Theory*, 55.

extinction? How do we cognize the murder of the ecosphere? What has caused it and what will obtain after? An enormity of interrelated factors, an unrepresentable totality with some nonetheless representable intensive tendencies: profit-maximization, extractivist ideology, inattention to the future. To begin to think of literary contributions to addressing ecocide, we might start at these biggest registers: literature, as the making of something more than the phenomenal world, is inherently speculative in ways that attune it to futurity; literary language, in its estrangement from ordinary language, harkens value systems other than the most instrumental or the most efficacious extraction; literary counterfactuals, fictional worlds, alternate signifiers provide infusions that check extractivism. Such interjections afforded by the literary in principle must of course be enacted in specific works and judged in specific readings, but keeping the general potential in mind can expand the ways we appreciate the contributions of literature and art beyond the literalist options.

Mediacy is the renewable resource that literature offers our resource crisis. This promise has been impressively indicated by Nathan Hensley and Philip Steer in their introductory essay "Ecological Formalism," which sets aspirations for their edited volume by arguing for the coordinating, synthetic function of literary form, practicing the linkages among components of a system or temporal locations in history that are necessary for fathoming ecological destruction. In their account of the power of the novel specifically, the form seems to name a capacity *for* ecology, form-as-ecology: novels construct organized, structured, dialectical situations, grafting personal to social, local to global, past to present, quotidian to systemic. This ecological thinking resplendent in the form supersedes referential or thematic ecological content. Instead of reading for content then, literary critics inclined to ecological questions ought to read for form. In a crisis wrought of extractivism, it would be good if our critical methods were not themselves extractive, mining thematic ore from broader ecosystems, seizing on stray references in the margins. Rather, our specific skill as literary critics, and the specific force that literary works tender in social cataclysm, is an interjective making, the composing of thoughts, the mediacy of formalization.

What are the literary critical processes—and the apt literary objects—that can fulfill these aspirations? In pursuit of this ecological form, this essay takes up a novel that works outside the literalist paradigm, seeding its thought with neither the subjectivization of environmental degradation, nor with the prime coordinates of plausible contemporary atmospheric experience, but with the particles of past worlding that objectively precipitate our present ecocide. Lydia Millet's *How the Dead Dream* (2008) conjures early 1990s Los Angeles as an epicenter of automobile fetishism, real estate speculation, animal cruelty, and social alienation, and weaves these relations together through a third person narration centered loosely on an obtuse, repugnant man. Refusing personalization and circumventing direct reference to climate crises, the novel resounds its different formal components of setting, narration, and figure into a devastating representation of resource recklessness and extinction.

Its shard-like lyrical prose and short total span compress these many aspects of environment and relationality into a literary thought that reckons with the truth of the irrevocable: a few decades ago, the American mania for oil-propelled land development reached a point of no return, that now imperils animals and humans. The peril is unevenly distributed but also random; man-made human extinction is the ultimate untimely death. *How the Dead Dream* articulates this concept of the causes and effects of climate crisis without referential dystopian scenes of displacement, without carbon facts, without words like "atmosphere," "greenhouse," or "fossil fuel," and without any likable victims courting our identification. It uses the concatenation of novelistic form to objectivize this concept, to activate it figuratively and mediately rather than iteratively and immediately. This is how literature thinks. Close reading embraces this thinking, asking of literature not literalism but mediacy, and giving in return not extracted direct messages of immediate salience, but affirmative regard for the constructions of alternative conceptuality.

Objectivity functions as a name for the aesthetic and conceptual project of *How the Dead Dream* in three ways that I will explore here. One, an intensified, problematized evocation of setting. Two, an impersonal "anti-protagonist" presented in third-person narration. Three, an elliptical narrative mode including constant elisions, eddying figures, and an ambiguous ending. In each of these vectors, the novel works to actuate dimensions other than the immediate, the personal, the literal. And the multidimensional object formed by the conjuncture of the vectors actuates the dialectic that cognizing ecocide and synthesizing alternative modes of production in the ecocorpse requires medicacy, impersonality, and figuration. Reified and habitual ways of seeing will not enable our response to the enormity of climate destruction. Prevailing authentications of literature as self-writing and autofiction will not tap the creative objectivity that must fuel our making. The imagined communities, extraordinary logics, defamiliarized signifiers, and alternate universes in literature open portals to different dispensations. Literary critical enterprises in the environmental humanities predicated on offering anything less short sell the crisis and the vivifying, vital role of imagination, clever synthesis, and originative form for outpacing technocratic solutions and extractive paradigms.

If literary studies do not generally explore objectivity, this is no doubt because subjectivity has long been the celebrated epistemic virtue of both literature and literary study. On the side of the work, we find elaborations of the author's intent, of the specific refraction of specific social context, of the unparaphraseable, of the singularity of the literary event, of the resistance to theory, of the right to represent, of negligible sample size. On the side of the reader, we find reader response, affect theory, the right to recognition, MRIs, the passion of the critic, and the sympathy industrial complex. Across these disparate methods and movements in literary study, the field is determined by its unrestricted, roving, catholic approach to itself. Thus, some critics argue that epistemic pluralism, while grounds for frequent disagreements, is what makes literary study important, and others argue that the subjective basis of the discipline has enabled the public at large to believe they simply don't need the kind of knowledge we offer. Whether or not one believes it is possible to produce a coherent account of our method and our object, the fact of the debate thereupon contributes to the positioning of our field as subjective, not subject to syntheses, context-dependent (with larger political, economic, and cultural forces driving the intellectual trends and methodological innovations, rather than the core object or consistent discipline). Our findings are not replicable.

This methodological subjectivism entails of course the frequent thesis that literature itself does not exist. There are genres but not forms, there are institutions but not literariness, there are specific works but not a general category. Read and unread texts are equally promising for the scholar; manuscripts and journals and letters, to say nothing of train schedules and city records and magazine advertisements, all warrant consideration in interpreting a text; the written word dating before the invention of disciplines or the rise of fiction is as ripe for analysis as Netflix original content or Instagram poetry. We understand texts as expressions of an author's subjectivity, characters as having a right to be represented by those who share their social location, and the function of literary creation to be empathogenesis.

Often literary critics connect this emphatic sense of the subjective and the singular to ethical and political positions. Following the lead of our objects, we understand our own knowledge as situated, constructed, and ephemeral. We understand the force of our cumulative knowledge as nuancing, qualifying, hybridizing, and de-reifying, moving against broader socioeconomic forces of abstraction and reification and broader epistemic tendencies of generalization and quantification. The task of the critic, we so frequently argue, is to linger with the fleeting, to cow before the sublime, to host an encounter, to resound intimations. Aesthetic judgment has long ago been forsworn as elitist, so our expertise should not culminate in it. We even undermine the hard-won authority of our own interpretations with constant declarations that literature is inexhaustible and will always court new alternative elaborations.

If this sketch of the contours of overarching notions in literary critical method and literary reception convincingly suggests the pervasiveness of subjectivist orientations and outcomes, it perhaps becomes clear why it is counterintuitive to think of literary study as trafficking in the objective. While this essay does not want to argue for objective method (since the computational turn has culminated that impulse), it does want to argue for the objectivity of the literary. Literary texts compose ideas in nonpropositional fashion. The specific mode of the novel is to produce this composing through the interrelation of different formal registers: setting resounding plot, point of view reinforcing figure, characterization repeating temporality. Novels implicitly pose the question of how their many pieces fit together, and this fabricated whole is a projection of the integral world they precipitate.

1 Part One

How the Dead Dream channels heightened energy into its craft of setting, inverting normal ratios of background–foreground and ordinary unadorned surveys of property. Hyper-attunement to and figurative description of landscapes, roadways, locations, buildings, windows, doors, design materials, blueprints, gardens, staircases, forests, parks, yards anchors the narrative, which also curiously suspends colloquial identity. For some time, no known setting is wholly named, even as a continuous movement between interior and exterior divines an interpenetration between construction and consumption, endeavor and environment, bespeaking anthropocenic earth writing in another tongue. The novel's first sentence refers to an American president but no more specific location is given, until after around twenty pages, when the partially named protagonist (known only by an initial, T.) goes to college in "North Carolina"; eventually it is implied that his home town is on the east coast (of his mother the narrator relays: "She had grown up in a southern climate and the winters were long in Connecticut"[8]), though the banal fact in an independent clause is rather detached as a location. Both of these are states without cities. Eventually T. moves to Santa Monica, the independent municipality on the Los Angeles County coast, and the momentum of the plot takes off once the terrain of southern California becomes activated as the environmental domain. Though most iconic of Hollywood celebrities and the hegemonic cultural matrix, Los Angeles less directly but still viscerally evokes the capital of cars, the westward frontier, and the territory of artificial irrigation, a mirage of habitability in a superhighway desert. Later, an unspecified Central American country trafficking in many languages becomes the site of a resort development, of a surprise storm, and of the novel's ambiguous ending.

Within its diffuse environmental scope, the novel also precipitates a kind of historical uncertainty, a plotted temporal axis to complement its obscure spatial one. The events take place before cell phones, but that absence is the only clue for the first quarter of the book. Neither politicians ("the faces on the small screen were interchangeable") nor wars are named (53); branded technology, like the Mercedes S-Class that is T.'s beloved car in Santa Monica, puts the action after 1972 but not more pinpointed than that. Only a full third of the way through the book, when T.'s mother is convalescing after a stroke, does a nurse query ("can you tell me what year it is?"), revealing "1990" as an unconfirmed answer (68). The deferred establishment of time suggests a bidirectional relationship to the origin of the story—on the one hand, consistently anytime after 1972s oil crisis and the end of Bretton Woods, the American capitalist leadership class made catastrophic energy decisions leading to twenty-first-century ruin; on the other hand, the early 1990s specifically accelerate those decisions in individual consumer activity (desert homes, SUVs, personal debt). Coupled with the eccentric occlusions of

[8] *How the Dead Dream*, 19. Hereafter cited parenthetically in text.

T's familial origins (his mother in an emotional and cognitive fog, his father disappearing and reappearing as queer), the novel asserts a probing, suspended relation to origins and causes, a managed confusion as to our atmospheric coordinates. How did we get here, and how can we get clear? These probing questions of orientation and origin, of destination and destiny, of the present and its causes, are aroused by the book's figurative system, and accretively answered in its ultimate figurative fusions.

2 Part Two

The uncertainty of time and even space is redoubled in the impersonal tenor of the narration, an aesthetic engineered not only by the ambivalent and exteriorized relation to the problematic protagonist but also by free indirect discourse. Imparting a figure for its own approach, a moment of transition from T.'s attributed mentation to the generalized abstraction of free indirect discourse intones: "a car interior should be smooth and well-ordered, not festooned with hopeful signals of the driver's personality" (89). T. emits little identificatory appeal and the narrative purveys little characterological depth, casting instead a generic type, ubiquitous, normal, indicative. T. is an agent of destruction of the planet, but not out of personal malice, just out of business as usual. He wants to leave a mark on the world, and like all the capitalists of the great acceleration, he appraises that mark in economic rather than ecological terms: "It wasn't that he needed to be well-known—he would be happy to be the gray eminence behind a publicly traded logo—more that he wanted to have a hand in the revolutions of the market itself, in the ebb and the flow" (31). He wants—and even the wanting is not a personal failing but an impersonal drive for ease. The generic and flawed protagonist refigures the uncertain and accentuated setting: what matters in this book is not the precious person, but the environment he has had a hand in casually destroying for future dispersed persons unknown.

The novel's opening quickly roots T.'s representativeness in his political economic drives, and wastes no time telegraphing that its focal character is no hero. The first sentence conjures a subject of indeterminate age and no proper name, with a puerile affection for genocide: "His first idol was Andrew Jackson." As the opening unfolds, the "his" becomes a "he" who attends school but with few geopolitical coordinates; his mother is minimally contoured as "the sole Catholic" on his block and eventually he comes to be referred to as "T." (with no referent for the abbreviation). A monster without a name, his only affections evidently for dollars and cents and ever foxier means to amass them, T. is an intriguing focal point busy with extortions, thefts, and schemes, underneath which rests only a blank of the personal; "it was crucial, he believed, to learn which aspects of his character to make available to sight and which to keep hidden" (15). A statement indeed of the novel's own characterization strategy, this studied partial perspective propels the action indifferently to identifications of or with its own protagonist. Riveting representations of sensitive environments and marauding men need not hinge on subjective attachments.

The first very large development project T. undertakes illustrates the novel's framing of the impersonal quality of his endeavors:

> In the desert subdivisions would spread…in the distance homeowners in the settlement would be able to make out in the night sky the hulking shape of the Panamint mountains, the lights of the naval base winking beneath.
>
> And in the morning, as the sun rose to the east over the national monument, automated sprinklers would come on and begin their twitching rotations, misting the putting greens and the fairways and the sculpted oases of red-and-yellow birds of paradise and palm, bringing songbirds out of nowhere to perch in the mesquite and palo verde trees lining the courses.
>
> Hundreds of units were already presold.
>
> […]
>
> Was it not a decent way for life to end, in the peace of all that slowness? That he would not wish for an end like that himself was irrelevant. The buyers were not him.
>
> Never pretend to know better, had been the first lesson of real estate. His own preferences were only a private luxury. (60–61)

This sequence does not reveal what end he would wish, what his own preferences entail. Instead it shuttles between a conditional and a present, constructing in the current timeline of the future visions. Such shuttling is an exercise in ecologic: appreciating the ramifications in the future of the projects in the present. Because it is housing rather than commercial properties that T. develops, from his first minor transaction to his first huge venture, these passages also link the elementary relations of dwelling to the problematic enterprises of desert irrigation, asphalt composition, and transportation infrastructure. Humans unquestionably need places to live, but at what scale, of what material, to what ends?

As the impersonal narration progresses, it frequently pivots, at passages of potential personal pique, into second-person pronouns, transmuting back into generic implication. When, for instance, T. has recently had a nauseating encounter with a customer in one of his developments demanding to pave over desert plants with asphalt, for ease of not having to turn the steering wheel when parking, the revulsion inspires shameful revelations of his and our own, species-generic, similarity:

> He had never, he realized one night, been away from a road before, never in his whole life been out of sight of pavement [...] What place would that be, a whole world without roads. It was a panicking thought. A world without roads! He would go nowhere in such a place. He would be trapped where he was, he would have lived out his life only where he was born.
>
> And the world outside the roads was not straight or smooth [...] it was whirlpools and washes of soil and the mass of the clouds, dispersing into each other and leveling distinctions. It was trying to invade him and he should be alarmed. He was in danger. What you needed more than anything, for the purposes of ambition, was certainty, was a belief that the rest of being, the entirety of the cosmos, should not be allowed to penetrate and divert you from the causes—the chief and primary cause, which was, clearly, yourself. (130)

T.'s deep thoughts are slashed as little other than self-promotion, social climbing that existentially defines a group smaller than the species but larger than an individual: the subset of wealthy, powerful, oblivious humans who have precipitated its extinction.

Aptly, reflections on the land and animals, rather than on human failings or human suffering, anchor this novel's few telegraphic statements on climate crisis. Ledgers of degradation ensue not personally but interspeciesly: upon learning that regulators will require one of his developments to set-aside "a mitigation" (a small plot of land to maintain a habitat for a rare rat species), T.'s thoughts again objectivize themselves in free indirect: "Cities were being built, built up into the sky, battlements of convenience and utopias of consumption—the momentum of empire he had always cherished. But under their foundations the crust of the earth seemed to be shifting and loosening, falling away and curving under itself" (125).

The interaction of these two dynamics we've thus far explored—intensified setting and impersonality—generates much of the objectivity effect. Emotional states are presented not in vocabulary of the interior, but through exteriority. For example, when T. is grieving the sudden death of a girlfriend, his affective state is less described than his fluctuating attunement to his environment.

> He worked in order to keep up the pace and the focus, worked hard and steadily, and gradually the usual texture of rooms crept back - rooms, buildings, streets and the sky. In the office he watched as elements of the lobby lost their alien particularity. Turning to background again were the file cabinet, the phone, the television with ticker tape running across the bottom. In his own office was a relief map of the Mojave project; he put his hands on the hollow ridges of the mountain and felt the plastic peaks digging into his palms" (100).

Notably, the state of grief is figured here not as indifference to environment, everything is a blur, the bereaved often say—but rather as unusual texture, over-sensitivity, alien particularity of the streets and the plastic peaks. Grief and loss, the sequence seems to say, evince themselves not in intimate reflection or personal worship (there is virtually nothing said of Beth and certainly nothing of her particular qualities in these sequences), not in subjective experience, but in objective attunement, in the contours of objects and the totality linking file cabinets and maps to streets and the sky. In a typically lyrical moment, this environmentalized grief transfigures the ecosphere itself: "He thought of her then, watching flotillas of leaves drifting and bobbing on the surface, and it was less difficult than before -as though the shock, once absorbed, had spread so thin and wide that it was only the skin of the world" (113).

That skin fleshes out so many wounded relations. From childhood, T. stands estranged from other people. His father disappears near the beginning of the book, and it takes months for an adult T. and his mother to discover that their decades-long marriage was, as the father puts it, "only a dream" and that he has commenced a new life as a gay Floridian without further ceremony (50). The mother is an obsessive, condemning catholic among protestants, who attempts suicide and then descends into dementia and trichophobia. He has no friends but suffers the company of an abusive bigot because Fulton invests in T.'s developments. He has two principal employees, one of whom he appreciates, and when she gives him a ride to the car dealership, he meets her daughter Casey, whom a bad car accident has rendered paraplegic. At an investor cocktail hour, he meets Beth, an investor's assistant; "she did not give her last name" and little of their exchange is relayed, but soon she becomes T.'s fond companion, and soon after that she succumbs to "sudden cardiac death" (91). In an accounting of dead relatives, orphans, and "estranged or distant" connections, "he tried to enumerate family members and came up with almost none" (195). A dog he uncharacteristically adopts is subsequently kidnapped and tortured, perhaps by Fulton, necessitating amputation. After a strange friendship ensues with Casey, she makes an advance on T., but when she detects a post-tryst flinch, she shuts him off instantly, including moving out of her own apartment. All the maimed and the lonely, the disaffected and the abandoned, evoke so many failed relations, doing everything wrong from the familial and the intimate to the professional and the societal. Personalizations and intimate scales will not clear the haze of the violently wet environment and the rapacious denialism; personalizations are also where those start. Every tie, every dreamlike alliance, every usurious partnership already encodes the private, instrumental, optimizations that rationalize carbon modernity.

3 Part Three

Although narrative is often celebrated as a vehicle for exercising links between causes and effects—and therefore as the framework of causality and consequence for uniquely reticulating the known facts into a pressing message—part of the strength of *How the Dead Dream*'s modality of environmental objectivity is its delinked and even elliptical form. The book uses chapters to segment the action (two hundred fifty pages spanning ten parts), but it markedly also uses, at variable intervals, dinkuses for transitions unmade, and even more frequently, simple double breaks dividing paragraphs for gaps, skips, aversions. Via these ellipses, major transformations in T.'s projects, his thinking, and his relationships are often produced rather than narrated. Leaps between events and obscured decisions pitch the text over a set of questions: why these projects? Why these places? What motivates these or any people? Most shocking of all of the ellipses is the fading away of the action in the novel's final pages, after T. has gotten lost in a forest, his guide stricken dead in his sleep, and he lays down to sleep himself, shivering, starving, dehydrated, evidently dying.

The novel does not conclude so much as drowse, adopting a delirious cyclicality in place of its previous sharp leaps, and T.'s bed becomes shared with an unspecified animal:

> He would let go, but never give up. A name, a life, the street he lived on when he was ten: goodbye then, soon, to all of them. This was what was occurring all over, as the world dwindled and its colors were stripped from it. People kept busy on their surface, but underneath it they were sleeping, sleeping in their billions. They were sleeping simply, as the other animals did, sleeping and dreaming of the life that might once have been.
>
> As the animal slept its way through time until the end of it came, so would he.
>
> [...]
>
> Back to the beginning, and on to the end—home was flesh, was nearness. Poor animal. It thought he was its mother, but its mother was gone.
>
> As, after a while, all the mothers would be.

T. sleeps, and may not awaken (that the novel some years later inspired a sequel, after other intervening books, and further a threequel, makes the question all the cloudier). The decrepit trope of death as sleep has been prefigured by the novel's title, whose twisted temporality denominates the failures of no-future thinking. The dead do not dream, they are not sleeping. But if they did, they would rehearse the occluded causes and partial objects that brought them to death. While human beings have been alive, a very small percentage of them—in the boardrooms of fossil fuel corporations, in the most powerful statehouses, in their asphalt driveways suffocating desert plants—have dreamed up a way of life that will mean only death for most. Untimely death ordained by the Haut Monde has for centuries been the fate of the poor and wretched of the earth, and thus scholars feverishly debate whether the present ecocide can have any distinction.[9] In consigning its obtuse, impersonal car-loving land-developing protagonist to uncertain undeliberate death in the deformed wild terrain after a hurricane, in an unspecified southern country, around 1990, *How the Dead Dream* hazes over a generic humanity and the specific class of humanity that has caused the current extinction event.

[9] Notably, Kathryn Yusoff, Dana Luciano, Donna Haraway.

How the Dead Dream thinks via setting, impersonality, and ellipsis. It isn't set in the future or even the present, but in that absolutely transformative period of the great acceleration, the early 1990s, and its intensified and problematized production of setting invites a lot of slow processing about when and where we are, and why. Similarly, it isn't personally narrated (not in the first person, like so much contemporary fiction, and not promoting identification with its sociopathic focal point), which is essential for making appear the privatizations fueling carbon modernity. *How the Dead Dream* asks us to laminate impersonality and estranged/attuned ecology, it asks us to read for connection and cause, to cognize the ecocide, to end the destruction. The novel's elliptical quality intricates these connections, while also sharpening our focus: this is not an international saga coordinating lots of locales Babel style, but a winnowed, harrowing concentration on the place and people that matter as the causal force: wealthy Angeleno real estate scions and their investors. Ecocriticism often cherishes complexity and interpenetrating agencies; *How the Dead Dream* offers the simplicity of conceptualizing fault, underlining what must be therefore unambiguously transformed.

Literary objectivity promotes this fathoming of causality, the very intellective modality refused by the Latourianism of most ecocriticism. The problem of ecocide is enormous, but rather than the complexity of distributed agency and nonhuman–human continuums, this enormity poses the simplicity of rapacious, nihilistic capitalism practiced by a very small number of specific humans. Literary objectivity perceives connections of this structural sort; literary form works by the whispered insistence that its elements belong together, and asks for criticism to say out loud the syntheses and abstractions intoned by the formal interrelation. Such syntheses are vital for integration, imagination, and projection—the intellectual praxis for political determination.

How the Dead Dream's paradoxical title alludes to paradoxical intellection: not only dream logic, but the impossible temporality of unconsciousness after death, a modality of thinking unavailable in ordinary phenomenality. This literary objectivity obtains not through iteration of current conditions or probable futures, not through literalistic mimesis of rising tides and fossil fuel executives, but through the uniquely novelistic ecology of interfused setting, character, figure, and narration. *How the Dead Dream* intercalates its elements into a proposition that unplanned exurban development, private profit, psychic obtuseness, and the supervalence of the automobile cause untimely death, animal cruelty, human disfigurement, and ecological abandon. With this thought, the novel's intervention in the world isn't sugarcoating facts, but tendering aesthetic objectivity, ideas which require contemplation to actualize. For what comes next, for promoting flourishing and for mitigating war, for any hope at all, we need entirely new syntheses, different vocabularies, structures of feeling, scaffolds of meaning, and world infrastructures—the very resources literary objectivity stores.

References

Adorno, Theodor W. *Aesthetic Theory*. Translated by Robert Hullot-Kentor. New York: Continuum, 1997.

Buckley, Cara. "Why Is Hollywood So Scared of Climate Change?" *The New York Times*, August 14, 2019. https://www.nytimes.com/2019/08/14/movies/hollywood-climate-change.html.

Daston, Lorraine, and Peter Galison. *Objectivity*. New York: Zone Books, 2007.

Ghosh, Amitav. *The Great Derangement: Climate Change and the Unthinkable*. Chicago: The University of Chicago Press, 2017.

Haraway, Donna. "Situated Knowledges: The Science Question in Feminism and the Privilege of Partial Perspective." *Feminist Studies* 14, no. 3 (1988): 575–99.

Millet, Lydia. *How the Dead Dream*. Mariner Books-Houghton Mifflin Harcourt, 2009.

Ryzik, Melena. "Can Hollywood Movies About Climate Change Make a Difference?" *The New York Times*, October 2, 2017. https://www.nytimes.com/2017/10/02/movies/mother-darren-aronofsky-climate-change.html.

Afterword

CHAPTER 14

Let's Hear It For Janus: Looking Behind and Ahead

Heather Dubrow

1 Reading *The Work of Reading*

The title of Derek Attridge's Introduction, "Criticism Today: Form, Critique, and the Experience of Literature," gestures toward what this impressive collection has indubitably achieved—and toward continuing problems and potentialities confronting both its contributors and subsequent critics. How, for example, does one negotiate the divergent ways "close reading" and the very experience of reading are represented within this book and, indeed, within our whole field? And if, as Attridge indicates later in that Introduction, many articles here are united by their focus on "the work of art," how shall we address controversies embedded in the very concepts "work" (as opposed to, say, "text") and "art"?[1] How do questions like all those reflect both the politics of our discipline and the larger political issues in which they, according to the essay by

[1]For valuable assistance with this essay, I am grateful to Thomas O'Connor, Jahan Ramazani, and Jane Rickard.

H. Dubrow (✉)
Fordham University, New York, NY, USA
e-mail: hdubrow@fordham.edu

A. Sridhar et al. (eds.), *The Work of Reading*,
https://doi.org/10.1007/978-3-030-71139-9_14

our co-editor Mir Ali Hosseini, are embedded? Accompanying valuable contributions to such subjects in *The Work of Reading: Literary Criticism in the 21st Century* are many debates about even broader issues, notably what the critic's obligations should be and how and by whom meaning is made.

My brief initial hope of supplementing the analysis of contemporary criticism in Derek Attridge's valuable introductory essay with an overview of principal issues like those, thus as it were bookending the book, soon crystallized the problems of doing so. Indeed, as my opening paragraph suggests, the author of an Afterword must negotiate metacritically in that essay many challenges the authors in question themselves explore. And an Afterword needs to address another challenge discussed in some of those articles: balancing generalizations with nuances and qualifications. I will return to a further dilemma confronting generalizations about this book, *The Work of Reading*: the differences between our discipline in England, as well as other English-speaking countries, and the United States. Indeed, the observation that the English and Americans are up against the barrier of a common language is apt for the language or rather languages of literary criticism. This Afterword itself at times devotes more attention to practices more common in the United States than elsewhere, though it attempts to encompass other cultures as well.

Acknowledging such difficulties, I do not aim for a comprehensive summary of the very varied essays collected here, instead concentrating on a representative group of issues. Nonetheless, an overview of the achievements of this collection, though not a panorama of its principal arguments, readily emerges. Many contributions here demonstrate the inclusivity that often characterizes literary criticism at the point when this book appears. (Inclusivity is, of course, a value currently also celebrated in a very different form and sphere, the long overdue heightened awareness of racism today, and is relevant too to the mistreatment of adjuncts and other temporary faculty members today). The versions of that value more immediately germane to these essays are variously manifest in many of them: in the breadth of their critical methods, their dialogues with other critics, and their selection of texts. First, methodological capaciousness in the work of a given critic often distinguishes criticism today from many practices in the later decades of the twentieth century. Among my own war stories: during that period one reader rejected a book manuscript of mine, citing prominently among its limits the use of too many critical methods and urging me to select and ally myself with one camp or another (fortunately, a reader at an equally distinguished press shortly afterward recommended publication, singling out for particular praise the range of critical methods). But if that breadth is a valuable option for individual critics and a useful shift in our discipline, it is not a sine qua non for effective criticism: some of the essays above instead effectively favor by precept, example, or both a particular critical approach.

Although the book illuminates many cutting-edge issues and adduces many currently prominent critics, also evident are references to and extended dialogues with critics of earlier generations, no doubt encouraged by the reservations about and rejections of critique in the sense of antagonistic rebuttal often expressed here.[2] William Rasch revisits T. S. Eliot, who also appears more briefly elsewhere in the volume, to develop a revised and updated version of dissociation of sensibility. Ronan McDonald's study of Frank Kermode exemplifies a sensitive but never servile relationship to earlier generations in our profession in not only its representation of how Kermode influenced him but also its explicit emphasis on continuity and its identification of earlier members of the field, notably I. A. Richards, who had influenced Kermode himself. A reference to defamiliarization in the work of Anna Kornbluh demonstrates continuing respect for the Russian formalists, who arguably never received quite the attention they deserved earlier. And of course very evident throughout this book is the impact of numerous Marxist and materialist critics, notably, as one might predict, those exemplars and critics of the movements in question, Theodor Adorno and Louis Althusser.

In short, Oedipus got into a lot of trouble. In our relationships with our professional fathers and mothers, like so many other subjects, we need not think in terms of either/or. Doug Battersby tempers his stress on newness and transformation with a warning against undue dissatisfaction with the old. We can, indeed must, acknowledge and when relevant incorporate what we learned from our predecessors while developing newer approaches, such as the ecocriticism central to Kornbluh's valuable readings. Although Dr. Leavis was hardly an exemplar of measured responses to other members of his discipline, his advocacy of a "Yes, but" response is

[2] Given the extent of recent and older criticism closely related to these overlapping subjects, the footnotes in this Afterword can provide at best a very limited sampling. For further bibliography on the principal issues in this volume, consult the excellent endnotes in the essays it includes and the "Works Cited" and "Bibliography" sections in some major books in the discipline, such as Leighton, *On Form* and Wolfson, *Formal Charges*.

worth recalling. It's also worth registering one reason "Yes, but" is often appropriate: what goes around comes around, though often in a different version. Thus today's formalism should indeed be read as in dialogue with its analogues in the twentieth century rather than just being defensively contrasted with them; at the same time, it remains true that not only the increasing emphasis on history and culture but also the inclusion of forms like genre fiction that would have been dismissed as sub-literary, not worthy of study in universities, represent significant differences.

These types of approach to the past can enable us to develop our own critical approaches more appropriately. For example, we should acknowledge that the intersectional was widely practiced in the twentieth century though without that label: rather than reinventing that wheel, we can valuably reinterpret some developments in that earlier work and resist ones that no longer seem relevant. Has ageism been unduly neglected in many discussions of intersectionality? But as I write we are reminded of a far more pernicious factor in intersectionality: the murder of George Floyd is generating invaluable new perspectives on race and calling some older ones into question.

Although one might perhaps have wished for additional textual analyses in the volume, those that do appear, notably Susan Wolfson's brilliant (not a word I use often or lightly) interpretations, are incisive, and the range of literary writings discussed in this book further demonstrates inclusivity. In the acute readings that often characterize it, *The Work of Reading* draws, of course, on canonical texts like *Hamlet* (it's not easy to get more canonical than that). But this book also serves its readers by introducing a few writings with which some will probably have been unfamiliar, notably Rachel Cusk's *Outline* and Lydia Millet's *How The Dead Dream*.

Seconding Rasch's emphasis on the importance of prose style, I list that among the other achievements of many contributions to this collection, which includes a number of essays graced with splendidly witty and apt phraseology. For instance, I delighted in Ellen Rooney's "Oxymoron is a canny fool who speaks a pointed truth to make possible the impossible" and her wordplay in "As she tries to face down or face up to her own libidinal investments."[3] And Rachel Eisendrath's prose is not the least of her essay's many strengths: witness, among a host of other examples, her title

[3] Chapter 4, 67–90.

"Polonius as Anti-Close Reader" and her subtitle, "Towards a Poetics of the Putz." And, as the inclusion of "putz"[4] testifies, this volume demonstrates that a more informal style of critical prose has become accepted, even favored in many circles, perhaps encouraged by Jeff Dolven's notable experiments in this area.[5] And Eyers's contribution to this book exemplifies the potentialities of styles informal and conversational enough to make my principal thesis director turn in his grave.

In its recurrent discussions of how and by whom meaning is made, the collection as a whole introduces three principal and sometimes overlapping arenas: the reader, the author, and form. The perspectives on all three differ strikingly and suggestively from essay to essay. For instance, a number of articles, such as Attridge's splendid introduction, draw on affective criticism, while a few others attack it. Attridge himself compellingly emphasizes three perspectives on the experience of reading: its singularity, its otherness, and its inventiveness. Kornbluh, in contrast, advocates for objectivity. Another suggestive anatomy of the role of the reader results from Rooney's emphasis on surprise, an experience discussed from a range of perspectives elsewhere in the book. Eyers analyzes readership by developing a new category for narratology, the "non-I."

In contrast and opposition to such arguments, Henry Staten asserts that the author, not reader, makes the poem through *techne*, a concept also explored from different perspectives by Sridhar. A complex term in the work of Aristotle and others, this word can roughly be translated as "craft" and that, indeed, has important connections with the way creative writers refer to craft, another point to which I'll return.[6] In some other contributions to the collection, too, the agency of authors is not neglected, indeed receiving more attention than they probably would have garnered around the turn of the century in a comparable collection. But authors would still trail readers in any poll based on this book. This comparative ranking may well not be as true, or in any event not as marked, throughout the profession, especially in the United States, and arguably the race between writer and reader may still be too close to call in some circles there; the rebirth of the author has been evident in a great

[4] Informal North American expression for wasteful activity.

[5] Dolven, *Senses of Style*.

[6] Compare my emphasis on *techne* in Dubrow, "Foreword."

deal of criticism in English-speaking countries and, indeed, in a couple of books recently published in Germany.[7]

The book is also characteristic of the period in which it appears in its emphasis on form, which until fairly recently I had been describing in presentations and papers as the f-word of the profession.[8] As that riff would suggest, I certainly agree with the many contributors who stress that form was submerged, even in many circles reviled, until around the turn of the century. (It is suggestive if understandable, though, that in this book as elsewhere critics who celebrate the survival or return of form often associate that revival with their own favored methodology.) In any event, on the subject of form like so many others, the essays demonstrate divergent approaches. A few contributions address it in relation to narrative, reminding us that the dramatic, narrative, and lyric modes were often seen as a central model of form; as noted above, Staten discusses form in relation to *techne*; many other critics, such as Attridge and Rasch within this collection, relate form to the reader's experiences. The best evidence of how conceptions of form diverge is the range of opinions on its relationship to historical questions: is this a sine qua non for discussions of form today or one option, however significant?

My discussions of the roles of the reader, the author, and the form suggest a promising variation on our usual literary histories. Such narratives typically and understandably focus on what is widely perceived as the dominant school and its key concepts—power in the heyday of new historicism, linguistic indeterminacy during the reign of French poststructuralism, and so on. But it would also be helpful to unearth and unpack concepts and approaches that appear simultaneously, often in related but in distinctive forms, in coexisting movements. For example, the New Criticism of the 1950s and the Freudian literary criticism of the same period share a preoccupation with the concealed but implicit and a drive toward closure and resolution. In the 1980s in the United States, those rivals new historicism and feminism both explored the assignment of predetermined roles and their performance. To the credit of our discipline today, it would be hard, as I have emphasized, to identify a single dominant school, but questions about readership allow for fruitful comparisons and contrasts.

[7] Jannidis et al., *Die Rückkehr des Autors*.

[8] Among the best discussions of the rejection and reinvigoration of form are the essays in Wolfson and Brown, *Reading for Form*, especially Wolfson, "Introduction"; and in Burton and Scott-Baumann, *Work of Form*.

As I have suggested, in scrutinizing the work of art, many essays in this volume also scrutinize the work of its critics. The book demonstrates the revival of close reading, though often in versions many earlier New Critics—themselves a more varied and on occasion contentious group than discussions of the movement usually allow—would not have countenanced. Like Reuben Brower, the leader of Harvard's often embattled practitioners of the trade—or rather perhaps adherents to the faith—Eisendrath compellingly argues for thinking—and teaching—in terms of slow, not close reading. The adjective in question better describes the process—and draws attention to its value in a culture where practices like scrolling on one's devices and tweeting on one's social media privilege rapidity over reflection. I return to these questions below.

The recurrent emphasis on surprise in this volume is another marker of our critical moment. Rooney's powerful analysis of it, for instance, relates to her approach to critique, which she defines more broadly than many other essays in *The Work of Reading* do, seeing not suspicion but surprise as one of its key markers. Many other critics who emphasize that marker in so doing implicitly converse with, and argue with, many of their predecessors, though generally implicitly. Deconstruction, for instance, traced how texts surprised and unsettled us, yet on another level discovering that words were saying the opposite of what they seemed to say was predictable, not surprising, however dazzling the exposition was. As these comparisons suggest, many works of art introduce surprise in some ways and modulate its effects in others, another pattern where we can explore the various agencies of reader, author, and form.

2 Future Rereadings of *The Work of Reading*

The conclusion to this Afterword looks backward at the essays preceding it and forward to what we may achieve—and what we should avoid—in future written studies and discussions. Many such issues revolve around critique in the widespread sense developed in seminal writings by Rita Felski and Eve Sedgwick, among others; that is, suspicious attacks on literary and critical texts that at their worst descend to a delight in "gotcha."[9] (As I just noted, however, Rooney does not define critique in

[9] Comments on Felski's work from a range of critics may be found in the "Theories and Methodologies" section of *PMLA* 132, no. 2 (2017).

terms of suspicion, emphasizing surprise instead; and the concept of political critique is potent in many quarters and occasionally appears in these chapters.) In supporting the more collegial and indeed genial approach often labeled "postcritique" here and elsewhere, I myself am certainly not advocating bland and yes, sometimes blind acceptance of positions with which we disagree: many essays in this collection also exemplify productive and sometimes sharp disagreements. But those disagreements can be compelling, sharp in several senses of the adjective, while still avoiding condescension or vitriol. (Battersby's proposed alternative to such attacks, judging a methodological approach by how it contributes to our readings of a particular text, is liable to the objection that some such approaches might fail as dramatically for one text as they succeed for others—but his thoughtful alternative to polemical denunciations, examining how a given method may illuminate some writings, could fruitfully remind us how New Criticism enriched our understanding of metaphysical poetry, for instance, and thus temper the pro forma condescension to that movement still common in many circles.) A recent collection of essays, *Ekphrastic Encounters: New Interdisciplinary Essays on Literature and the Visual Arts* offers both an analogue to and extension of arguments in our volume: its editors endorse the growing emphasis on reading ekphrasis in terms of often congenial encounters between the visual and verbal rather than the winner-take-all competition often associated with the *paragone,* in so doing also supporting such encounters among members of the academy.[10]

Further examinations of why our profession may encourage unproductive mischaracterizations of opponents can help us to continue to avoid them.[11] Does the common and too seldom interrogated praise of "smartness" encompass judiciousness as fully and frequently as it should? The competitiveness encouraged by the training in many graduate programs in the United States and exemplified by some, fortunately by no means all, people teaching in them no doubt breeds a long-lasting temptation to conflate the incisive and the snarky. Might not England promote a similar temptation though through different channels? That is, the emphasis on originality in the current Research Excellence Framework, successor but not solution to the preceding Research Assessment Exercise, may perhaps

[10] Kennedy and Meek, *Ekphrastic Encounters*.

[11] Also see the discussions of how and why movements discredit their rivals in Graff, *Professing*, esp. 240–41.

invite negative valuations of other critics. Moreover, many if not most careers even of those fortunate enough to have the all too rare permanent appointments have been threatened earlier by some obstacles, including, for example, those rivalrous colleagues or gendered prejudices. Whether or not one rejects his other paradigms, Freud was quite right about *fort-da*, that is, reenacting versions of past losses in order to assert mastery over them; not the least danger of this process is demeaning the work of others. And as my emphasis on "what goes around comes around" would suggest, teleological models are frequently more appropriate for the STEM fields than literary criticism; but they are too often enlisted to celebrate how an author demolishes their misguided predecessors. The good news: some of the most distinguished people in the profession are also among the most generous, and the work by these and many other critics repeatedly demonstrates that identifying limitations in another critic's approach does not preclude also observing and in many situations commenting on its strengths. Among the characteristics Simon Grimble attributes to an ideal critic are open-mindedness and flexibility; such approaches can encourage the "affirmative voice"[12] that he persuasively advocates.

How else, then, can we ensure that we approach the critics and writers we discuss from angles that are always open-minded and judicious—and always incisively critical in the senses of that noun encapsulated in the concept of critical thinking yet never critical in the senses of self-congratulatory or what can only be called nasty?[13] First, we need to identify and avoid straw men, remaining alert to the convenient temptation to reduce a movement monolithically to a single practitioner of it or an essay that is not typical of its author's entire career. Rasch demonstrates how Eliot uses Tennyson as a straw men, and comparable practices too often characterize criticism. New Criticism is not infrequently dismissed through attacks on a single practitioner, notably Cleanth Brooks, thus neglecting the complexities in his own work that Wolfson unpacks so well and also the range of other approaches not only in England (William Empson of course overturns many common generalizations about that movement or rather movements) but also within the United States.

[12] Chapter 9, 173–191.

[13] On the dangers of misrepresenting one's predecessors, also see Dubrow, "Foreword," ix–xvi.

We should also beware of generalizations conveniently based on a single essay or book that may not be typical of its author's position elsewhere. Although new historicists emphasize form in a few articles and one or two books, it was certainly generally neglected. Moreover, a particular essay may not reflect how its author's approach shifted in later writings; Edward Said questioned and modified some of his earlier assertions, but they remain foundational and unquestioned in postcolonialist writing by many other critics. In addition, we will judge the work of others better if we recognize the investments that shape and might at some points misshape our own critical positions. Attridge's essay is, again, exemplary when he writes, "I welcome this fresh attention to issues I've been interested in for several decades, though it remains important to subject the newly-emerging accounts of literary form and affect to careful assessment."[14]

Space theory can gloss how we approach both our own critical writings and those of others. The twin processes of gathering in and excluding that it explores so incisively recur when we attempt to control the space of literary criticism.[15] Grimble's observation that close reading can produce an in-group is justified by the history of that movement but equally applicable to many other critical approaches for our own ends as well. The in-groups in literary criticism often gather in their adherents through distinctive vocabulary, citations of each other's work, and the process of identifying and excluding the unwashed. Because studies of the work of art and the very concepts behind both those nouns vary among themselves, and because, as observed above, many people dovetail a range of critical methods, the possibility of gathering together an in-group comprised of the many people addressing the work of art is ameliorated. But the possibility is still a clear and present danger for, say, people approaching that work through distinct types of close reading or affective criticism, among many other methods.

Although Barbara Kiefer Lewalski is primarily respected and even in some circles revered for her scholarly contributions, not the least of her legacies involves the tones and assumptions with which we approach the work of our colleagues. Discussing the decision not to award something to a candidate, she observed, "Well, he isn't ready for it yet, but who

[14] Chapter 1, 1–19.

[15] On gathering and excluding in space theory, see Casey, "Space to Place," esp. 24–26.

knows where he will be in a few years." Her intense consciousness in this and many other situations that people change and, in particular, grow intellectually models the value of generally attaching most negative comments, if they are called for, to a specific work or a specific period in someone's career.

My observations about differences between critical practices in different countries may alert us to the risk that the contemporary and laudatory emphasis on the global carries with it, the possibility of neglecting differences between and within particular nations when considering subjects central to this volume, including conceptions of the work of art and the workings of forms like narrative and lyric. Editor of *The Cambridge Companion to PostColonial Poetry*, Jahan Ramazani has impeccable credentials as leader of the study of what he terms "both literary flows across national borders and global historical convergences and affinities across discrepant spaces."[16] But despite—and more to the point because of—his many contributions to shaping that field, he has repeatedly enjoined bridging the study of the national and global rather than submerging and even shedding the former. Thus, in discussing modernist and postcolonial authors, he insists that "both poets fashion a locally responsive poetics, paradoxically, by virtue of a bypass through the global. Nourished by poetry's cross-national and ever-mutating storage house of forms, techniques, genres, and images, individual poems give expression to locality at the same time that they turn formally, linguistically, allusively in other directions."[17] And shortly afterward, he broadens that argument to a warning against the misuse of globalism: "The effacement of newly articulated minoritarian and postcolonial identities under the all-flattening sign of an undifferentiated globality would be particularly unfortunate—hence my emphasis on the muddy footprints of the *trans*national and the *trans*local."[18] In these and many other instances, Ramazani's work, yet another instance of a both/and approach, not only models bridging the local and global but also offers an exemplary instance of two goals of this Afterword and many other contributions here: disagreeing with predecessors and contemporaries without hostility and dovetailing generalizations and nuances.

[16] Ramazani, "Lyric Poetry," 102.

[17] Ramazani, *Transnational Poetics*, 10.

[18] Ramazani, 13.

The preoccupations of many essays in this book exemplify the need for distinctions between and within cultures and within movements often represented as monolithic. The influence of Dr. Leavis and the movement to which he gave his name was very limited in the United States. And the impact of I. A. Richards has been far deeper in England than the United States, with his work still current in certain circles at the University of Cambridge in particular, not least because of his presence in the legendary courses given by an academic also mentioned by Attridge, Jeremy Prynne (one should note, however, that Reuben Brower, a dean of American New Criticism, was a student of Richards).

In short, as Ramazani compellingly argues, the valuable centrifugal focus on globalization should be accompanied by a centripetal emphasis on differences between those linked in terms like "Anglo-American," "Anglophone," and "English-speaking."[19] Admittedly, the increasing participation of scholars from the other side of the Atlantic in conferences like the annual Shakespeare Association of America convention and the Modern Language Association's recent addition of a conference in Europe may well be diminishing some of those differences. But they still call for attention. This collection can suggest one promising case study: playing Grimble's and McDonald's analyses of the workings of theory on the English side of the Atlantic with the same question in the United States. Other instances come to mind; for example, arguably cognitive literary study assumes different forms because the United States is less likely than England and Canada to offer large-scale grants for collaborative projects in that and other fields, funding that facilitates the involvement of neuroscience, psychology, and history in literary discussions of the cognitive. (One always should recall that Canada is too often ignored in overviews of our discipline.)

The history of New Criticism, a movement that was far from monolithic even within a particular country, is the best touchstone to why that centripetal movement accompanying the centrifugal energies of globalism should also address internal distinctions as well as those between Anglophone countries.[20] The Wolfson essay incisively crystallizes these and many related issues, while differences in foci among essays here that advocate and practice it to recall earlier differences. Should close reading

[19] I thank Mary Thomas Crane for useful observations on the issues in this paragraph.

[20] On those differences see, for instance, Strier, "Formalism," esp. 208.

be especially alert to words? Or imagery? Rhetorical practices? And, as we all know, the reassurance that texts end on resolution and unity distinguishes many earlier members of that tribe from the practitioners of deconstruction.

Moreover, it is not hard to find telling exceptions to the often-unchallenged generalization that New Criticism rules were the absolutist sovereign of literary criticism in the United States in the 1960s and 1970s. It was literary history in the sense practiced by Douglas Bush and his many heirs and assigns that ruled the roost at Harvard during those decades and had, dare one say, something to crow about in its English Department, where the adherents of close reading were a determined but often embattled minority. And to move to the country as a whole, psychological criticism remained prominent in some venues throughout those decades.

A sidebar of memoir, two nouns that can rhyme in more senses than one in contemporary criticism, is relevant here. As an undergraduate, I had the privilege of one-to-one honors tutorial in consecutive years with two of the most impressive close readers of their generation. My deep commitment to that approach, bred by my undergraduate education, contributed to a delay in learning the other methods and skills that had become prominent by the beginning of my professional career. As someone else nurtured in close reading observed to me, we had to learn techniques of argumentation, which are at the core of so many other types of criticism, belatedly. But if I paid this price, it was well worth it: a continuing, deep engagement with the nuances of texts has interacted with the other critical methods to which I have turned, and, as many have observed, however they may evaluate close reading in theory, in practice many teachers find it invaluable in the classroom.

The Work of Reading also gestures toward promising directions for subsequent work on another subject that arises in the Sridhar essay and is very relevant elsewhere: the relationship of creative writers and literary critics both within particular departments, where it varies considerably, and in the profession at large. Creative writing has been taught at universities much longer in the United States than England, although undergraduates' interest in it is now rendering it a growth area in the latter country as well. But in both areas its relationship to literary criticism and its practitioners has often been tense and contestatory. Full disclosure: I wear both hats. And I still remember the distinguished critic who greeted my explanation that I was returning to writing poetry while also continuing my work as a critic with virtually these words: "But Heather, you're a successful scholar of early modern literature. Why would you want to spend your time writing poems?" Indeed, many academics of my generation were forced to see those two paths as another of those either/or choices; one explained to me that he did his doctorate in folklore rather than literary criticism because members of the latter cohort were so unsympathetic to his plans to continue his creative work as well. Tensions were often intense in the heyday of French poststructuralist criticism, whose proponents were wont to dismiss the creative writers in their midst as touchy-feely, while the writers dismissed those benighted opponents as out of touch with how writing really worked. And funerals for the death of the author were not welcomed by those who considered themselves alive and well members of that cohort.

In many quarters, such prejudices on both sides have been ameliorated but by no means completely resolved. The essays in this volume gesture toward though generally do not pursue routes toward further resolution via an examination of the work of art. The allusions to *techne,* a concept that in many of its manifestations corresponds to writers' celebration of craft, is one route to a rapprochement. And the respect for the writers implicit in the very term "work of art" and by no means necessarily erased even when one sees the reader as the primary agent making meaning could help build bridges between creative writers and critics.

Not only the collegiality of department members who variously identify as creative writers and critics but many other aspects of our discipline would be enriched by pursuing certain perspectives on that triad of author, reader, and form. Future studies of reading in general, and close reading in particular, could fruitfully expand Sridhar's valuable point about groupings of poems. The emphasis on the single, isolated text is among the regrettable legacies of certain versions of close reading; its limitations demonstrate the interaction of that methodology and current questions about readership. How—and how securely—one text is linked to the other may be determined by the agency of the reader, the writer, the form, other agents such as the printer, or some combination. Often that process demands the informed and careful judgments that many essays in this volume both advocate and exemplify. If, for example, we read Donne's "Hymn to God My God in my sickness" as a reassuring answer to "Good Friday. Riding Westward," we will shape—and some may argue, misshape—the meanings of the former poem.

Certain literary forms also variously mandate or encourage links among poems so strong that they should not be interpreted as separate units; witness, for example, the corona of sonnets, where the last line of one poem becomes the first line of the next and the final lyric repeats a line from the first one. Authors may of course connect poems in many other ways, such as repeated images or titles that refer to each other. The catchword, the first word of the succeeding poem that printers in the early modern period insert at the bottom of the previous one, creates a different type of link. Compilers of commonplace books and of anthologies often implicitly or explicitly link poems. On this subject like so many others, the process advocated above, creating more bridges between creative writers and critics, would benefit both groups. Again, we should think in terms of neither an either/or choice between the isolated text and an amorphous grouping but rather a range of possibilities.

Acute analyses of the reader's impact should certainly be linked, as many of these essays have done, to the influence of Bruno Latour's development of actor-network theory, the psychological studies behind affective criticism, linguistics, and many other current approaches. But clearly the current emphasis on the reader also reacts against the adulation of the author that characterized the less acute criticism in preceding decades. Texts triumphantly achieved their goals, according to this model; forms and authors always had their acts together. I am certainly not recommending a return to either that model or suspicious reading in general, but an interest in the processes of authorship can and should include the recognition that Homer and his heirs and assigns do occasionally nod.

Yet more to my purposes here—and more to the benefit of our discipline—let's also dovetail the interest in readership that runs throughout so many essays in this volume with more attention to how the creation of forms demonstrates an author's struggles, and often the successful resolution of such battles. Yes, I again have a horse—or rather a Muse—in this race. Admittedly, it is not uncommon for poets to present their poems as sui generis in the most literal sense of that expression; for example, at his readings the distinguished poet Paul Muldoon often uses phrases like "the poem wanted to be a sonnet." But Muldoon would surely not disagree that any author who has struggled to write in a challenging form like a ghazal or sestina, or indeed, a sonnet, contributes to its successes or, when relevant, its failures, in ways that should not be underestimated. To return to actor-network theory demonstrates the diffusion of agency in this and many other situations—and the prominent inclusion of the author.

But if reading is one of the major foci of the essays in this book, arguably it is also the area where those essays invite further work and on occasions further revisions of their own revisionist stances. Critics have not neglected the differences among reading a book in the traditional sense and examining the text on another device. And many university teachers have considered the differing effects of various types of books—in the United States, for example, what happens when a student encounters a given poem in the Norton Anthology as opposed to some book less weighty in several senses? But we could profitably do much more with that issue and especially its implications for our pedagogy. Today's students are deeply affected by the devices on which they read a text.

Affective criticism and close reading that emphasizes slow reading, as well as several other approaches, crystallize another pedagogical challenge, especially acute in institutions in the United States whose demographics include students with spotty training before they arrive. Many of those less advanced students today envision the goal of reading as finding an answer to a predetermined question, hence a process that should be completed as rapidly as possible. That process often carries with it the assumption that both questions and answers will be and should be brief. Tweeting and its analogues in effect become the norm. Sometimes expectations like these are indeed appropriate and even valuable, especially perhaps in STEM fields. And sometimes rather than fighting them we should adapt them; for example, my students have responded positively to comparing and contrasting couplets with tweets.

But Eisendrath's condemnation of Polonius as a hasty reader warns us that the types of reading many students practice can build bad habits, dangerously inimical to what we hope to accomplish when they approach most literary texts (in the capacious sense of "literary" that would include, for example, graphic novels and political speeches). So how can we encourage our students to adopt alternative reading practices as well, ones that will generate the rich experiences traced by many essays in this book? Recognizing the expectations they may bring to reading and talking about it in terms of its range of potential forms and processes, each with its distinctive purposes and challenges, is an important first step. Scrolling needs to be balanced and sometimes challenged by pausing, and scrolling back to where one was before. Reading aloud can develop good approaches to reading silently as well. Assignments involving memorizing—Maynard Mack, Jr. has long advocated for the alternative term "learning by heart"—can also encourage slow reading.

Addressing these challenges in the classroom may well alert us to a challenge that we face ourselves when assuming and analyzing the readerly role discussed in so many essays in this book. For all the other differences that distinguish them, many discussions of reading focus largely or entirely on the initial encounter with a text. But we need to talk less about a single, particularized experience of reading and more about the interplay among repeated experiences, whether they follow consecutively on the same occasion or are separated by days or weeks or years. How does this complicate though not obviate the element of surprise? How does the revision—in the several potential senses of that word—of earlier judgments and interpretations affect—or is it sometimes effect?—our agency as readers?

Not the least advantage of negotiating such questions about reading is that they alert us to a comparable, and comparably neglected, process in writing. In discussing texts, critics too often envision the process of composition as occurring at a relatively brief and often readily identified period of time. Dates are imposed on poems and affiliations with historical events and texts by other writers traced with assumptions about such a period in mind. But in fact, writers often return to poems or prose compositions or fragments of them that were rejected or put aside some time ago. What went cold on a back burner often lends itself to rewarming and transforming. And it is not uncommon to extract and reconceive fragments of something written earlier to very different ends.

This collection, too, invites us to revisit, reread, and sometimes reconsider its thought-provoking contributions.

References

Burton, Ben, and Elizabeth Scott-Baumann, eds., *The Work of Form: Poetics and Materiality in Early Modern Culture*. Oxford: Oxford University Press, 2014.

Casey, Edward S. "How to Get from Space to Place in a Fairly Short Stretch of Time: Phenomenological Prolegomena." In *Senses of Place*, edited by Steven Feld and Keith S. Basso, 13–52. Santa Fe: School of American Research Press, 1996.

Dolven, Jeff. *Senses of Style: Poetry Before Interpretation*. Chicago: University of Chicago Press, 2017.

Dubrow, Heather. “Foreword.” In *New Formalisms and Literary Theory*, edited by Verena Theile and Linda Tredennick, vii–xviii. Basingstoke, Hampshire: Palgrave Macmillan, 2013.

Graff, Gerald. *Professing Literature: An Institutional History*. Chicago: University of Chicago Press, 1987.

Jannidis, Fotis, Gerhard Lauer, Matías Martínez, and Simone Winko, eds. *Die Rückkehr des Autors*. Niemeyer: Tübingen 1999.

Kennedy, David, and Richard Meek, eds. *Ekphrastic Encounters: New Interdisciplinary Essays on Literature and the Visual Arts*. Manchester: Manchester University Press, 2019.

Leighton, Angela. *On Form: Poetry, Aestheticism, and the Legacy of a Word*. Oxford: Oxford University Press, 2007.

Metzlersche, J. B., and Carl Ernst Poeschel, eds. *Autorschaft: Positionen und Revisionen*. Stuttgart: Springer-Verlag, 2002.

Ramazani, Jahan. “Lyric Poetry: Intergeneric, Transnational, Translingual?” *Journal of Literary Theory* 11, no 1 (2017): 97–107.

———. *A Transnational Poetics*. Chicago: University of Chicago Press, 2009.

Strier, Richard. “How Formalism Became a Dirty Word, and Why We Can’t Do Without It.” In *Renaissance Literature and Its Formal Engagements*, edited by Mark David Rasmussen, 207–15. New York: Palgrave, 2003.

Wolfson, Susan J. *Formal Charges: The Shaping of Poetry in British Romanticism*. Stanford: Stanford University Press, 1997.

———. “Introduction” In Wolfson and Brown, *Reading for Form*, edited by Susan J. Wolfson and Marshall Brown, 3–24. Seattle: University of Washington Press, 2006.

Index

A. Sridhar et al. (eds.), *The Work of Reading*,
https://doi.org/10.1007/978-3-030-71139-9

CPSIA information can be obtained
at www.ICGtesting.com
Printed in the USA
BVHW011156200521
607799BV00002B/34